# *Improvising:*
## *My Life in Music*

Published in 2007 by
Backbeat Books (an imprint of Hal Leonard Corporation)
19 West 21st Street, New York, NY 10010
www.backbeatbooks.com

Book design and production by Dovetail Publishing Services.
All photos are from the author's personal collection.

Library of Congress Cataloging-in-Publication Data is available upon request.

ISBN-13: 978-0-87930-826-1
ISBN-10: 0-87930-826-5

Printed in the United States of America

07 08 09 10 11   5 4 3 2 1

*To my mother, Cora May Hanson Coryell,*

*my stepfather, Gene P. Coryell,*

*and to my real father, whom I never*

*knew, Lorenz Albert Van Delinder II*

# Improvising:
## My Life in Music

## Larry Coryell

Backbeat
Books
New York

# Contents

# *Prologue*

YEARS AGO, WHEN I WAS IN HIGH SCHOOL, one day I was walking down George Washington Way in my little hometown out in the boondocks of southeastern Washington State, and I was fantasizing about being dressed up like Barney Kessel on one of his album covers, wearing a black shirt and a white tie. I already had the glasses. That was my dream.

A few years later, when I'd learned some more about playing jazz guitar, I was talking music with a fellow jazz fan and college co-worker. "You can play, all right," he said, "but you'll never play with the likes of someone like Dave Brubeck."

And so I went on with my life, a college student studying journalism in the early 1960s, just a guy wanting to do the right thing as a member of a safe, conservative American society. But the music never strayed far from my consciousness, and that music—improvised music as played by people like Barney and Dave and Charlie Parker and John Coltrane, to name just a few shining examples—took over my inner life.

I would go to the library to study and start composing bebop lines instead. There was no jazz program at the university, so I went out into the surrounding city and soaked up every jazz sound and met every jazz musician I could. I got into appreciating folk and classical musicians, too. I listened to everything that had "magic." And there was a lot going on—the magic was unfolding—it was the '60s.

During all this inspiration and aspiration, I never thought I'd actually get to know someone like Barney Kessel or Dave Brubeck. Maybe I'd meet one of them sometime, like I met Oscar Petersen in a camera shop one day. I freaked out—to this day, I can recall the sound of my voice rising two octaves when I tried to say something to him.

One time, I ran to B.B. King's hotel on the day after one of his gigs, hoping that he would give me a guitar or a lesson or at least some encouragement—but he had already checked out. I went back downtown the next week and heard James Brown—wow! That was a trip—this was a whole new culture, radically different from what I had known. I really liked it—I felt at home. But still I had no thought of being a professional musician myself—no, not me. When my friends told me I should get out and play with more advanced musicians, I told them they were crazy.

But then I started getting gigs with better players, and I liked the steady work, and I liked what I was learning from the older musicians. There was so much in the music that was subtle, but it was all learnable and it was all possible—I just had to keep listening, practicing, performing. Finally, in the summer of my 22nd year, I couldn't stand it any longer. I couldn't learn any more where I was. I had to go to New York. So I went.

Pretty soon, not only had I met Barney Kessel—I'd toured opposite him in Europe. I met Dave Brubeck's sons and eventually got to play with the whole Brubeck family. I was listening to and meeting some of the most amazing musicians to ever touch an instrument, like Ornette Coleman and Keith Jarrett—and there was Coltrane, sitting in the Village Vanguard listening to me—and there were Eddie Daniels, Roland Kirk, Jeremy Steig, and whole orchestras full of top-notch players—and there were Mingus and Miles and Sonny Rollins and Archie Shepp and Jack DeJohnette and my hero, Wes Montgomery. I became a full-fledged member of the amazing community of people that was such a creative force in the middle part of the 20th century. What an honor that was!

I think back to that walk down dusty George Washington Way, with the sticker-burrs on the ground and the tumbleweeds being pushed by the sandstorms against a backdrop of dun-colored, low-lying mountains, and I say to myself: "Coryell, I didn't really think this was going to happen, but you made the grade!"

Today, I'm a player and a composer and, to my surprise, an educator, too. I've made a difference (I'd like to think). If I hadn't gone through all the struggles for my music, fighting to develop my style of playing and my concept, then perhaps some people never would have been reached by the magic of music. That, I see now, was my mission—and it still is.

Here's my story.

# Improvising:
## My Life in Music

# *Chapter 1*

*The little whippersnapper makes his entrance on the scene
in Texas, of all places, has to do it in the middle of
a war—the nerve of some people—and where's Dad?*

DURING WORLD WAR II, a little girl in Texas named Dorothy McNeir got
a gift she remembers well. It was Easter 1943, and her Aunt Cora had
crocheted a "charming dress" for her, with a matching crocheted cap. "Although
she was busy making the layette for her first baby, whose birth was imminent," says
Dorothy, "she found time to crochet an outfit for her niece."

Dorothy goes on: "That Easter morning in Galveston was sunny and mild. I
remember feeling mystified when someone handed me a basket and instructed me
to place in it the colored eggs that were turning up in the oddest places. Although
I didn't understand what was happening, memory holds that I felt smashing in the
outfit created for me by my Aunt Cora."

Dorothy's Aunt Cora was my mother, who gave birth to a son on the evening
of April 2, 1943, around 9:30 CWT (Central War Time). His name was Lorenz Albert
Van Delinder III.

Before I continue with my story, I should mention that I was born deaf in my
right ear. My mother always said it was because she had some kind of virus when she
was carrying me—and that was most likely the cause. Be that as it may, when I was
11 or 12, she asked me if I wanted to have an operation that might be able to fix the
problem with my ear. There was risk involved, and as a scared pre-teen I said "no" to
the operation. Do I regret it? Honestly, I still don't know. Sometimes my "monaural by
default" hearing bugs me, and it's especially awkward when I'm trying to hear a stereo
playback. I've also noticed that when I see myself speaking on film I seem to favor one
side of my mouth—but I guess having one good ear was, in the final analysis, okay by
me. I could still hear the music, and the music is what I'm all about.

But let's get back to 1943: at that time, Dorothy's family was going through
some changes—not B♭7 to E♭maj7 to Abmaj7♯11; that would come much later.
No, these changes are the kind that are called "the vicissitudes of life," and they
happen to everybody. It's just that these changes occurred when I was too young to

remember them—so, for this part of my life, I have to rely on what I've been told by my beloved cousin, Dorothy.

When I was just short of four months old, a hurricane hit Galveston. The McNeir family survived the storm, but their house did not. After taking up temporary residence in nearby Arkansas, where there were good shrimp beds—my Uncle Watie was a shrimper—they purchased a two-story house at 1909 Avenue M 1/2 in Galveston.

Galveston is flat—not good terrain to defend against hurricanes. It's on an island, with the Gulf of Mexico to the east and Galveston Bay on the other side, to the west, towards the Texas mainland. The houses in our neighborhood were not terribly elegant—they were functional, made of wood or stucco, box-like, usually two-story. Nothin' fancy, but the architectural monotony was offset by the subtropical vegetation that dominated the streets and yards. There were lots of flowers, trees, and bushes, including one flowery shrub called oleander, which my grandmother loved, especially when its pink flowers were in bloom.

The Gulf dominates the Galveston landscape—the city is basically a long beach, and after the devastating hurricane the town built a seawall. As a boy, I loved going to the beach and bathing in the Gulf. Galveston was a major port at the time, because the Houston ship channel hadn't been dug yet. There were rail lines that ran into the city from the mainland, with lots of industrial and agricultural products being transported in and out. I remember going down to the railroad depot and seeing bales and bales of cotton stacked high in the open warehouse by the depot.

At first, Cousin Dorothy's future first-grade teacher and her husband occupied the upper floor. After a short while, they moved out—and my Grandmother Sadie, my mother, and I moved in. We needed a place to crash, as it were, because of the events that had taken place during the first six weeks of my life.

Cora and her husband—my father—had gone up to Peoria, Illinois, after I was born. My father was named Larry Alberts, and he became known to me, later in my life, as a womanizer, an alcoholic, and a musician. He played piano and sang, and he walked with a limp due to some sort of accident earlier in his life. He was of average height, had medium-brown hair, and was good-looking—but not "pretty-boy handsome." He had married my mother in New Orleans.

All I know about Larry Alberts is bits of information that have trickled down to me over the years. My grandmother, when she was still alive, told me very little about my father. Sometimes, when I pushed her, she would relent a bit, saying he was a strong man—"he had a strong back." She also mentioned that he had a beautiful singing voice and played the piano. That was about it.

Mom said part of the reason she hooked up with Larry Alberts was to learn more piano—she could play pretty well in her own right, especially in E-flat. There were some photographs in a baby album that got passed on to me after my mother passed, but all the photos with my father had been torn out. Later on, in the 1960s, I found a federal census listing for a Lawrence Van Delinder who was living in Hornell, New York, in 1930, but the trail stopped there.

When I was born, Larry came down to Galveston for the event. Dorothy's dad had taken my mother to Galveston to get the divorce after Larry had abandoned us in Peoria. I was told that he died in an influenza epidemic, but that may not be true. According to official records, L. A. Vandelinder, birth date 18 May, 1913 (a Taurus!), died on the day before Christmas in 1988, and his last known address was in Rockford, Illinois. I have played a lot of gigs in Rockford over the years, but I think most of them were after 1988. It probably doesn't make any difference—there would have been no way for us to connect anyway.

Soon after they arrived in Peoria, Dad impregnated another woman and subsequently moved in with her, leaving us high and dry. The marriage of Cora and Mr. Alberts was destroyed, which is why we moved back to Galveston, to my cousin Dorothy's house, in the summer of 1943. (On my first solo album, for Vanguard Records, I had a tune called "The Dream Thing"—but the original title of that opus was "My Cousin Dorothy.")

My mother had to start her life anew. "It was a daunting time for Cora," says Cousin Dorothy, "but she gallantly rose to the occasion. Eventually, when Larry was about two, some new apartment housing was built, and Aunt Cora, Sadie, and Larry got their own place. In the meantime, for about a year, we enjoyed their company in our new home."

Around this time, music entered my life. My mother needed to support us, so she went to secretarial school. According to Dorothy, she "sailed through" the course and landed a good job with the Union Carbide Company. "Things were looking up," says Dorothy. "Cora and several friends from work formed a singing group called the Carbidears, and she often sang at home. I can still hear her lively renditions of 'Mairzy Doats,' 'Swing on a Star,' 'Buttermilk Sky,' and my favorite, 'Wabash Cannonball.' "

So there I was, a small child in this strange corner of the state that my fellow Texan the late jazz guitarist Ted Dunbar called "The Crack." (I think it got that name because that section of the Texas Gulf Coast is more or less a straight line up from Corpus Christi, but Galveston has a bay—i.e., it's a crack in the coastline.) I don't remember anything about that time, but here's what Dorothy has to say about my mother: "Cora was very pretty, smart, and personable, with an attractive natural vivacity. She had sparkling brown eyes and long, dark hair, which she kept coifed in the styles of the day. Hats were important articles of everyday dress in those years." (They were important, I'm told, because when a young woman was not wearing a hat, the local sailors assumed it meant that she was a hooker.)

Dorothy continues: "Ladies who worked in offices usually kept their hats at their desks all day, as an essential part of their business ensembles. For a dollar or two, one could buy a hat base and decorate it with artificial flowers, artificial fruits, ribbons, net, or in whatever way one felt prompted by imagination. Aunt Cora's beautiful dark hair was set off with the prettiest hats in town, usually of her own creation, but Mama [that would be my Aunt Louise] told us of an Easter Sunday when Cora went hatless to church. It was really unusual then for a lady not to wear an Easter bonnet to church on Easter morning. It was an example of the freshness of Cora's ideas—she and the other women of her Sunday school class had donated their Easter bonnet money to the poor."

I can see now that I got of lot of my concern for others directly from my mother. I've always supported the underdog, always tried to be sensitive to the suffering of others and respond accordingly, exercising compassion and discretion—in other words, I've tried to be a decent human being. Even though it hasn't always worked out that way.

My mother was also resourceful. Because many materials were in short supply during the war, she developed exceptional sewing skills. She put together inexpensive clothes that looked great, and she made stuffed animals for me. She also did crochet—she was good at that kind of handwork, and one thing she gave me before she passed was a tapestry, crocheted, of the 23rd Psalm. She made it for my daughter Allegra, and it hangs on the wall of her room in her house in Florida.

Sometimes, my mother made something out of nothing. Dorothy tells this story: "Before the war, adult women's 'better' stockings were made of silk. Around the time when the U.S. entered the war, nylon was beginning to replace silk for hosiery. It was a culture shock for the ladies when silk was no longer available and nylon was diverted to the parachute factories. So, when stockings could not be obtained, Aunt Cora and other young women with pretty legs tanned them—easy in sunny Galveston—and then they painted a seam-like black line up the backs of their legs. At the time, young women also favored ankle bracelets as an expression of femininity, and I remember that Aunt Cora continued wearing them for many years. Young women in her age group wanted to look their best, just as they do today, but the effort Cora made in those unusual times was not just about looking good. It was about using one's creative talents to fight back against adversity and about making a spirited stand for a decent life."

Okay, so my background is kind of "square," but this is my family and the story of how and where I was reared. Texas is a bizarre and contradictory place, but it was my earliest environment—no Parker, Gillespie, or Ellington; that would come later. Most of all, I look back and revere and respect the kind of person my mother was—Cora May Hanson, born of Alf and Sadie Hanson, in Detroit, November 6, 1919. Bless her heart for nourishing and teaching me. She passed in July of 1999. May she rest in peace.

The next interesting development in my early life came at the end of the phase when Cora and I were just a twosome (along with Grandma Sadie). Cora met a fellow—a chemical engineer, an ex-Army Air Corps pilot who had flown 26 missions in Europe during the war. He was born in Houston in 1919, on April 7 (the same birthday as Billie Holiday and Freddie Hubbard), and he had gone to high school in Wisconsin and college in Oklahoma. His name was Gene Phillip Coryell.

Gene was about 5'10" and had dark hair, a handsome face, and a compact body—pretty much a straight-ahead "white guy." He read copiously and encouraged me to do the same. One time when I was about 12 he came into my room late at night, and I was reading something "risqué," so I hid the book under the covers. Gene told me I didn't have to do that—"I don't care what you read," he said.

Gene was a quiet man, and he had a tendency to be a bit grumpy, due to his demanding hours at work—he often worked the graveyard shift. He had been injured in a parachute jump during the war and had back problems his whole adult life, of which we children were very aware. He would occasionally tell a joke, albeit one with a sarcastic tinge, and he had a habit of drawing in his breath quickly as he reached the punch line—kind of like a cue for you to laugh. I've never heard anybody else do anything quite like that.

Gene had written a few short stories during the war, and he had a heck of a scrapbook of war photos. He had flown in a B-26 Marauder, and the most frightening photos showed the big black puffs of anti-aircraft fire (known as "flak") exploding near the airborne bombers. Gene had one photo in his collection of which he was extremely proud; it was taken during furlough, and it showed him and a couple of his buddies in a small boat—maybe a speedboat—with the entertainers Bob Hope and Jerry Colonna. Gene said that during that period near the end of the war, when the Allies knew they would win, he and his buddies drank steadily but moderately. "Just enough to keep a glow on," as he put it. That was the only time that he ever spoke about drinking alcohol.

Coryell was and still is an unusual name, and I acquired it in 1948 when Cora and Gene got married and Gene legally adopted me. My new name was Larry Van Delinder Coryell.

When I was about 12, my parents came to me and said there was something I should know. "Gene is not your real dad," my mother said. I remember replying, "Oh, yes, he is." He was the only father I had ever known—and the life lesson from this karma is very clear: family love doesn't have to come from the bloodline; it can spring from the hearts of those with whom one has a cosmic connection. I must have had a deep universal connection with Gene Coryell because, unlike most parents who want their kid to have some stable gig to "fall back" on, he simply encouraged the hell out of me to excel at what I loved—music.

I recall a night when Gene came to see me play at the House of Entertainment in Seattle, in the early '60s. The place was rockin' and swingin' with people of all creeds and colors. He looked around and saw that scene and said to me, "Hey, these people love your playing." I beamed. I think that was also the night when, as I walked up to the bandstand, a brother sitting at a table said to me, "You sure don't look like you can play." But I could. I could play—I can play—and that is the most valuable gift I've been given. It never leaves me, as long as I don't abuse it, and as long as I practice and try to play new things. Yes, I've blown it on some occasions—underestimated the situation, gotten too cocky—but I would like to think I've learned from my errors. Never rest on your laurels—that's what every mentor in my life, in and out of music, has emphasized.

But hold it—let's get back to Texas and the second major turning point of my life. The first was being adopted in '48; the second was when we made the big move to the Northwest.

# Chapter 2

## *Let's get the hell out of Texas and go someplace even more ridiculous*

In the late 1940s, Gene was selling insurance and doing what he had to do to make ends meet while he looked for work in his main field, chemical engineering. He even did a stint selling shoes at J. C. Penney's. By then, there were two Coryell children: my sister Gloria had been born in June of 1947, the same month as the noted Texas City Disaster, which is one of my first clear memories. (Another early memory, from when I was four years old, was harmonizing on "White Christmas" with Mom.)

We had moved to Texas City, which is slightly inland from Galveston, not long after my sister was born. On that June morning, I was at the dry cleaners with Mom when the explosions started. We found out later that there was some highly flammable material stored on some of the ships in the harbor. A spark had started a fire that spread quickly, and then it was just boom!—like a chain reaction, going from one ship to another. The series of explosions went on all day and into the night, and windows were blown out in houses ten miles away. Gene was among the first of the spontaneous outpouring of rescuers who headed for the scene of the disaster. He never spoke about the details, leading us kids to think that it must have been too gruesome for dissemination.

Another traumatic event from around that time was when Gloria, still a baby, got really sick. She came down with some kind of pneumonia that required a complete change in her blood, which Gene donated. Fortunately, she was only about a year-and-a-half old, so it didn't require all that much blood. The emotional part for me was seeing her confined in quarantine, in a glass enclosure, in a situation neither one of us could understand. Why couldn't I be with my sister? She was howling and crying like crazy during those visits. I never forgot that. She was in there for about a month, but when she came out she was as good as new.

As luck would have it, Gene found a new job working in atomic energy—and the position required a move up to the State of Washington. Gene went ahead of us. He had everything in order by the late summer of 1950, so we boarded a train in Houston and took off for Richland, in southeastern Washington, one of three metropolitan areas near the confluence of the Columbia and Snake rivers in what is called the Tri-Cities area.

I was seven years old and a proud Texan. Somehow, in my short life, I had become inculcated with the pride of being a son of the Lone Star State. So the move to Washington was something of a shock.

Before we left, we went from Texas City over to Houston and stayed for about a week at the home of a Canadian friend of the family, a Doctor Gardiner. It was while we were in his house that I first saw television, and all I remember was the wrestling—my first male media role models. I also saw my first escalator at a department store in Houston.

I remember Grandma Sadie accompanying us to the train in the big rail station there in Houston, but I don't remember hearing the conductor sing out, "All aboard!" But Grandma Sadie heard it, and she got off the train and went back to her home in LaMarque, and we took off.

A day or so later, in the sleeping car, my mother woke me up to show me the Rocky Mountains, thinking I'd glance at them and go back to sleep. But once I saw the mountains, I stayed up and stared at them for a long time. Texas had been very flat, so those mountains were a real eye-opener. I recall seeing Denver pass by the window, but that's about the only other clear memory I have of the journey.

We disembarked in Pendleton, Oregon. Gene was there to pick us up, and it took about two hours to drive to our new home in Richland.

The move was life-changing in the sense that I had left the South, where the warm weather had been nice and I was nearly always barefoot, for a place where there were four seasons and the winters could get severe. I loved the snow, but not the wind—riding one's bike to school in January against a hard, cold wind is not particularly pleasant. It was also an area of foothills and mountains, nothing like the flat coastal plain near Galveston. We had been near the Gulf in Texas, and in Richland we were still near water—but it was the wide, powerful Columbia River, which was just across the street from where we lived, at 1819 Hunt.

Our house was what I guess you call a ranch house—one story, no upstairs, but with a basement—with a driveway on the side and some bushes in front. The little boy who'd lived there before me had left a BB gun in my room, but it didn't work—or maybe I just couldn't get it to work. We had a rather spacious yard out back, bordered by a row of tall poplar trees, and off in the distance was Rattlesnake Mountain. Man, I was out in the sticks!

I might have been in Washington State, but I still thunk and tawked like a Texan—proud and braggin' to the bone! Plus, both Gloria and I were deeply suntanned, and I recall some of the neighbors making strange statements about our skin color—my first exposure to prejudice, I guess. Mom just laughed it off. Running around barefoot for my first seven years had made the bottoms of my feet impervious to penetration, so I got some comments about that as well. I recall some of the older children who became my friends saying, "You're from the South," because of my accent, but at that time I didn't have a clue about that.

# *Chapter 3*

*The young feller gets some exposure to music, mostly country & western, but here comes rock & roll!*

D URING THOSE EARLY YEARS in Richland, beginning in the fall of 1950, I developed a work ethic. I had a paper route and mowed lawns in return for a little bit of money; I also participated in sports like swimming, diving, baseball, football, and track rather religiously. I must have displayed some characteristics of a perfectionist; I know that I did like to work hard at whatever I did.

I also became more aware of the music around me. It really started around the time my brother, Jim, was born, in January 1952. Mom composed a song about him in his first year because he had an eye situation that need to be surgically corrected. She wrote a beautiful and sentimental melody about little brother Jim—and whenever she sang the line about "angels in heaven" knocking the "spoon right in your eye," she would burst into tears.

My main musical influence—other than what was sung around the house or at school or church—was the radio. Most of what I heard was country & western music; in the Tri-Cities, that's about all you could hear aside from really sappy pop music. I bought the single "The Naughty Lady of Shady Lane" by the Ames Brothers, and I remember Eddie Heywood had a simple, pleasant instrumental called "Canadian Sunset." I didn't know he was a black man until much later—back then, they kept that all hid.

One recording artist who stood out for me was this guitarist named Chet Atkins—his playing seemed more polished than the other instrumentalists, and he had a great fingerstyle technique. The first LP I owned was his *Finger Style Guitar*, and I must have been 15 years old when I bought it at Korten's music store in Richland, which was where I would take my first guitar lesson. The record started with "Swedish Rhapsody," and the liner notes said that Chet "played all the parts himself at one sitting," an obvious attempt to distinguish his music from the brilliant multitracked guitars of Les Paul, who was also big on the airwaves at the time. The people at RCA (Chet's label) wanted us, the audience, to know there was a big difference between their guy and Les, who was on Capitol Records.

Soon after that, I ran out and bought another Chet Atkins record called *Hi-Fi in Focus*. On that one, Chet played some material that was jazz-related—there was a solo version of "Walk, Don't Run," the great Johnny Smith composition, and his take on "Lullaby of the Leaves," played with his patented counterpoint style.

So—I was deep into the guitar thing long before I knew what jazz was. I was just taking in all the music I could get my ear on. If it moved me, I dug it—especially if it was played on the git-box.

Then rock & roll hit. It was 1955, and we were still living in Richland. I remained loyal to Texas, though, so I talked Mom into putting her three kids into the car (a Buick, I think) and driving down to Texas to visit relatives. My chauvinism as a Texan really motivated this trip—I was looking forward to being outdoors in the hot summer sun, leaping off diving boards, runnin' around and havin' fun. (Semi-naked pictures of Kim Novak were also starting to get my attention.)

That summer, as we traveled through Texas, the radio started to sound different. There was Shirley & Lee singing "Let the Good Times Roll" and Fats Domino and Elvis—yeah, Elvis. I heard this music and thought, Hey, this is some different stuff. What really grabbed me was hearing Bill Doggett's "Honky Tonk" late at night—"Part Two," with the long sax solo doing the call and response. And the Billy Butler guitar solo from "Part One" would soon be "required reading" for all the guitarists in my neck of the woods.

I didn't realize it at the time, but it was African-American, or African-American-influenced, music that was most appealing to me. It didn't matter initially, because I simply loved the music. Later on, I came to understand the history that spawned the culture responsible for the unique qualities of the music that had so deeply touched my life. That was to be an important part of my training, as it were, and I eventually came to see that (happily) I was not alone. There was a whole slew of cats—my contemporaries—out there digging B.B. King and James Brown and the like. And Dave Lewis—I'll tell you more about Dave Lewis later.

Back in Richland, I was in high school. I did well in English and Spanish, and I worked on the school newspaper. I was into sports, too—I was a pole vaulter on the track and field team, and did pretty well. I set a school record of 13 feet 2⅜ inches that lasted a few years, until it was broken by a vaulter using a more springy pole. I made a real study of it, getting my hands on everything to do with vaulting, and even kept a diary of my track exploits in my junior and senior years.

When I was about 14, I started looking through these catalogues that would come to our house and noticing the guitars. The catalogues were from Sears and Montgomery Ward. They had all kinds of stuff in there, but I would skip the clothes and tools and whatnot and go straight to the musical instruments. I think my first guitar was a solid-body black Silvertone that came from the Sears catalogue. (Those Silvertone guitars, I would later learn, were made by Danelectro). I ordered that guitar and an amplifier and waited and waited for my merchandise to come. After a couple of weeks—that's how long they said it would take to get out to Washington State from Chicago—I started calling the warehouse every day. Where's my guitar and amp? After what seemed to be an interminable amount of time, the boxes finally arrived. I took my new guitar and amp into the back room at 1819 Hunt and played "Whispering" all day, with the tremolo on. I was overjoyed that the amp had tremolo—I loved that sound.

Soon after that, I started studying jazz guitar with the teacher at Korten's, John LaChappelle. I went in for my first lesson with that hideous little solid-body Silvertone. My mom had been involved in a local civic organization's production of Pajama Game, which was performed at Chief Joseph Junior High School; I had seen the show, so I asked John LaChappelle to teach me its signature song, "Hey There."

John devised a beautiful chord solo for "Hey There" that I can almost remember by heart—but the hallmark of that lesson was the chord diagrams he wrote out. I marveled at the beauty of a performance piece that would have a different chord for nearly every melody note.

By this time I must have been around 16, because I remember being able to drive to my guitar lessons. There was another guitar teacher at Korten's named Danny Love; he was a wheat inspector in his "day gig," but he taught Chet Atkins-style at the music store. I enjoyed studying with Danny very much—I loved trying to do that Chet Atkins style, playing the bass part along with the upper chords and melody, but I really couldn't get the hang of it. I found myself gravitating more toward the jazz chord-melody way of playing—and, from John, I learned how to play scales that went all the way across the neck. The first scale John taught me in that way was C major, starting with C on the eighth fret of the sixth string, up one octave to the C on the tenth fret of the fourth string, then up another octave to the eighth fret of the first string. I recall working out a picking sequence for myself and calling John at home one night to tell him that I'd discovered a way to pick the two-octave sequence by not using strictly alternate picking, which was what he had recommended. So—I was beginning to adapt to playing in my own way, in my own style.

Another thing John did was take me to Kennewick one evening to hear this guy on violin he was backing up, Joe Venuti. I had no idea who he was, but if John said it was important, it was important. I don't remember much about the evening except that Joe Venuti could definitely play his instrument—but that was about it for me at the time. John was in the trio that played behind Venuti; John told me that Venuti's manager came up onstage and told him, "You better bring Joe on pretty soon, while he's still able to play." I guess maybe Joe might have been hittin' the sauce—I don't know, but later on in my life I was able to identify with that scenario. . . .

When I was 16 or 17, I bought a sunburst '59 Fender Stratocaster that had belonged to a guitarist named Johnny Hensley for $330 at Korten's. What a guitar! I should have kept it, but I had no idea that Strats were going to become collectors' items. Soon after I got it, a group of young musicians came down from the booming metropolis of Yakima to audition me for their progressive rock & roll group, the Checkers. It was progressive because they had a blind piano player named Mike Mandel. He strolled into Korten's and proceeded to blow my mind—a cat my age who could really play. He ran through one of the current hits, "What'd I Say" by Ray Charles, and I noticed he was playing it in the key of E. I thought it was in F, but Mike confirmed it was indeed in E, and from this I learned how the piano had its own personality for blues and funk. E was so much funkier than F, and the sound was "sharper" (the timbre, not the pitch)—I dug that.

The guys liked the fact that I could play Chuck Berry's solo from "Oh, Carol" and the guitar part from the Nat Cole hit "Send for Me." I didn't need guitar lessons to learn any of that popular music—that was stuff I could learn simply from the records, or from hearing it on the radio. Then I laid a little bit of Duane Eddy on 'em and followed that with the solo from a Connie Francis record, "Lipstick on Your Collar." (Many years later, I learned that the great George Barnes did that solo.)

I also played some of James Burton's solos from Ricky Nelson's recordings. Burton was one of the first guitarists to use banjo strings (lighter gauge) in order to bend the strings more, getting a sound almost like a steel guitar. Later on, Mandel called me from his home in Yakima and raved about how much he liked string bending using those light-gauge strings. Banjo strings were the replacement of choice at that time; we didn't have the comprehensive array of strings in all kinds of gauges that are available to guitarists today.

I told the Checkers about how I was also listening to jazz players like Tal Farlow—no string bending to speak of in his style. The reason I knew about Tal was because of John LaChappelle. During the course of studying with him, we got kind of tight, and I'd go to his house. He kept his best guitar at home—it was a big archtop Gibson with three pickups, an ES-5 model. It was very impressive to see a real jazz guitar like that.

While I was at John's house I looked over his record collection, and he lent me some of his jazz guitar discs—Les Paul, Johnny Smith, Barney Kessel, and Tal

Farlow. I played those LPs on my record player and tried to take off solos from each guitarist. I did pretty well with Les, Johnny, and Barney—but Tal was another story. His lines were too complicated to transcribe completely—he played very fast. His chord style was a bit different from the others, too; he would (I later learned) tune his sixth string down to A for ballads like "Autumn in New York." Tal also played—and John taught me how to do it—artificial harmonics. I was playing them was I was 16 or 17, and this would serve me well as I developed my style. Without knowing that technique, I never would have understood how to play in the Lenny Breau style, with its alternation of normal notes with artificial harmonics.

I was trying to cover all the musical bases in hopes I might be able to work as a studio musician someday. John LaChappelle had started to hip me to the studio scene. We'd hang out in Korten's and look at the records that had come in. I recall John pointing to a player on an album cover and saying, "Hey, I think that's Kenny Burrell." I was also learning about studio players from reading the liner notes on the back of the albums—there would be references to, for example, Barney Kessel, doing a serious jazz project as opposed to studio dates, which, I was able to discern, were a way to augment one's income as musician.

To become a studio player, I would have to be able to play many styles, read music well, and adapt quickly to any musical "short order" situation. I had heard that good jazzers like Barney, Howard Roberts, and Dennis Budimir were working as studio musicians in L.A.—and that sounded good to me.

Well, to make a long story short—the Checkers hired me. My first gig was at a school dance in White Swan, Washington (near Yakima), for which I was paid the grand total of five dollars. I drove Gene Coryell's late-model Chevy Biscayne up to White Swan that winter evening, played the gig, and on my way back slid off the road into a ditch. I had the radio on at the time, and I remember they were playing a new instrumental from Santo & Johnny of "Sleepwalk" fame. (Forty years later, I checked with the real Johnny—Messina or Farina, I think; Dick Clark would know—and he said there was no follow-up to "Sleepwalk." How weird is that!)

I was scared but unhurt. And, fortunately, the car wasn't damaged—there was just some dirt on the bumper. Somehow I got it out of the ditch unscathed and finished the drive home. I remember that Gene asked me about the dirt the next day. I don't know what I said, but I don't think I told him the truth—I think my plan was not to say anything.

About this time, I snagged my first girlfriend—or, I should say, she snagged me. She was Georgia Derrick, who lived in Pasco. I would drive over to her house, about a 20-mile trip, and after a while, needless to say, one thing led to another.

We'd take the Biscayne and go "parking" in the Welch's vineyards when we were supposed to be at church. It was during one of these newly-discovering-love soirées that I picked up radio station KSL from Salt Lake City. A DJ named Bowen was playing some great jazz, including tracks by this new guitarist on the national scene, Wes Montgomery. I was flabbergasted.

# Chapter 4

*Not-so-little Larry gets himself in some hot water,*
*but 40 years later all's well*

NOT ALL THAT WENT ON in Gene's car was music appreciation, and one day Georgia passed out in her kitchen. That was mystifying to me until she told me what had caused it: she was pregnant. Here I was, a junior in high school, and my girlfriend was pregnant. Oh, what a scandal.

I was also starting to go out on the road with the Checkers, and I skipped school for about a week while we were on a trip that took us down to Phoenix. My mother freaked out. I didn't call her for quite a few days—it was the most hurtful thing I ever did to her. I had to make tremendous amends to Cora after that—and Georgia's dad was furious with me, too, as you might imagine.

My best friend, John Day, drove me up to Yakima so I could tell a minister what was going on—so much shame. The clergyman got in touch with Georgia's parents, George and Lila, and there was a big meeting at our house. The upshot was, rather than have me marry Georgia, her parents sent her to live with relatives in Missouri. After the child was born—a girl—she gave it up for adoption. This was difficult for everybody, especially Georgia. I used my small paychecks from the Checkers to pay Georgia's expenses, and I also wrote her letters faithfully, addressed to her parents' house. They (understandably) didn't pass them along.

For 41 years I wondered if that baby was okay. I never knew anything about her, and I didn't have any luck trying to find her through the Internet. I lived with guilt, shame, and remorse—until, finally, after much prayer, I got an e-mail one day when I was in Seoul, South Korea. The e-mail was from a social worker who worked for the State of Missouri, and she asked if it would be all right for them to give my e-mail address to a woman named Annie White, who was my daughter. I said yes.

I received a beautiful collection of photographs of Annie with her husband, her parents, and other relatives. There was one picture of her dancing for joy at the Camden Yards baseball park in Baltimore; I really liked that one and was amazed by Annie's stunning resemblance to her mother.

I got to meet Annie in December 2002, when I had a gig in the D.C. area. Later on, Annie and her husband came down to visit me where I live in Florida. My son Julian also came out from L.A., and we had a few days of jamming music and playing tennis and golf. All the guilt and shame I'd felt since 1961—gone. Annie said she was going to cut back on her work—she had a job in the U.S. Senate—so she could concentrate more on her music. Her singing is especially promising, and with a few top-notch vocal lessons—hey, you never know. We'll see what happens. I support her 100 percent.

Finding Annie was unlike any other revelation I've experienced. Things really do work out if you have faith in the positive aspect of this mystical experience called life.

Larry's mother, Cora Coryell.

A young Cora being shown to the new colt by her great-uncle Paschel. This farm is still there today and owned by Larry's cousin Dorothy.

Gene Coryell, Larry's stepfather, in the cockpit of his WWII B-26 Marauder, *Spare Parts*, and his crew.

Larry as a one-year-old, and handprints from his baby book.

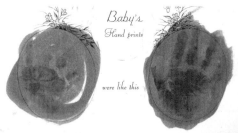

The Coryell family: Larry (top left) at 15 or 16; Gene, stepfather (top right); sister Gloria (bottom left); brother Jim (center); and Larry's mom, Cora (bottom right).

Larry's first guitars (1958) and his first band at Richland High School, July 1958. Larry is at left.

# Pasco Wins Subdistrict

## Col-Hi Ace Sets Vault Standard

By HAROLD CARR

Pasco provided a big surprise and Richland pole vaulter Larry Coryell turned in the individual heroics yesterday as the Bulldogs topped the field at the Yakima Valley Subdistrict Track and Field meet at Bomber Bowl.

Coach Bill Mayberry's Bulldogs, who hadn't won a track meet this spring, used its depth in the hurdles, pole vault and broad jump along with eight second places to spring its upset victory over its rivals Richland and Kennewick.

Pasco scored 75½ points, Richland 66½, Kennewick 54, Prosser 15, Kiona-Benton 4 and Connell 3.

CORYELL ATTRACTED the most attention as he vaulted 13 feet, 2⅜ inches to obliterate his previous Bomber Bowl record of 12-8½ and continue his superiority in the Yakima Valley district.

The annual subdistrict was noteworthy for below-par field marks and slow times on a loose track. Richland's reorganized mile relay team, running together in competition for the first time, turned in the best Valley time of the season with a fast clocking of 3:37.7.

Richland's Jack Glover ran the low hurdles in 20.8 seconds, which equals his previous best for the season. The effort is only two-tenths of a second behind the top Yakima Valley mark.

Kennewick, which was expected to battle to the wire for the subdistrict title, lost important points

CORYELL SETS MARK — Richland's Larry Coryell broke his own Bomber Bowl pole vaulting record and continued his lead as the Yakima Valley's top vaulter yesterday at the subdistrict track meet in Richland with a vault of 13 feet, 2⅜ inches. Coryell's performance highlighted the meet, and was the only new record established.

In the broad jump, high jump and discus and couldn't make them up in the track events.

PASCO JUMPED TO an early lead as Rich Jimerson grabbed first in the high hurdles, and Pe Lorain and Ray Avery pulled first and second in the 440. Wi nine events completed the thr Tri-City schools were separated only three points.

Coryell's performance creat the most excitement and attrac ed a large crowd around the po vault pit. The hard-worki Bomber senior missed once at feet, then easily cleared the ba Coryell set his new mark on h first try at 13-3 (later dropped 13-2⅜ after measuring). He mis ed three attempts to clear 13

Glover poured on the steam the second leg of the mile rel to get Richland its lead ov Kennewick, and the Bombers ne er relinquished it. Miles Wils led the Bombers' Kurt Johnson the first lap, and Chuck Thu moved 15 yards in front of Glov soon after the first exchange.

GLOVER LET THUOT set t pace around the first turn, sh by him on the back stretch a finished 20 yards ahead. Hig stepping Dave Warren increas Richland's margin on the thi 440 leg, and Jim Demand, althou hard pressed by the Lions' S Francisco, finished strong to i sure the Richland win.

Kennewick's Ed Alden won bo the 100 and 220. The century tu ed into a photo-finish as Ald won it with a lunge at the fini line to nose cut Richland's D Ott.

The first and second-place w ners in the track events, the top three finishers in the field com petition, and the best two relay teams now advance to the Yak ima Valley District Meet Satur day at Pasco's Edgar Brown Memorial Stadium.

Larry sets a pole-vaulting record of 13 feet 2⅜ inches.

High school graduation (1961).

Georgia, Larry's first girlfriend and mother of daughter Annie.

Georgia (right) and Annie.

Zach, Larry's third grandchild; son of daughter Annie.

"The Flames," 1961. Larry is on the far right.

Larry and Steve "The Count" Marcus, late '60s.

Larry as a member of the Gary Burton Quartet at the Berlin Philharmonic, 1967.

Larry at the Village Gate.

Central Park, June 1973. Notice that Larry's belt buckle is off to one side, done on purpose to protect the Super 400. Also in the far background is Mike Mandel's girlfriend, the late Mona Leibowitz.

Larry playing with the Eleventh House Band, Vancouver, B.C., 1973.

Mike Mandel, an early influence on Larry's musical awareness, pictured here as a member of the Eleventh House Band.

The Eleventh House Band, Europe, 1976, with Teru Masa Hino on trumpet.

Westport,
Connecticut,
1976.

Larry on a German television show with Airto Moreira (not shown) in 1985.

# Chapter 5

*A crewcut Bill Cullen look-alike moves from the*
*Tri-Cities to Seattle and discovers the blues*

I GRADUATED FROM HIGH SCHOOL in 1961, and the next day I moved to the booming metropolis of Yakima and joined a rival band of the Checkers called the Flames. My bandmates were mostly Mexican cats. I "knocked apples" during the day (you could see the snow-capped peaks of the Cascades to the west), and at night, mostly on weekends, we gigged. I was a working musician—playing the hits, rock & roll, and an occasional original.

I had been accepted by the University of Washington, so that summer in Yakima was my transition from Richland to the even more booming metropolis of Seattle, where I showed up as a college freshman in the fall of 1961.

Where I had lived in Richland was a desert environment—brown and dry— but Seattle was green and wet. It was quite a change, and I was also stunned by the beautiful UW campus, with its red-brick neo-Gothic buildings set in a beautifully designed arrangement that blended architecture and nature. In the spring, apple and cherry trees bloomed on the quad, and behind it all there were amazing vistas of Mt. Rainier to the southeast.

It was a great place for learning, but I was more interested in bebop than biology and sociology and all the other things that freshmen were supposed to be studying. Even so, at first I did well with my academics. I also got a job working as a houseboy at a sorority in what was known as "Greek Row." As you entered this area, the first house on the left had been the home of the Brothers Four, a folk group that had made some successful recordings; as I recall, one of their big hits had been "Green Leaves of Summer" in the early '60s. Not that I was interested in folk music—I would tell anyone who would listen that "folk music is for folks." It was jazz I was after.

So there I was, living in the basement of a sorority with another houseboy named Leo. Leo was from Utah, and he was a jazz fan. He knew about Bowen at KSL. Sometimes, when the drawing room was empty, Leo and I would go upstairs, and I would play the grand piano. One day Leo said, "Hey, you sound like Les McCann." I didn't know who Les McCann was, but it sounded like a compliment.

Leo and I would talk about jazz, and one time he said, "You're good, Larry, but you'll never be good enough to play with somebody like Dave Brubeck." At the time, that didn't mean much to me—except that I felt challenged to practice more. And many years later, I did get to play with Dave Brubeck (and his sons, too).

Now I'll tell you about Dave Lewis. When I was still in high school, we would make forays to Seattle now and then, and I had met the guys in a band called the Dynamics. They didn't care much for the band I was in at the time, but they liked my playing, and I figured a gig would be waiting for me after I got to Seattle. The Dynamics' piano player, Terry Afdem, was one of the first musicians to turn me on to using seventh chords in places where I hadn't thought of using them—and I realized later that Jerry got the idea from Dave Lewis.

Now, these guys called me a "cowpuncher" because I was from "east of the mountains." They knew I could play, but they wanted me to go to Birdland on Capitol Hill, in the black district, to hear the Dave Lewis group so I could get hip to the sophisticated music in Seattle. So I went down there with them one night, and as we drove to the club, they were all talking about this Dave Lewis tune called "Jive Ass Terry," which was dedicated to his guitar player. I was thinking, Okay, what's so great about this tune? When we got to the club, the band was playing this very tune—called "JAJ" for short—as we walked in.

I was destroyed. It was so R&B and so funky—only seventh chords—plus it had a bridge that went through the circle of fifths (or is it fourths?). I remember thinking at the time that Dave's music reminded me of a cross between Chuck Berry and Ray Charles (once again, a sign I was getting most of my music through radio), but it had an added quality that was derived from the Northwest. This latter characteristic can't really be verbalized—you have to hear it, you have to feel it.

I know now that I was fortunate to immerse myself, like a baptism, in the African-American culture that was developing so fast at that time. There were so many names, so many good recording artists, like Ike and Tina Turner, John Lee Hooker, and, of course, B.B. King—but there were also James Brown, Bobby "Blue" Bland, Earl King, Mongo Santamaria, and a new star, a 12-year-old kid named Stevie Wonder.

A few months later, the Dynamics recorded "JAJ" for the Bolo label, and it became a regional hit. I played a rather simple solo over the blues form (I didn't improvise on the bridge; I wasn't ready for that circle of fifths), and we used Terry's younger brother, Jeff, on baritone sax to double the bass line. Voila! Pretty soon, we were hearing our record on the radio—a big thrill for me, at the age of 19, especially since I was putting myself through college working as a lowly houseboy in a Jewish sorority, Phi Sigma Sigma (you're no enigma).

On the flipside of the Dynamics' "JAJ" single, there was a small sign of what lay ahead: it was a version of "Moonlight in Vermont," sung by Jimmy Hanna (whose father owned Bolo), with me playing a few jazz chords.

For my sophomore year, I moved into a dormitory. I still had my passion for music, but I was also a journalism major and working on the college daily—doing pretty well, until a couple of things happened. The first was that I realized I definitely wanted to be a musician, not a journalist. The second was my introduction to drugs. The latter was no small event—especially since, up to the point when I first got high, I had thought that drugs were bad. That's the way I'd been raised.

Due to the influence of a couple of musicians whom I considered "hip"—and in spite of my Protestant upbringing regarding the evils of drugs and alcohol—I acquiesced to smoking grass, because I was tempted into thinking I could play better if I got high. And, boy, did I want to play better! The first few times I smoked, nothing happened. But on the day when marijuana's reality-altering properties finally kicked in, I happened to be on the street in the Capitol Hill district of Seattle, and lo and behold two girls from my high school class who were also going to college in Seattle happened to saunter by. They took one look at me and asked, "Larry, are you drunk?" I thought that was the funniest thing I had ever heard in my life. That was my "welcome to the club" moment.

After that first high, and under the continuing influence of the cats who turned me on, I became a big proponent of the druggy lifestyle. I would tell anyone who'd listen that grass was a good thing. As a musician, I felt it helped me. I thought I understood jazz better while high—I thought the drugs opened the door to the essence of the music; I was able to really feel what Bird, Coltrane, Miles, Monk, Hampton Hawes, Art Tatum, and Ornette Coleman were communicating.

As I write this, I see the total fallacy of this attitude about drugs and music. But at the time—I was 21 years old—it became my philosophy. I started hanging around with my fellow users, cats who were hip because they got high and were into music. More and more, I neglected my studies and spent time in pursuit of mind-bending chemicals. Pills soon came into the picture, and LSD would be waiting for me when I got to New York City.

As a result of this decadent regimen, I started screwing up in my daily life. The culmination of that was an article I wrote for the university daily about an economics lecture, where I got all the facts ass-backwards! I was stoned. It might be funny now, but back then there was no small amount of criticism hurled at me (deservedly) by the newspaper bosses on the first floor of the Communications Building.

Ironically, the same issue of the paper that had my ass-backwards article also contained a story about me as a budding jazz guitarist. I was pictured with a really nice Guild electric archtop, which I soon sold or traded on my way to a Gibson ES-175, which I then sold or traded to buy a Gibson Super 400.

My days as a straight-life, middle-class, goody-goody college student came to an end as my drug usage progressed. By this time, I was playing in a number of bands; I was still with the Dynamics, but I had also joined a kind of lounge band, consisting of slightly older cats who got good gigs and were able to play standard tunes. That band was called Chuck Mahaffay & the Individuals, and the attraction there was that Jerome Grey, my jazz teacher, had played in the band. That was good training for me. I was also sitting in with an after-hours band led by a pianist/arranger named Overton Berry—and that was a kick. Overton was the first musician I had ever heard use the word "concept" in talking about music, and that blew my mind.

# *Chapter 6*

*Gabor comes to town—"Where'd you get the grass?"*

Cats from out of town who were appearing at Charlie Puzo's Penthouse would come down to the club where I was working with Overton Berry's band, the House of Entertainment on First Avenue, and I heard some amazing jam sessions. One night drummer/bandleader Chico Hamilton came down to sit in, and he brought his bassist, a young talent named Albert Stinson. Albert was from L.A., and his playing was reminiscent of the legendary Scott LaFaro, the great bassist who had been in the Bill Evans Trio. I had never seen a bassist play like that, with so much facility and so many phrases played in the upper register.

Later, in 1969, when I was living in New York, Albert would join my band, but his stay would be brief because he died during our first gig, in Boston, from an overdose of narcotics. Albert was a great bass player and a great guy—he was very humble and totally dedicated to the music. When he was with Chico, the band also included the saxophonist Charles Lloyd and Gabor Szabo on guitar.

Gabor was Hungarian—he had come over to the U.S. after the Soviet crackdown in 1956. Gabor loved to say that his earliest guitar influence was Roy Rogers, because he had learned about the States by watching cowboy movies. After he arrived, he attended Berklee College of Music in Boston and started gigging around. Gabor told me that early on he wanted to play like Tal Farlow, but as time went on he became more interested in finding his own voice. I remember standing outside the Penthouse (I was underage), looking through a hole in the wall at Gabor onstage. He was playing a Martin folk guitar with a DeArmond pickup, soloing in a way I had never heard before. It was boppish, but there were none of the usual jazz clichés—and he used the open strings, ringing free with other single notes, to get a sitar-like effect. It was exotic and unique.

The crowd of players I was hanging out with all dug Gabor's originality— and his personality. He had that Hungarian accent to go with a Bohemian bent, and he seemed to be an easygoing guy. We asked him over to our houseboat on Lake Union, just to hang. There was my roommate Rich Dangel (guitarist with the Fabulous Wailers), trumpeter Mark Doubleday (later to play with Mike Bloomfield in the

Electric Flag), Gabor, and me. The first thing we did was get Gabor high on grass. He got the full thrust of that, and in a few minutes he was serenely plastered. Then he said, in that inimitable Dracula-like accent, "Where'd you get the grass?" We thought that was hilarious—we hadn't been around too many Hungarian hipsters. We cracked up.

After we'd settled into this jovial mood, we got out our instruments and I asked Gabor what chords he played for Charles Lloyd's "Forest Flower." He showed me, and what got me was that his chords contained only the essential notes—for example, tonic, third, and seventh for a major-seventh or minor-seventh chord. Also, he chose positions a bit higher on the neck than usual, to get a different sound for these chords.

Some guitarists didn't like his sound so much, but I dug it. Moreover, I listened carefully to his musical philosophy—he had very specific and clear ideas. For example, he told me (as if to help correct my current direction) that the music came first, the instrument second. He looked at my Super 400 and said, "You're playing the Cadillac of guitar"—the point being, I think, that one's sound should come from within, not from the particular instrument. He also shared his approach to ballad playing: he said he would learn the lyrics in addition to the melody and chords, so he could interpret the tune better.

I never forgot the principles that Gabor laid on me, or the impact of his playing. When I had seen Gabor and Albert play "What's New" at the club (viewed through that hole in the wall), the emotional depth of the performance had blown my mind. I couldn't bring myself to record "What's New" until 2002, because I felt I hadn't really understood the lyrics until then. (I also loved the way Johnny Smith did it, so my version on *Cedars of Avalon* is a tribute to both those influences from my youth.) Where would we be without these heartfelt influences? Bereft of any depth, for sure.

Gabor died quite a few years ago. He did have a fondness for drugs, and I've been told he eventually drank himself to death. It was sad to hear he was gone, but when I think of Gabor—especially that day on the houseboat—I get happy. When I go to Budapest, I always visit his grave, pray for his repose, and leave one of my picks on his gravestone as a gesture of respect.

As my sophomore year progressed, I went from student to ex-student in short order. All I wanted to do was learn jazz, be around jazz musicians, and do what jazz musicians did—which was, I thought, get high and hang out and play the fool.

Bad perception! But that's what I thought it meant to be a jazz musician, and that misperception stayed with me for a long time—many lessons that I would need to learn were ahead of me. Little did I know what the real deal was. They talk about "payin' dues" and say that's how you get "soul," but from the standpoint of my life as it is now, I see that we are always payin' dues—it's a continuous process. And, most important, it's not about getting high and playing the fool. The music has to come first.

In the midst of all this half-learning and mis-learning, at least I was sincere about the music. I knew I could play a little bit, but I knew very well that I was a long way from really playing. This became evident when bands from the East would come through Seattle—especially ones like Wes Montgomery with the Montgomery Brothers, Dizzy Gillespie with James Moody and Kenny Barron, Cannonball Adderley with his brother Nat and Joe Zawinul, and the great Stan Getz with Gary Burton on vibes. Also, in 1964 or '65, Randy Brecker came out to the University of Washington for a summer program. We met and hung out, and one afternoon at the Penthouse jam session he walked onstage with his trumpet. They called "Nardis," and my mind was blown—somebody my age playing that well. Randy later told me he had never played that tune before—could have fooled me!

Hearing all of these heavyweights made me realize that I had to get out of Seattle. Plus, I wasn't having much luck at relationships with the opposite sex. I felt as if I was somehow cursed in the area of love in Seattle, so the idea of changing locations for musical reasons also held out the promise of an improvement in my ability to attain more rewarding experiences with the ladies. It was going to be either L.A. or New York. After a brief trip down to Los Angeles, where it seemed that very little was happening—especially because I drove down there with a bassist who loved cough syrup—I decided to go to New York City, alone.

Moving to New York was a fantasy at first, but it became a real possibility as other musicians started to tell me that I was "the best guitarist in town." I didn't put much stock in that—I didn't think I was the best at anything, but I did think about what the jazz environment of New York could offer me. The best players in the world were there.

The problem was my naïveté. My more experienced and wiser musician friends could see that my drinking-and-drugging lifestyle was going to be a liability. In New York, it's really better to be sober. The rule there (as I would find out) is "take care of business," and if you can't t-c-b, brother, heaven help you. You may not be fortunate enough to have someone do it for you, especially at the beginning of your career. I was 22 and sincerely thought it was my destiny to move to some big city jazz scene because one of my heroes, Barney Kessel, had done it when he was about the same age. Barney had left Oklahoma for L.A., so (it seemed to me) I should leave Seattle for New York.

But I would need to save some bread, which I did on a gig—my first as a leader—at the Embers in West Seattle. I had an organ trio and lived in a rather Spartan apartment just up the hill from the club. (Of course, "Spartan" in Seattle was, and still is, "lap of luxury" compared to New York.) I bought a blue VW beetle on time from the local dealer, and I was in business. I even had a dog, Benny, although he was later dropped off at my parents' home in Tennessee as I made my way to the Big Apple.

# *Chapter 7*

*Larry stows away and meets the great Wes Montgomery*

While I was doing the bread-saving thing, I had an opportunity to meet Wes Montgomery, who had been invited for a private cruise on Lake Washington. I'm not sure who invited him, but Seattle was like that. There were patrons of jazz, and some of them had a little bread—and they were very hip. I found out about this special event from the mother of Pete Borg, who was the bassist in the Dynamics. Her name was Marwayne Leipzig. She was a great gal, loved music, cared about musicians—and she was like a surrogate mom to me when I was living in Seattle.

The cruise featured vibist Elmer Gill and pianist Jerome Gray (we called him Jerry at that time); they would play for the pleasure of the Montgomery Brothers and the other passengers. I stowed away down in the hold, with my guitar, and waited until we were out in the middle of Lake Washington before I came up on deck. I found Wes and was all over him—I told him how great he was, and then I played his solo from "West Coast Blues," very poorly but with respect. He seemed to dig it. He even took my guitar and pick and proceeded to play in that fashion (he normally played with his thumb, sans plectrum), just for kicks.

While we were talking, Wes shared a detail about improvising: he said that he envisioned each note "a fraction of a fraction of a second" before he played it. I never forgot that. He also said he didn't like any of the records he'd made, but he did like the one he'd just done, *Full House,* which was recorded in Berkeley, California, with "Miles's rhythm section." He was very pleased that drummer Jimmy Cobb, pianist Wynton Kelly, and bassist Paul Chambers had played with him. Saxophonist Johnny Griffin was also on that date. It was a live performance, and I have to agree with Wes that, more often than not, the live stuff makes better jazz than the studio efforts. He even played for me his original, the title tune, "Full House." The memory of that day on the boat still makes me say, "Wow!"

Jerome Gray, who was playing piano on that cruise, was my teacher. He showed me the details and subtleties of playing jazz, and he really encouraged me. I'm not sure how long I studied with Jerry; I tried to make every lesson, but I didn't always succeed, which bugged him (understandably). Jerry had a no-nonsense approach to working with me—we dug right into things like time feel, odd time signatures, and composing. He didn't mess around, and he had some strong opinions about jazz, which was good for me at the time. I needed a mentor with strong feelings about the music.

Just before I left for New York City, we played at a friend's house—just the two of us. That's another golden memory for me. I'm still in contact with Jerome—he's still a mentor, and as his disciple I have to check in with him every now and then to return to the basics. I think that's important for all artists in all fields of creativity.

That friend whose house we played at, by the way, was bassist Chuck Metcalf. He used to have jam sessions at his beautiful home in Seattle, late at night after the clubs closed, and all the national acts would come over—what a great thing that was for an aspiring player like me. I met so many cats there, like Gerry Mulligan, the Jazz Crusaders, a great pianist from L.A. named Mike Melvoin, the bassist Victor Sproles, and many others—I can't remember them all.

What I do remember from those sessions was the camaraderie among the musicians. This was another world—an esoteric universe of players who understood the language of jazz. Chuck knew Ron Carter, so when I did my first gig with Chico Hamilton in Philly in 1966, with Ron on bass, I told Ron I was from Seattle, and we talked about Chuck. Several years later Chuck would move to New York, and we worked opposite each other at the Village Gate one time, when he was with Dexter Gordon, and I was doing a solo.

As I was finishing up my time in Seattle, I was jamming one weekend afternoon at the Penthouse, and Dave Bailey, the drummer with Gerry Mulligan, heard me. He recommended me to John Handy, a Mingus alumnus, for a new group he was forming. Ridiculous as it seems, I turned down the gig because I was set on going to New York and Handy was based in the San Francisco Bay Area. As it turned out, he hired a hell of a guitarist, Jerry Hahn, and Handy's quintet was the hit of the 1965 Monterey Jazz Festival. The recording of their set, *Live at Monterey* on Columbia, was trend-setting because it featured the guitar a lot, and Jerry was playing some forward-looking music. Their version of "Spanish Lady" is still a classic.

Being in John Handy's group was not my destiny, but as soon as I got to New York I looked up Dave Bailey and expressed my gratitude. He said my playing had reminded him of Grant Green. What a compliment—George Benson had just been in Seattle with Jack MacDuff, and George was raving about Grant. I had told George that my man was Kenny Burrell; George said Kenny was beyond cool, he was great, but that I should really check out Grant—which I would soon do in Gotham.

# *Chapter 8*

*Leaving Seattle—finally—and driving to New York in that blue Volkswagen, thinking about Kenny Burrell and Grant Green*

AFTER I FINISHED UP MY RUN at the Embers, I took the money I'd saved and stuck it in my pocket. Then I grabbed the dog, my two amps (an Ampeg and a Magnatone), and my prized Super 400 and crammed everything into the VW. It was the second week of August 1965, and I was on my way.

It was a gorgeous day—blue sky, no clouds, and a bright sun. I drove over the floating bridge that connects Seattle to Mercer Island and headed east. As I drove toward the mountain passes that take you up and over the Cascade range and into "the rest of America," I felt sad, very sad, to be leaving such a beautiful place. I must be crazy, I thought, to leave this paradise and roll the dice for my shot as a jazz player. But something deep inside told me I had to do it. So there I was, starting on a cross-country journey—and with virtually no grass. I hadn't had time to score; all I had were some sticks and stems that I ground up and smoked in a corncob pipe. I had an orange Dexedrine tab or two to help me keep going, and I got to Denver in about a day and a half. I stayed at Bruce Horiuchi's parents' house—lucky for me. Bruce was my dorm-mate from my sophomore year at UW. He was also a budding jazz guitarist. I stayed in Bruce's room because he was out of town, and I noticed in his record collection a Chico Hamilton album called *A Different Journey*, and there was a Charles Lloyd composition on it titled "One Sheridan Square." The liner notes said that is where Charles lived in New York.

I met Buddy Miles in Denver. What a drummer, what a guy—we met when I was making the rounds of the organ-trio gigs in town, and we started jamming. We played up a storm for a couple of days, and then I had to push eastward. I found Denver to be a really cool town, and I never forgot the day of my departure. It was late morning or early afternoon, and the weather was really beautiful. Buddy was standing on his front porch, saying "goodbye" and "hope we can hit it again"—little did I know that in a few months he'd be joining Wilson Pickett's band, and I'd see him in New York, under much different circumstances.

The drive from out of Denver was bittersweet because I kept thinking I should just stay there for a while and maybe start a band with Buddy Miles. . . . that would have been memorable, to say the least. But it wasn't to be: Buddy Miles was headed for—down the road of music destiny— an encounter with Jimi Hendrix. So off I went, heading due east, sloping down the mid-Colorado plateau towards Kansas and beyond. I'd been across the country before but never alone—I felt like Charles Lindbergh flying across the Atlantic all alone for the first time. I entered the Great Plains and started picking up powerful-signal AM radio stations like one out of Oklahoma City that was blaring Lonnie Mack's "Memphis" in rotation at the time. The other songs that were dominating the airwaves were "Hang on Sloopy" (with guitarist Rick Derringer) and Bob Dylan's "Like a Rolling Stone." Of the latter there was something out of the ordinary, a break with traditional radio. It was music unique to our generation. I really didn't care for the musicality of "Stone" per se—it was folky, rocky, sloppy—but the message was new.

I stopped off in Oak Ridge, Tennessee, to see my family and to drop off Benny with my brother, Jim. My mother gave me one of her "utterly deadly Southern pecan pies" to take with me when I started out of Tennessee for New York. I drove most of the day and stopped in the middle of nowhere—a place called Hungry Mother, Virginia—and pulled off the side of the highway and ate practically all of the damn pie. I felt some sadness as well, knowing I was out here in life's no-man's land, totally on my own—but the pie did help, and the radio stations along the way up through Maryland and Virginia continued to blast '60s rock & roll music.

I stayed the night of September 2nd in a little motel near Harrisburg, Pennsylvania, wondering when I was going to finally hear some jazz music—I certainly wasn't getting it from AM radio! Interestingly enough, when I got to New York City and was going up East Side Drive for the first time in my life, I turned on the radio (that was a strange feeling, hearing radio in NYC—how different was it going to be?), and the DJ started to spin a record and said, "This is the number one song in the country"—it was "The In Crowd" by Ramsey Lewis. I said to myself, Hey—that's a jazz musician, but he's not so esoteric that he can't reach the masses—that's cool!

# Chapter 9

*Uh oh, this is really New York and the big city is
daunting—but you look like you belong there*

I ARRIVED IN NEW YORK CITY on September 3, 1965, at noon. I came in
through the Holland Tunnel and was immediately rear-ended at a red
light. When I stopped, I was a little bit over the pedestrian walkway line, so—as we
would do in Seattle—I backed up. Wrong! You don't back up in the City, bro.

I had never seen so many buildings built right next to each other, with no
alleyways in between. Plus they were tall. And old looking. Then there were the
people—they were all moving quickly, and there were a lot of them.

I drove uptown, towards Greenwich Village. I saw a copy of the *Village Voice,*
and Bob Dylan's picture was on the front page. Yeah . . . I was starting to think I was
in the right place.

After a few more blocks I was on Seventh Avenue, and there was the Village
Vanguard. I recognized it from album covers. I parked my car in a garage (so expensive!) and went down the stairs, and there was Max Gordon, the owner. I introduced
myself, said I had just blown into town, and that was that. Max said that Charles
Lloyd's group was playing there that night—it was a Friday.

Charles Lloyd—wow—he was one of the reasons I had moved to New York.
I had seen him at the Penthouse in Seattle, and he really stood out, especially when
he was guesting with Cannonball Adderley's group. I had also seen him with Chico
Hamilton (and Gabor), and I remembered that on one of Chico's albums Charles had
a tune called "One Sheridan Square"—that was his address in the Village. Of course I
remembered that "One Sheridan Square" was where he lived—I wondered if he was
still living there. I drove over and Charles was in his apartment. He answered the
bell when I rang. I went up, and he opened the door and said, "You're just in time,
I'm moving." He handed me some suits on hangers—I was connected! I spent the
rest of the day helping him move to another part of the Village, not far from where
the present day Blue Note is located.

Charles suggested some places I could stay, and after a short search I
grabbed an SRO—that stands for "single room occupancy," a tiny place where the

bathroom (and/or shower) is out in the hall—on West Third Street, a block or so down from Charles's new apartment. It was funky and soulful and, yes, I was glad to be there. I read an article about bandleader Claude Thornhill by Michael Zwerin in the *Voice* and then made it down to the Vanguard to hear the group. Gabor was on guitar and Albert Stinson was playing bass. The drummer was Pete LaRoca—I knew his name from albums, but I had no idea that he would dominate the Lloyd quartet with drumming that struck me as being more Tony Williams than Tony Williams. He was amazing.

The group sounded as if they were getting "lost" together. You couldn't really tell where the downbeat was when they played uptempo; it was as if they were combining Miles-level straight-ahead with the more rhythmically free avant-garde style that was emerging in jazz at that time.

The force and impact of LaRoca's drumming didn't really hit me until I took my first subway ride the next day—the sound of the train was polyrhythmic and loud and angular, with other rhythms coming into the picture from unexpected places. That was the sound that Pete had captured.

That first night was extraordinary. I met Charles Lloyd and hooked up again with Gabor and Albert—and I also met a young guitarist who would become one of my best friends, Joe Beck. All I remember was telling Joe how much I admired Gabor, and Joe's reply was something to the effect that that was okay, but he didn't really like Gabor's sound that much.

I was off and running. I went back to the Vanguard a few days later to hear Jim Hall's trio, and when I went into the kitchen to meet Jim and tell him how much I loved his playing, there was Jimmy Raney over by the sink, drunk. Years later, in Nice, Jimmy would be the sober one and I would be the drunk—but that's another story.

# Chapter 10

*Okay, Coryell, dig Grant Green and you might just*
*learn some music*

Whar I had been in New York for about a week, I went up to Wells' Bar to hear Grant Green. It was September, absolutely beautiful, and the ride up to Harlem from where I was staying downtown was stunning—the cab ride cut right through Central Park.

When I went in, there was a dude at the bar. It was Larry Young; I knew about him from records, so I struck up a conversation. I told him I was new in town, the whole nine yards, and he was very friendly. Larry was playing in Grant's trio; the drummer was Candy Finch, I think. Before they took the stage, there was a promo man from Blue Note Records pushing some of Grant's recent sides. There was no stage—the promo man, like the band, was situated on floor level at the far end of the club, but that didn't stop him from doing his thing.

The band started off with a Larry Young composition, a 3/4 blues called "Tyrone." It was done at a pretty fast clip, and I think Larry took the first solo. I watched Grant comp; he had said in the liner notes to one of his records—I think it was *Green Street*—that chords hung him up, but on this night his comp-chords were short, sharp bursts of percussive and harmonic support for Larry's solo. Larry played solo lines not unlike Coltrane, so I was captivated by the thought of what would take place as the improvising unfolded—but I had no idea what was about to hit me when Grant started to solo.

He started out playing simple funk phrases, but the way he played those phrases threw me for a loop—he was really anticipating the time, pushing it forward in a way I had never heard before. He kept working with the same idea, varying it, developing it, moving it forward until each chorus of blues became a spontaneous cry of freedom, filled with hard-core soulfulness and a musical intelligence that only comes out of a certain kind of life experience. In short, he was burnin' up the bandstand. I remembered what George Benson had told me: "Larry, Grant Green plays a whole lot more shit live than on his records. When you hear him in person, you won't believe it."

Right away, I saw what George had meant. Grant just tore the place apart. His timing was so precise that he carried the trio on his shoulders like some kind of powerful philosopher-king. His technique was flawless; his articulation was as clean as a samurai sword cutting through a submissive foe. He played a semi-hollow Gibson and the sound was incomparable—Grant's tone was deep, his attack was percussive, and his notes had sonic edges on them that drilled right into the center of my body.

"Welcome to the East Coast"—that's what Grant Green's trio said to me that night. "Here's something for you to shoot for." I don't recall what else they played that night. I can't remember anything except "Tyrone." It made me say "Wow!" to myself, and I was glad to get the chance, three years later, to record that tune, at Apostolic Studios on Tenth Street, during the sessions for *Spaces*. (It didn't come out on *Spaces,* but was released on *Planet End,* a follow-up album that used the leftovers from that session.)

I returned a few months later to hear Grant's trio again, at another club in Harlem, the name of which escapes me. It was still amazing—the tightness of the trio and the hard-driving virtuosity of Grant. About two years after that, he came downtown to Slug's Saloon on the Lower East Side, where I was playing with my group, the Free Spirits, and played one of the greatest, if not the greatest, jazz versions of a Beatles tune—"I Want to Hold Your Hand"—that I ever heard.

At that time in New York, in the mid-'60s, there was a real dichotomy between interest in the straight-ahead, four-beat jazz I had been trained in up to that point and different, more radical things that were outside of the traditional jazz literature. Charles Lloyd had a lot to do with that "different" approach, and I wanted badly to play with him. I was hanging out with Gabor, and I remember him playing me a tape of what was, I believe, a Town Hall concert of Charles's group. The balance wasn't very good—the guitar was under-recorded—but the important thing was that it all sounded really good to me. Although the guitar was way off on the side, sonically, I was able to hear what Gabor was doing—inside/outside types of lines with a tremendous esoteric aspect to the whole thing. I really liked it, and I think I tried to pattern my playing, consciously or unconsciously, on what I heard on that tape.

Gabor's playing at that time predated his more "commercial" phase, when he was blatantly trying to get into a pop-jazz bag—no, this was some interesting stuff. Many of the scales he was playing were outside of the chord but still relevant to the harmony. Plus he was still playing his Martin guitar with the DeArmond pickup—that was unique to Gabor. I liked it. I also liked the straight-ahead, more mainstream playing of Jim Hall and Tal Farlow—Eddie Diehl, too. But what really attracted me to Gabor and Charles was that they were trying to do something different.

This desire for difference spilled over into what Charles was doing "on the side." He was hanging out with Robbie Robertson, Bob Dylan's guitarist, and snorting some strange powder. I was just getting into acid myself. What a disaster that was, but I was an addict, so it was a destiny thing. I took acid one night when I had been invited over to Charles's house to play just with him. Boy, I was energized—everybody was supposed to take acid; Tim Leary and all that jazz—so I got caught up in it. All I remember from that night is that Charles's wife, Joan, was very nice, and Charles finally got tired, and I went home. But at the time, I felt as if I had just played with Christ himself.

When Charles was cutting the album *Dream Weaver,* he invited Robbie Robertson and me over to Atlantic studios off Broadway (near where Lincoln Center is now) to play on a rockin' blues. His regular group was there: Cecil McBee on bass, Jack DeJohnette on drums, and the insufferable Keith Jarrett on piano. Robbie had a girl with him, and I was alone—on acid . . . whew. Robbie also needed a guitar string. How I managed to find a spare E string and give it to him, in my state, I'll never know.

So I'm peaking—the acid is really kicking in—and the quartet is checking out a take they had just done. Keith is listening intently to the playback and really digging it. He's also putting out a vibe that says he doesn't like having these long-haired guitar players in the studio. I could dig that—recording is a sensitive, personal, and private process. I felt as if we were intruding—and on acid, every feeling is hugely exaggerated—so maybe you can imagine . . . .

We get in there, Robbie and I, and I have my Gibson Super 400, and he has his Telecaster, and he plugs in and turns up really loud. Robbie has this great technique where he uses the pinkie of his right hand to manipulate the volume knob; he'll have the volume off, or way down, and then he'll hit a note and quickly ratchet up the volume, so the note has an otherworldly, swelling effect. Well, I'm on acid, so you can imagine what that sounded like to me—it was like When Worlds Collide or Invaders from Outer Space. The notes sounded as if they were backwards on tape—the Beatles and others at the time were using that effect—and they had a sitar-like aspect as well.

Here I am, tripping, with all these players that I admire. Robbie has his amp cranked up to gargantuan volume and is playing these blues phrases that sound like they're from outer space filtered through Kashmir, and I'm trying to find something to go with that. I try one weak bebop phrase (I think we were in the key of A), and it falls on its butt. I'm not loud enough (thank goodness) or, more important, coherent enough.

Forget it—I was out of it, the whole thing was crazy, and I don't think it was ever used. It was probably erased. Charles is to be commended for trying to do something different, but on that day it was to be more bizarre than long lasting. C'est la vie, c'est la musique du fusion . . . .

Fortunately, I would get the chance to return to that studio and do several other projects, all of which were good enough to be released—included the wonderful (for me) *Three or Four Shades of Blue* project of Charles Mingus, recorded in 1977. That was a great experience, especially the work that trumpeter Jack Walrath did, helping Mingus—who was dying from Lou Gehrig's disease—with the arrangements and orchestrations. That session was a who's who of New York players: Mike Brecker, Lee Konitz, Steve Gadd, Charles McPherson, Ron Carter—the list goes on and on.

# *Chapter 11*

*Ah, the upscale tawdriness of the Lower East Side—and then the acid hits*

IN MY EARLY WEEKS AND MONTHS in the City, there was so much going on I didn't know what to do. Here I was in a place where there was, side by side, the best and the worst of everything. You would see some famous rich guy standing at a street corner right next to a homeless person. And there was so much music: great pop music, great ethnic music, great folk, classical, jazz. There was also an insane element, because it was the '60s; the drug thing—the widespread acceptance that everybody who wanted to be hip needed to drop acid—was deeply embedded in the scene.

So there I was, hangin' with the hippies on the Lower East Side, and there would be interesting events—like the time I was stopped by the cops while driving my blue VW. They looked at my Washington State driver's license and registration, ran it through their surveillance system, made me wait around for a while, and eventually let me go. Then there was the time when I was jamming on the street with some like-minded individuals, and one of the dudes told me he was sure I had taken acid, the way I was behaving.

At that point, I actually hadn't taken LSD, but it wasn't long before I did. As I said, I did that crazy session with Charles Lloyd under the influence of acid. I can't remember who gave me my first hit—it might have been Chip Baker—but when I took it, all hell broke loose inside my mind. It was the autumn of 1965, anti-war vibes all over the place, peace and love messages abounding. When the acid hit my brain, my perception of everything changed abruptly—it was as if I was looking at things through a microscope.

I stared out through a window in somebody's apartment and studied the patterns of the window itself and the vines on the wall on the other side of the window. It was beautiful; it seemed to manifest in a secret sort of visual way the universality of all patterns. And that included the marvel of symmetry, the repetition of lines in, say, a spider web. Colors were intense and truly amazing.

During my first trip, I went over to Washington Square Park and watched the trees swaying back and forth. It was as if they were doing the "Freddie," a simple, silly dance made popular by a group called Freddie & the Dreamers, where you would kick out your right foot, then the left, and flap your arms—like a zany kind of warm-up exercise . . . . Whoa! Trip city! Boing! Boing!

I stayed up until dawn (sometimes called the "early morning fear") because of the energy the acid generated. So this was the psychedelic experience! No wonder Jimi Hendrix would come along soon and ask, "Are you experienced?"

Earlier that evening, as I was sitting in Chip Baker's apartment, gearing up for my trip, I had met a fellow who had just driven in from Atlanta with a real nice Gibson acoustic guitar—a flattop, round-hole affair. His name was David Baker. Unfazed by his long drive from the Southeast, he settled in quickly and played a 16-bar blues. I had never heard a 16-bar blues before, but there it was—and David played pretty well. Then he handed me the guitar. By then, the acid was starting to build in my system and I was feeling some positive energy. I remember playing, but I don't know what—probably some bluesy-type stuff. I just remember it felt good to play that guitar. And David was digging it.

A few weeks after that, David and I took an apartment together over at 198 Eldridge Street, moving in with our respective girlfriends and having all kinds of adventures appropriate to those wild and crazy times in the period of 1965–66 in New York City.

David was an aspiring recording engineer, and he would be one of the first engineers to record me. He engineered *Spaces,* the notable album I did with John McLaughlin, and would go on to become one of the most sought-after and respected engineers in all of jazz. David was a great guy, and we stayed in touch over the years; he had a great memory for the insane things that we did.

In July 2004 our mutual friend Richie Okon approached me at Birdland and told me that David had died in his sleep. He had been upstate doing—what else—a recording session. The memorial service was held in a recording studio, appropriately enough. John Scofield, Dave Liebman, and many other of David's friends played, but I wasn't able to be there. A few weeks later, I got together with David's wife, Kyoko Baker. We had tea at a Starbuck's on the Upper West Side, near their apartment, and we talked about David. Both David and Kyoko had grown up without their parents, so their mutual destiny was somehow connected to their tragic childhood situations.

Kyoko didn't meet David until long after he and I were tight—after we had the apartment on Eldridge Street, took our trips, and engaged in a variety of sophomoric '60s activities. One time there was a small fire in the apartment; the fire department came immediately, but thanks to the cool head of David's friend Francis Mitchell, we had almost extinguished the fire before the firemen got there. Still, it was a traumatic experience because we were—at least I was—blasted out of our brains. We lived in near-poverty but were sure we were somehow going to make it in this crazy business of music. Well, David made it all right—he became one of the top jazz-recording engineers. He made his mark; he completed his mission. Word was that he died peacefully—he just didn't wake up.

# *Chapter 12*

*I know some Spanish, but I can't understand*
*that Puerto Rican accent, Cabron!*

TO ME, ONE OF THE HALLMARKS of the era when I was living on the Lower East Side was the surprising importance of pop music. It was the start of a time when popular music was having a profound, related-to-one's-life type of effect—a time when the messages in both the lyrics and the playing reached deep recesses in the mass psyche.

Spanish-speaking immigrants, mostly Puerto Ricans, were all around us. We lived in a fourth-floor walkup, dropped acid, chased women, smoked pot, went to the bodega to buy Yoo-Hoo chocolate drink and pint cartons of Tropicana orange juice. And I tried to remain a jazz musician while dressing as a hippie.

Opposition to the Vietnam War was quite strong, and all of us in the downtown neighborhoods felt we were part of a counterculture that was poised to produce some sort of revolution based on a new faith in humanity, one that would improve the lot of the generations to come. That was a good idea—the only problem was that drugs powered the whole mindset, so, ultimately, our good intentions would be misdirected into something other than what was intended. It took me a while to understand that.

With the growing popularity of the Beatles, Rolling Stones, Lovin' Spoonful, and Bob Dylan, someone with a jazz mentality could either completely ignore what was happening and stay the straight-ahead course, or try, in some way, to incorporate these new elements from pop music into the jazz spectrum.

I remember listening to the Beatles' *Rubber Soul* for the first time while on acid. Wow . . . the songs took on other meanings. When we listened to "I'm Looking Through You" while tripping, it seemed as if you could look through the person next to you, into his or her very essence. Unlike more "normal" songs, the message of the music was multi-level: there was the literal meaning of the lyrics, then there were the implied meanings. We might hear a George Harrison lyric that was ostensibly about a boy-girl relationship, but, upon further reflection, one could read an anti-war or pro-world-peace message into the song. All of this got me thinking about how much work it must be to write a really good song—a song that would be originally crafted plus have an extra "something" that was kind of magic, an element that would reach deep into people.

I collaborated with a songwriter/producer named Nick Hyams in 1966. I wrote the folk-rock-style chords (quite simple—no jazz), and he had some fresh (or at least I thought they were fresh) lyrics:

> *Hate ties you up*
> *In thin black thread*
> *Wraps itself*
> *Around your head*

Something like that, anyway. I dug it, at the time. The refrain went:

> *And in the early morning fear*
> *You just might suspect*
> *That once and for all, and all at last,*
> *Finally and much too fast*
> *God has really come at last!*

Those were really some acid lyrics. I could identify with the "early morning fear" because of the paranoia that would set in when you'd get too high from the acid or were simply coming down in a scary way—what later became known as a "bad trip."

# *Chapter 13*

*Trippin' in the Apple; the sidewalks and sidekicks
of New York lead to a new appreciation of the blues*

We HAD A LOT OF TRIPS in the fall of 1965 and into '66. They weren't all on drugs; sometimes we'd just get in the car and drive east, through the Midtown Tunnel and into Queens and Long Island, or sometimes Brooklyn. Chip, David, and me, with some young ladies—Chip's wife-to-be, Elaine (from Boston), and Jo Ann and Cathleen, two friends from Washington, D.C., who had moved to New York around the same time as I had. They had a strong connection with Mexico, for some reason . . . . well, pot, which came from Mexico, was a very strong reason.

Man, I was in Hippie Heaven—but what about jazz? Well, jazz was still everywhere in New York, but there was all this other stuff going on, too. Somewhere during that time I started toying with the insane idea of combining, say, George Harrison's guitar sound with the saxophone lines of John Coltrane. Crazy? You bet! But along came the Byrds, with Jim McGuinn's 12-string guitar sound that rocked the artistic sensibilities of a whole generation. McGuinn and the Byrds were aiming at a new sound, borrowing from whatever styles that would advance the music. On their first album they used an extended one-note motif as background (or middleground!) for a song, not unlike the way Indian musicians would use the drone of the tamboura as the foundation for their pyrotechnic modal improvisations.

Speaking of modal improvisations—we had been introduced to that genre by the seminal recording *Kind of Blue* by Miles Davis, where the players (Cannonball, P.C., Coltrane, Bill Evans) improvised using just one or two scales. There was very little II-V-I harmony. The II-V-I had been the basis of so much jazz improvisation for so many years, and Miles was making a move to break away from that. Some of the non-jazz players (blues players, plus rock players who were improvising using mainly the blues scale) picked up on that and began putting more emphasis on "blowing"—improvising.

This trend was evident on a record that was popular at the time, *East/West* by the Paul Butterfield Blues Band, out of Chicago. This was a nice discovery for me, having come from a pretty strong blues tradition in Seattle. I heard these cats from

Chicago, and it was some other stuff—it was good, especially the playing of guitarist Mike Bloomfield, whom I would soon get to know quite well.

I first heard Bloomfield on record when I was living on Eldridge Street. What I dug about what he was doing was the extended soloing over a vamp, using basically one scale. Later, when I met Bloomfield, I got a first-hand look at his total passion for and involvement in the blues. He was a student of the blues and a fan of the great blues players out of the Midwest, and when he was on, no one could touch him for the sheer emotion of a simple blues phrase. I recall watching him play a Les Paul through a Fender Twin, executing a popular minor shout-phrase. The phrase goes from the fifth to the fourth to the minor third to the tonic: DEEE-AH-AH-UUMM!

I would watch the Butterfield band rehearse in the basement of the Albert Hotel, and I admired the way all the members—especially Michael—showed their love for the blues. They'd bring in some "soul" horns for support on some tunes, and they'd go crazy when the horns did their thing. Michael was so passionate about the blues—he listened to everything and was very competitive, in the sense that he pushed himself to play better by comparing himself to other top players. He also got totally into the singing styles of blues and gospel, and it was through Michael that I first heard the Swan Silvertones. Bloomfield's brand of blues was obviously not as sophisticated as what Miles and company had done on *Kind of Blue,* but there was a connection, because it was still the blues.

Michael was crazy, but it was a good type of crazy—and he was great to hang with. The first time Michael heard me play, at the Café Au Go Go, I played some swift passages, and he dismissed me, to my face, as "just another 'fast' player." That was funny, because later we got real tight, and he found out I loved the blues, too.

During this period I was working on many things, but one of the chief projects was playing over vamps, or blues-related extended solo sections, and really saying something. You couldn't just go on and on—you had to develop your playing and come up with interesting ideas. Another thing was composition; instead of working on straight jazz composing, I was trying my hand at some pop-oriented tunes. I was also studying classical guitar, and that influenced me to use non-jazz chords and more open strings.

I would get up in the morning, smoke a big joint, have breakfast, and then pick up the nylon-string guitar and start playing the scales, Segovia's scales. The scales would start to sound a little like bass lines to me, because I was high . . . later, much later in my life, I was relieved to discover I didn't have to put all those chemicals into my "personal environment" in order to play. As a matter of fact, the further away I have gotten from drugs and alcohol, the better my playing has become—but down on the Lower East Side in late '65, I was fitting in with the New Wave of Being to the best of my ability.

I didn't have many gigs, but I went out and heard music a lot. I went to the Village Vanguard often, and one of the weirdest occurrences I witnessed there was when Archie Shepp "crashed" the stage on Miles's gig. Miles was leading his quintet, with Herbie Hancock, Ron Carter, Tony Williams, and George Coleman on saxophone. They were playing their asses off. All of a sudden, Shepp takes out his horn and strolls onstage and starts playing in a style different from what the quintet was doing. He was playing more abstract and unspecific—"out," in musicians' parlance.

Miles was taken aback—he got pissed off and left the stage. He hung around a bit, didn't dig what was happening, and just went home. The music drifted into a chaotic state. Tony was responding in an avant-garde fashion, which was easy for him—he didn't have to play any chords or melodies. But Herbie was literally trying, he later told me, to knock Shepp off the stage with his playing. He was really hitting the piano, playing dissonant chords, responding to the quasi-insanity of Shepp's musings with visible anger. He was miffed that Shepp had come onstage and played, uninvited. I'd never seen anything like that before, nor have I seen anything like it since. Only in New York—only at the Village Vanguard in the '60s.

# *Chapter 14*

*Larry gets a gig: Ed Sull-i-van! This "killer Joe" isn't from Benny Golson, but he'll do*

ROUND THANKSGIVING OF 1965, I got a call from an alto player named Dennis Brault. He said he had a gig for me playing in a band backing up a professional dance troupe headed by a cat named "Killer Joe" Piro. The first gig was backing the dancers on the *Ed Sullivan Show*. That was a strange and interesting experience. I didn't get to play that much—the band was there just to support the dancers—but this was an opportunity to show my parents that my move to New York was paying off.

So we go uptown to the CBS studios and rehearse, and then the day of the show comes, and we do it. No big deal, but my folks are watching at their home in eastern Tennessee. A few days later, I get a letter from Gene Coryell—something to the effect of "Your mother nearly fainted dead away when she saw you on national television with all that long hair. Why can't you just grow a beard; it's much more dignified."

Wow—I didn't expect that. What the heck, my hair was really long, and I looked like a dropout (which I was), and, well, this is what happens when generations clash. I felt bad for my parents, but I wasn't about to change my appearance. I was going to look like a weirdo or die trying.

And, hey, we got a gig out of that appearance on the *Ed Sullivan Show*. Killer Joe was hired to appear nightly at the Drake Hotel, and the band had steady work—not bad, when you consider how difficult it is to make ends meet in the Big Apple. This was a steady gig, and of course I got a crush on one of the dancers, who happened to be black. I had had crushes on African-American girls before, in Seattle—a couple of sisters—but when something like that happens in New York, it's much more serious. That's just the nature of things in New York.

My attitude and lifestyle were such that I caused a lot of unnecessary problems by being sexually permissive. I was expected by this lady's family and friends to take responsibility for the relationship, which I did not. She tried to jump out a window one night because of me, and I just sloughed it off. I had no ability to face the unpleasantness of daily life, especially anything involving a relationship.

I gradually slid out of any declared or undeclared commitment to this girl. (She was beautiful, very youthful looking, but she was old enough to have a teenage daughter—nevertheless, I still think of her as a "girl.") What was really crazy was that my old girlfriend from Seattle came to New York to visit, with romantic intentions, but I found myself having stronger feelings for the dancer. When it was all over, I realized that I should have gone with my Seattle girlfriend—she would have been much better for me. However, at this stage of my life, I simply had zero wisdom in the ways of the heart; my attention was focused on playing music—that was my true love.

Inasmuch as I made mistakes with people during this insane time, well, that's the way the cookie crumbled. I made errors, and my vision was clouded by the chemicals I was ingesting; that's not an excuse—I'm accountable for everything. I always look at the things that have gone haywire in my life and see there's no need to blame anyone except myself. I've done things that have produced damaging results. I've caused emotional pain to myself and the people around me. I hope I've learned—I think I have. I eventually started to think about the consequences of my actions at some point—but not in 1966.

The Drake Hotel thing wasn't all horrors and disasters, and having regular work and some bread coming in gave me a chance to start composing some folk-rock-type material. I would go across the street to the bar there, where they had a piano, and sometimes I would get up and accompany myself on the piano and sing a bit of Mose Allison–type blues. I had gotten this idea in my head (rather tragic to some) that I should sing, if only to better compose words and music. In 1966, the world was bursting with emerging singer-songwriters—there were people like Paul Simon and Jimmy Webb and Jimi Hendrix writing tunes with lyrics. The Beatles, the Stones, and Dylan had set the pace for this new take on songwriting. None of my attempts amounted to anything commercially, but I think it helped me in later years when, as an instrumental improviser, I was better able to interpret a tune because I understood the lyrics as well as the harmony.

# Chapter 15

## *I run into Bob Dylan and stand outside Joanne Brackeen's door, listening*

A LOT OF THINGS HAPPENED in that first year in the City, good and bad. The blue Volkswagen I had bought in Seattle was repossessed—no surprise, since I wasn't making the payments. I was so far away from Washington State, why should I bother with car payments? Besides, part of being an unofficial member of the counterculture was behaving irresponsibly. Looking back on that now it seems ridiculous, but it went with the mindset of being a hippie . . . grown-ups and grown-up values were bad.

On the upside, I saw Bob Dylan. Yeah! He was coming in the front door of the Chelsea Hotel as I was leaving. He kind of half-smiled and waved at me. (Years later—on October 27, 1981—I took my son to see a Dylan concert in the Meadowlands; a guitarist friend of mine, Fred Tackett, was in the band.)

I would go to the Village Vanguard on Monday nights to attend jam sessions hosted by the legendary reedman Roland Kirk. He could really play, whether it was doing his trademark multi-horn thing—playing three at once—or just soloing like a banshee on tenor. At one of those sessions, I scrambled up onstage and managed to play a blues. The jazz guitarist Attila Zoller was there that night, and he encouraged me.

There was a family living downstairs from us, and the husband was Charles Brackeen, a tenor player. He sounded good, and he'd ask players to come over and jam. His wife was named Joanne, and they had a couple of kids—I used to babysit the kids from time to time, taking them to a park by the East River near the end of Houston Street.

I was leaving the building one afternoon and heard what I thought was Cecil Taylor playing piano in the Brackeens' apartment. I knocked on the door and discovered it was Joanne—unbelievable. I was amazed but not amazed, because that was New York in the '60s. Of course, she went on to become a very successful, world-class jazz pianist—that's the Universe of Jazz. She played a lot of interesting music in that pad. I used to stand outside the door for a few minutes almost every day to check out her ideas.

That was how I learned. Those early experiences in the City taught me about music and about life. Although I was unaware of it at the time, that mix of the creative with the mundane was shaping an emerging musical concept. What I wanted from music was to be able to express ideas that were sublime and deep, but at the same time I didn't want to forget about the blues. I wanted to be a soaring virtuoso, but I never wanted to be too far from the earth. I wasn't really aware of thinking this way; I think it was more intuitive.

When I practiced, I went back to the basics, keeping in mind that no original concept could emerge unless I woodshedded a lot. I don't know how many hours a day I practiced. It wasn't like my days as a college student, when, during the summer, I'd be in the basement practicing for eight hours a day—but I put in a lot of time. As I said, I started with the nylon-string guitar in the morning and did Segovia's scales, religiously. Then I'd go on to some exercises in La Escuela Razonada by Emilio Pujol. When playing those scales, slowly, I'd try to emulate a walking bass. Then I'd switch to the Super 400, using a pick (the nylon string is played with the fingers) and working on jazz stuff—quite often I'd try to play what I heard from the masters who performed around town, especially good horn players. I'd work on new phrases and scales that I'd picked up by ear, and try to play tunes I didn't know. That's the thing about New York: you have such a huge pool of players that there's always a cat out there who's got something to teach you.

I kept going out and hearing music, too. I heard Charles Mingus (with Howard Johnson—what a talent!) and Gerry Mulligan and Art Blakey and Kenny Burrell and, of course, Charles Lloyd. I was still living downtown and kind of drifting with the creative tide; I would often jam with guys my age in their apartments or in lofts. We'd play standard tunes, and sometimes it would sound okay—but most of the time, compared to the straight-ahead jazz I was hearing in the clubs and concerts, we were below par. We seemed to sound better when we did more of our own thing, more rock or blues-oriented, with modal improvising.

# *Chapter 16*

*Larry meets some friends who will change his life*

At some point, I met tenor saxophonist Jim Pepper and drummer Bob Moses. I don't recall the exact circumstances—we were all part of a loosely confederated downtown scene. What I do recall is that when I met Moses, he and Pepper had been dropping acid and playing long avant-garde jams in downtown lofts. "Mose" had a couple of these on a tape, and when I listened to it I was impressed. They were doing their own thing—not sounding like any established straight-ahead stars, not connected to folk or rock music. It was just balls-to-the-wall free playing. Full of emotion. Bereft of shallowness. Utterly intense.

I started thinking, How can I get the guitar to work in a context like that? That was my challenge. I don't think I ever got it together as well as Sonny Sharrock did, but I made moves into a more abstract way of improvising, by tapping the strings with the fingertips of my right hand (with the volume way up) and using feedback (with a big Gibson Super 400, that was easy if you were loud enough). Moses and Pepper also got me into using non-diatonic scales and atonality, but it was an atonality that had some substance, not just any random sequence of notes.

Pepper and I would hang out and get high, and he taught me tunes. One night—somewhere, in somebody's apartment—he showed me John Coltrane's "Naima." That was a revelation—what a beautiful tune! He also taught me "When Will the Blues Ever Leave" by Ornette Coleman. Pepper was totally into bebop, too, but he had developed an original approach through the avant-garde style, not unlike the sound of another tenor player on the scene at that time, Albert Ayler. Pepper loved Ayler. I remember listening to Ayler records, on the ESP label, in our railroad flat on Eldridge Street. That music was not the standard four-beat jazz that I'd cut my teeth on in Seattle. I'd heard some avant-garde there, especially from the alto player Carlos Ward, but when you listened to this cutting-edge music in New York City, played by true masters of the idiom, it took on a more profound quality. It was as if the players needed the hardships and obstacles they encountered while struggling to make it in New York to be pushed to their highest level.

I like to think that atmosphere still exists in the Big Apple today, which is why I usually tell talented young players to go to New York. You'll be burnished in that creative crucible. If you survive the fires of competition and intimidation, your sword will be forged into a strong instrument. Amen to that, brother.

Although I was ill prepared, emotionally and musically, I never regretted going to New York. I made all kinds of mistakes and nearly got screwed up beyond repair, but I seemed to know that this was the best thing for me. Maybe it was, maybe not—but one of the things that came out of my early years in the City was an enormous expansion of my understanding of life, especially through meeting outstanding people, many of whom were also great musicians.

You can get so deep into the totality of life experience that you don't know if it's the music that drives your life or your life that drives the music. Perhaps it doesn't matter. What I do know is that your goal, ultimately, should be to have the musician in you integrated with who you are as a person. But this may be an almost unreachable ideal. Some of the best players I heard were rather strange and surprisingly coarse as people. And some of the nicest cats couldn't play that well. The absence of an easy answer to this paradox is what makes the pursuit of that goal all the more compelling.

I was living with a strange creative dilemma. I was developing as a jazz musician, but I also listened to a lot of rock, folk, blues, and pop—especially the Beatles. And there were a lot of drugs around. Pepper, Moses, Chip Baker, and I were all living on the Lower East Side. Cathleen was now my girlfriend, and I was taking lots of acid trips, with Cathleen acting as my sober "guide" to make sure I didn't go too far out. One of the most mind-blowing occurrences was when, at the peak of the trip (the most intense part, where you're emotionally like a one-year-old baby), Cathleen drew a strange design on a piece of paper and folded it up. Then she asked me to open it. When I did, the word "EGO" popped out. Because of the fragile emotional state I was in, this fucked me up—like it was bad to have an ego, or something like that. But I got over it—it only took 20 or 30 years.

Another strange occurrence was when somebody from the magazine *The Realist* asked us to do a musical protest demonstration in the offices of *Esquire* magazine. We were supposed to be objecting to some new editorial policy. Moses and Pepper were there, and we took the sacrament—LSD—and then cabbed it up with our instruments. We went up to the floor where the offices were and starting playing outrageous, free-form, avant-garde music—disorganized noise to the people who were hearing it. The editorial staff was quite upset and called the police, and I remember a big, blue-suited cop coming into the room and grabbing the acoustic guitar out of my hands. The abrasiveness of the cop's law-and-order discipline was too much for my acid-soaked psyche, and it gave me a bad trip—a "bummer." The whole thing was over in a minute or two, and then we got back into a cab and went downtown. When I was finally able to speak, I said, "If I can get through this, I can get through anything." It was sort of true—in a way, the whole silly thing was some kind of a character-building experience.

Soon after that nonsense, we found another musician, a bass player named Chris Hills who had moved to the city from the Boston area. He was a good player and a great guy. At this point we had the makings of a band, and we called ourselves the Trees. Later, we found out there was a band in New Jersey (there's always a band in New Jersey) that legally owned that name, so we became the Free Spirits.

# Chapter 17

*Gary Burton and other free spirits appear—and the boy gets hitched*

WHILE ALL THIS WAS GOING ON, I was still hanging with Gabor Szabo, who was now on his own and doing a mix of styles—namely, jazz with a Ravi Shankar tinge. He emphasized the Indian influence by using open strings as drones. At that time, many guitarists in New York had an interest in Indian instruments like the sarod and the sitar. I knew, for example, that the pick used to play the sitar was called a mizrab. So when Gabor was looking for a title for one of his Indo-jazz vamps, he called it, at my suggestion, "Mizrab."

Our new band was on a collision course with Bob Thiele, who had produced records by John Coltrane, among others. After Gabor had heard Pepper, Moses, and me, he said he was interested in using us on an upcoming date for the Impulse label. Around that time—May 1966—I was hanging with a bassist from Memphis named Jack Gregg, who had actually been the first musician in New York to play with me. My girlfriend, Cathleen, had a friend named Maxine, who was married to Jack.

Gabor asked Jack, Moses, and me (I can't remember if he wanted Pepper or not) to be on his record. We got Moses's dad to drive us out to Rudy Van Gelder's studio in New Jersey, although we showed up so late that they had already done the date with other musicians. But Bob Thiele expressed interest in us as a band, and this led to our signing with ABC as the Free Spirits. Gabor's record—I think it was called *Simpatico*—had a photo on the front cover showing him on a motorbike.

For the Free Spirits' record, we put together songs like "Early Morning Fear" and a few collaborations between Chip Baker and me, plus some blues like "Cosmic Daddy Dancer" (a great title from Chip). We were ready to record—or so we thought—so we went back to Rudy's and recorded our book of folk-rock originals, with Pepper doing most of the improvising.

What happened with us happens often in music: you gather and organize material, rehearse it, and then record it. But when you go out in public and play gigs, the music evolves. Arrangements change, and you find better ways to play on the material. That's what happened to the Free Spirits. After our record was done, we went into clubs like the Scene in Midtown, and all the songs changed. New sections—for more blowing—emerged. I started improvising more. After we'd play the first chorus, instead of following the arrangement on the record we'd stretch out and blow—sometimes on the form of the tune, sometimes free-form. There's a recording of one of those nights at the Scene—a very poor recording, but a document of what we were doing nevertheless. We sounded raw, primitive, and contemporary all at the same time. Moses really sounded good; he had thrown off the mantle of being exclusively a jazz artist and absorbed some rock playing into his bag.

By then, I had kind of had it with trying to be an innovator on the fringe of jazz. I wanted to get more into traditional playing—no vocals, for starters—and when you play with vibes, that's unmistakably a jazz sound. No folk-rock either, although the GB Quartet did dip into the realm of rock and pop for material and styles; at one point, Swallow was featured playing a Bob Dylan tune. And we listened to the Beatles all the time. They weren't jazz, of course, but they were "happening." The Free Spirits were not happy that I left the group, but they changed their name to Everything Is Everything and had a hit record on a Jim Pepper-composed American Indian peyote chant called "Witchie-Tai-To." We went our separate ways, but later our lives would become intermittently intertwined, especially after I left the GB Quartet and decided to go out on my own.

We got pretty good—but, for me, it wasn't going to last long. Gary Burton, who had moved from Boston to New York, came down and saw what I was doing, and he decided that I could be the guitarist in a quartet he was forming. Gary was organized as well as being an excellent player, so I thought I should take the offer. It would mean I could get out there in the larger jazz scene, where the gigs would be better, plus I would learn a lot, since Gary was a good teacher. And he had Steve Swallow on bass and Roy Haynes on drums. Later on we had different drummers, and Moses ended up getting the gig at one point—that was nice.

Playing with the GB Quartet was a dream come true for me in the sense that it was a straight-ahead jazz situation that got a lot of media attention (including two articles in Time magazine). It was also an opportunity to work with someone who was really together: Gary was not just an excellent musician—he knew how to run a jazz group as a business. He had a mind like a steel trap when it came to details, and he had a tremendous work ethic. He also had great charisma within the network of connections he had made in the business, including record companies, club owners, and festival producers. (George Wein was managing him, more or less, throughout 1967.) And other musicians respected him because of his great playing.

Gary had a bent for researching a project. When he went to Nashville to cut a record for RCA that mixed jazz and country music, he examined a wide variety of country songs and artists for material and came up with an especially hip blues called "Walter L." The melody line was not easy to sing, but it was beautiful to listen to—a bit like Ornette Coleman's early work. Gary knew Chet Atkins and other important Nashville players whom he asked to play on that record, *Tennessee Firebird,* along with saxophonist Steve "The Count" Marcus. It was a brilliant musical statement, well ahead of its time, and it showed that jazz players could mix styles without losing the integrity of jazz.

Around this time—the summer of 1966—Gabor Szabo was leaving the Chico Hamilton Quintet and grooming me to take his place. I was phased in, so to speak; my first gig, in August, was at the Bijou in Philadelphia, with both Gabor and me on guitar, Tony Ortega on alto, and Ron Carter (gasp) on bass.

Among the people who showed up to hear us were the Jazz Crusaders (who were playing around the corner at Pep's), organist Jimmy Smith, and the parents of the Brecker brothers, Robert and Tiki. The Breckers were like parents to me on that first-time big gig, and they invited me to their house for dinner. They told me Randy was on an international tour with Horace Silver, which was why he wasn't around to hear me. I remember Robert saying, during dinner, that Randy's younger brother was coming along quite well musically—he said something to the effect that Michael would eventually play tenor better than just about anybody. And he was right . . . ah, the perspicacity of the patriarch!

While I was in Philly, I got a telegram from Gary saying: "Please confirm record date with Count." The date was for the aforementioned *Tennessee Firebird,* and Gary wanted me on it. I forget what happened, but I think it conflicted with a record date Chico was setting up where he was going to "introduce" me to the jazz public, as he had done before with other guitarists, like Jim Hall and Gabor. I was honored, so I took that date.

As fate would have it, the photo of me on the back cover of Chico's *The Dealer,* on Impulse (produced by Bob Thiele), was noticed by a young lady from New York who was living in California. She saw the photo, with me leaning back in a chair playing my Super 400, and said to herself, "I'm going to get that guy." Well, she did. She sent a note backstage at a GB concert at UCLA's Royce Hall saying, "For a unique experience in cosmic consciousness, please come to (such and such address) in Laurel Canyon." Her name was Julie.

Faster than you could play two choruses of "Cherokee" at bebop speed, Julie showed up on my doorstep at 36 West 73rd Street in New York, and after a few months of living together we were married in the backyard of our mutual psychiatrist. The date was September 28, 1968, and it was a lovely outdoor ceremony with the psychiatrist's son playing some great classical guitar and a pre-New Age folk-oriented guitarist named Peter Walker playing the sarod. Bob Moses and his parents were there, too. I don't even know what happened to the marriage license. I did things super loose back then—it was the temper of the times, combined with my addiction to controlled substances, and it produced the insanity that became my first marriage.

As horrible as this marriage experience was, I really have no regrets about all the craziness and pain because of the children—two sons—that were the result. What happens, happens—and like it or not, it is what it is. Thank goodness for the gift that helps us, if our attitude is right, to make sense out of just about anything. Both of my boys, Murali and Julian, grew up to be performers, and they have acquitted themselves well—they are eclectic musicians who have established their own voices in the business, and needless to say I'm button-busting proud of them.

But let's get back to 1968. I was newly married, yes, but outside of my personal life all hell was breaking loose. In the U.S., the Vietnam War was dividing the country along ideological lines. Those of us against the war were disappointed in President Lyndon Johnson, who was going through the emotional wringer himself—enough so that he decided not to run for re-election. The Democratic convention in Chicago was a huge mess, with riots in the streets, and all of it happening on national television. As a player none of this affected me too much, but for me as a private citizen, as a human being, it stirred up of lot of gnarly ethical issues.

I was so far from developing any emotional maturity that my way of dealing with it was just to keep getting high. For instance: On the evening of my wedding, I was performing at the Village Gate with Herbie Mann; as a wedding present, the musicians gave Julie and me a gram of high-powered cocaine. That's just the way it went down. And one of the cats on the scene that night came up to my wife and me, with his wife in tow, and expressed his condolences that we had just made a commitment to multi-year domestic misery. He may have been joking.

This is not to say that Julie and I had nothing but bad experiences during the time we were together. We both loved music, especially jazz, and there were many times when we were able to sit at the feet of the masters and learn from them and their music. One of those times was at the Village Vanguard, on a night when the GB Quartet was playing opposite the Bill Evans Trio. Bill's bassist was Eddie Gomez, whom I had met on my first gig in Boston with Gary, at Lenny's on the Turnpike, just outside the city. That was an unforgettable happening—Eddie could play faster on the bass than I could on the guitar, plus he was always saying something. It wasn't just a bunch of note-y nonsense.

Having been totally inspired by Bill Evans's recorded work before I moved to New York, I was doubly impressed and inspired to be in a club, three feet away from Bill at the piano. I sat behind him, at the end of the long bench that runs down the back wall of the club on the left side, for a whole set. Eddie was on bass, and it was Marty Morell, I think, on drums.

I was completely inside the sound of the trio. They played with no identifiable ego-manifestation—they played literally together, filling each other's open spaces, complementing each rhythmic motif as it became evident. Gomez was right inside Bill's phrasing, as if they were telepathic. They were the embodiment of a French Impressionist painting in the form of sound.

Quite often, when remembering Bill Evans, his admirers wax sentimental about his tenderness and his gentle approach to the keyboard. Yes, there was certainly some of that—but what I remember more was Bill's rhythmic aggressiveness, plus the amazingly dexterous interplay between the right and left hands. He was able to produce block chords in rapid repeated succession. And he was really able to reharmonize tunes, especially when he played the well-known ones from his recordings, like "Autumn Leaves," "Israel," "But Beautiful"—to name just a few—as he did that night.

Bill was a heroin addict. This needs to be mentioned only to explain some of the problems he had to deal with (because of his habit, his fingers would swell up like hot dogs) and to understand his quirkiness. One time he was so high when he came into the club that he sat down at the piano in his overcoat and never took it off for the whole set. Sometimes we must recognize and tolerate the eccentricities of genius.

I wish I could remember in more detail some of things Bill said when he talked to my wife and me. Between sets, he would sit on the steps that go up to the street near the men's room. It was a hanging-out area for the musicians when they didn't want to go into the kitchen. Bill would reminisce about his youth in New Jersey and his college days and share ideas.

There will never be another Bill Evans. I still listen to his recordings from time to time, and I recall how close his live performing was to his records. He was truly a stylist—he developed a style with its own parameters. It was not limiting in any way; in fact, the nature of his style insured unbridled freedom within the parameters he laid out. He was a true master of every aspect of the music—of harmony, rhythm, single notes, and chords. Most of all, he was a master of interpreting his material to the most heartfelt depths. I recall Father John Gensel saying at Bill's funeral that the quintessential song interpreted by Bill Evans was "But Beautiful." Read the lyrics and you'll get it.

The GB Quartet worked opposite another great genius at the Vanguard: Thelonious Monk. I remember him being a rather large and handsome man, always wearing a suit and one of a variety of really smart-looking hats. I used to hang with Monk in the back of the club, behind the bar, and he'd talk—sometimes to me, sometimes to no one in particular. On one such occasion he kept saying, "Wrong is right, wrong is right" in that gravelly-gruff voice of his. This was Monk's way of commenting on the folly of so-called "wrong" notes. (It took me a while to catch on that he was serious—initially I thought he was just trying to mess with my head.) Monk was saying that you could turn any "bad" note into something that was right. That opened me up a lot, since for many years I had always been encouraged to play "correctly" and avoid "mistakes."

Monk's attitude was: "Play anything—notes, chords, whatever you want. Just make it work." So from what I first thought were incoherent mumblings came concrete inspiration for something I could add to my music. After that encounter about turning wrong into right, I composed a tune, dedicated to Monk and the guitarist Jim Hall, that had a 33-bar form. I called it "Wrong Is Right."

Thelonious Sphere Monk was a humanistic and musical work of art. Whatever he did was cool—I loved the way he danced onstage when he wasn't soloing. He'd just get up from the piano bench and shuffle around the bandstand while his three bandmates wailed away. Monk was a little bit crazy and eccentric. One night, he played the head to one of his tunes by himself—solo—for the whole set. The band never played a note. That's the way it was in 1966 and '67—the jazz scene was vibrant, loose, and (in a positive way) off the wall. I hope it's still like that in the City—it's an ambience that rarely occurs anywhere else.

# Chapter 18

## *Barney Kessel*

WHEN I WAS 16 OR 17 and studying with John LaChappelle, I started learning solos off records, as close to note-for-note as I could. As I said before, I had a hard time with Tal Farlow's playing because he played so fast. Johnny Smith was easier, but his chord voicings were so smooth and silky I could never tell if I was getting the intervals right, because I could never match his sound.

Then there was Barney Kessel. John always raved about Barney the most; I couldn't understand what John meant right away, but I kept listening to Barney's records and trying to hear what John was hearing. I started taking off some of Barney's solos, both single-line and with chords, and I gradually began to see John's point. There was a certain clarity and directness to Barney's playing that began to emerge in my understanding.

I learned Barney's version of "Love Is Here to Stay"; it was relatively easy to follow, but it was good for me—that clarity again. I could hear the chords clearly, and his embellishments were very logical and "earthy," in the sense they were blues-based. Much later, I discovered that Barney had played on some of Billie Holiday's records. He was also the only white guy in that famous jazz movie called Jammin' the Blues, which was produced by Norman Granz and featured Lester Young, among others.

The more solos I took off Barney's records—like his chord solo on "A Foggy Day," another good one for me—the more I saw what John was talking about. This guy was special. At that time, Barney was at the top of the jazz guitar world—he was winning polls, everybody bought his records, and his rare personal appearances in Seattle were the stuff of legend. (One Seattle club where he played was called Pete's Poopdeck—all I remember about that club is that they spread peanut shells on the floor.)

Cut forward about ten years and, bang, I'm backstage in London on the George Wein tour, and Barney is playing his Gibson Charlie Christian model right at me as I sit in the dressing room. Barney had been the top studio guitarist in L.A. for many years and at that time—1967—he had gone back on the road to get back to his "legit" jazz roots.

On the first few concerts we did, starting with that night in London, Barney's playing didn't sound like it had sounded on the records. It wasn't until we got more than halfway through the tour and were in a little German town called Dinslaken, in the Koln-Dusseldorf area, that Barney was relaxed enough to open up and play at his best. His playing in Dinslaken sounded just like those records I had cut my teeth on. I was happy to hear it, because I knew Barney wanted to get himself back into top form, and, finally, he did.

At the end of that tour, in Paris, we went to a jam session. I played some standard jazz tunes, and Barney liked what I was doing. He could see that although I was playing in a rather strong avant-garde style in the GB Quartet, my roots were quite close to his.

After I left Gary's group and moved briefly to L.A., Barney came down to see me at Shelly's Manne Hole, and we had a "sit-down" one evening in the club before the gig. He counseled me, and it was a real privilege. He told me, above all, to enjoy life—and I needed to hear that at that time. He also said I should become knowledgeable in things other than music, like world affairs and politics—in other words, that I should continue my education as a human being. I deeply appreciated that he had appointed himself my temporary mentor. That he cared enough to assume this role touched me deeply. I had always wanted it to happen.

Barney had a stroke and experienced some other serious health problems that eventually led to his death in 2004. When he was ill, I called him in California. We had a short conversation, but he did remember me, and that was heartwarming. Shortly after that call, we did a thing at Birdland in New York to raise money for Barney's medical expenses. Howard Alden and a couple other guys played one of Barney's originals, "Sixty-Four Bars on Wilshire." Boy, that was a hard chart. Now that's some respect, for busy New York cats to play a complex tune like that—and they did it beautifully! At that same gig, Jim Hall played a gorgeous version of "In a Sentimental Mood" and shared an anecdote about Barney from when they were on tour together in Japan. John Scofield played the baddest version of "Gone with the Wind" I ever heard, after talking about Barney in glowing terms. It just shows you how deeply Barney's music had reached into these guys' hearts. I'm so glad I can say I knew this man.

# Chapter 19

## *Larry Coryell, meet James Marshall Hendrix*

IT WAS 1966–67. MARTIN LUTHER KING JR. was formulating his dream of bringing the brutal racism of previous generations to a halt and creating more positive and value-enhancing relations among the races. I was having my own dream, about the Next Big Guitar Thing that would emerge from my generation. My premonition was that this new king of the strings would be of mixed race and come from someplace remote, like Alaska. The perspicacity of my intuition notwithstanding, there did emerge from the Pacific Northwest (not far from Alaska) a young man of African-American and American-Indian heritage with a middle name, changed by his father after his birth, of Marshall. Yes, Marshall, as in the British mega-amplifiers—mystical!

Be that as it may, Hendrix was on the scene. I first met Jimi on the East Side of New York. We got wind that he was hanging out in somebody's apartment, so we went over. We were ushered into the back of the apartment, where Jimi was sitting there dressed as if he were ready for a gig, wearing upscale hippie garb, complete with a decorative scarf—all quite colorful, as was the fashion at the time. He also had some straight pins stuck into his pants—horizontally, not into his skin, mind you—as if to say, "This is my fashion statement."

I introduced myself as being from Seattle and started talking about bands that he would have known about—the Wailers, for example, and about songs that seemed to be popular only in Seattle, like "C'mon" by Earl King. When he heard me mention "C'mon," he perked up—we connected. A few months later, after I had moved to Nyack, New York, I heard Jimi's newly recorded version of "C'mon" on the radio. Maybe he had followed my suggestion that he record it.

Jimi was very friendly and generous to my wife and me. Whenever he was in New York, he would invite us over to where he was staying. Most often he'd hole up in the Drake Hotel—which I knew from my "Killer Joe" days—and we would get high, listen to music, and hang out with his bandmates, Mitch Mitchell and Noel Redding. I felt a strong kinship with Mitch because the way he played with Jimi was very jazzy—he even used brushes on some tunes—plus he mentioned that Elvin Jones was a big influence on him. With Noel, it was a bit different because he was actually a guitarist—he switched to bass to get the gig with Jimi—and he was a hard-core rocker. But we had a great friendship because of our mutual respect for each other. He was a real sweet guy, and I perceived that he was extremely conscious of his good fortune to be in a world-class music group.

A lot of our camaraderie was based on goofing off—we were all in our twenties, and it was New York City, and it was the swinging '60's. We were a bit foolish, but we did get to jam together at the Scene on several occasions. We played mostly blues and rock stuff, but it was really swinging, and at one point I thought that Mitch and Noel would join my band. But it wasn't to be.

We would spend hours at Jimi's suite in the Drake or eating after-midnight dinners at La Brasserie (which Jimi referred to as "the brassiere"). One night, when Buddy Guy was playing at the Scene, we all dropped acid at the Drake and decided to go down and hear him. Well, we walked up to the entrance of the club, and what did we see but Buddy himself, out on the sidewalk, playing the guitar! Turns out he had a really long guitar cable, and he had strolled from the stage downstairs up to the street. He was wailing away on his axe as we approached. Jimi immediately got kind of competitive and said "I'm goin' to cut him." After Buddy returned to the stage, Jimi did sit in, but I recall the performance being rather lackluster—he was tripping pretty hard. (With acid and playing, it was like throwing the dice. Sometimes you could really play some different stuff, but other times it was a disaster.)

There was another time when we were hanging out, early in the evening, and were, once again, stoned out of our brains. We were going from east to west on 43rd Street, I think, in a long black limo, with "Hey Jude" (the original) blaring on the radio. Jimi said something about how frustrating it was sitting in all the traffic—the difficulty of getting across town. Later, on *Electric Ladyland,* there was a tune of his called "Crosstown Traffic." (That was the track where he made his guitar produce some earthy, revolving sounds that could easily be interpreted to depict the sex act.) I wonder if that title came from that experience—pun intended.

Jimi was a really straightforward person. He was loaded a lot (like so many of us), but he was always sincere about the music. I remember hearing him for the first time on the radio in 1967. I was in a car with Gary Burton, driving across the Golden Gate Bridge. Thinking it was Harvey Mandel, I said, "That's a real good guitar player." The song was a slow blues, but what a slow blues—loud, screaming guitar phrases executed with incredible technique. It turned out to be Hendrix playing "Red House."

A few months later, when Jimi was exploding like a meteor across the music scene, Danny Kalb (a good guitarist from the Blues Project) and I sat in the back of the Scene and heard his first East Coast set. Jimi had a lot of problems with his gear during the set, plus he broke at least one string. The most interesting thing for me was that when Jimi dropped out to deal with these problems, the band sounded basically the same. Mitch and Noel were playing so strongly that you hardly missed the guitar. They were really tight, and the way Noel's electric bass drove the bottom end it covered practically the whole guitar sound spectrum, while Mitch was taking care of the high end with his drums. Danny and I were not impressed with Jimi, initially, but Mitch and Noel knocked us out! A few tunes later—I think it was when they got to "Hey Joe"—Jimi finally got his sound together, and Danny and I got a whiff of the exalted aura of Jimi's electric-overdrive wizardry. It just took a while.

One of the great things about that time period in New York was that the club scene was so tied in with the recording scene. You could play a gig, or go to hear someone, and then go to one of the many recording studios in Manhattan, and if you were a musician and the right people knew you, they'd let you check out what was going on.

One night, Jimi was working on Electric Ladyland at the Record Plant in Midtown. I think I was playing at the Scene, a few blocks away, and several of us—including my wife and some other musicians—weaseled our way into the studio, where Jimi was laying down tracks for "House Burnin' Down." It was obviously his response to the horrors of the war, and I really liked the tune, the tracks, and the lyrics. Jimi's way of recording, supported by a British engineer named Eddie Kramer, was to lay down lots of tracks, and then choose the best musical moments when they got to the mixing stage.

Later in that series of sessions, Jimi asked me to play when he was doing "Voodoo Chile" with Stevie Winwood and Jack Casady. I was not in the mood to sit in and passed, telling Jimi, "It sounds great just the way it is." People ask me about that—they wonder what might have happened if I had responded differently. I say it's moot. It doesn't matter, because I didn't take up the invitation at the time. The way it worked out was destiny, so, for me, no regrets. I'm just glad I was there to be witness to so much history. In "Voodoo Chile," for example, Jimi's guitar wailing, in the good old key of E (actually it was the key of D, since Jimi tuned down a whole step), was superb, especially the way he'd bend the A (G pitch) note on the second fret of the third string up to B (A pitch) before striking the string, and then release it down to the A (G pitch).

Jimi was a sheer genius. He knew music, and he knew the technology. He practiced the wah-wah pedal for hours. He read a lot of books and magazines, and he listened to all the music his contemporaries, including Cream, were making—he was pretty much up on all the relevant goings-on. And he had—as Eric Clapton said one time when I was jamming with him in London—"strong fingers." Starting with that strength in the hands, Hendrix branched out into areas where previous blues and rock players had never ventured, especially in the processing of his sound through pedals, like wah and distortion, and also just the sheer volume of the wall of Marshalls that he plugged into.

Jimi's string-bending and vibrato were the best; thanks to those "strong fingers," he had impeccable control over every nuance. And he wasn't just a single-note, lead guitar virtuoso; he had a great sense of chords and how to use them. On top of that, he accompanied himself beautifully during the vocals and created an almost big-band coherence with precise interaction between what he sang and the support-response phrases from the guitar. He was a left-handed player, which meant that on many occasions, if he wanted to jam, he'd have to turn a borrowed right-handed guitar upside down, and from this he probably developed more alacrity with regard to his fretboard visualization.

We were on the stage of the Scene together once or twice in an awkward situation. "Awkward" because Jimi had to play a right-handed guitar—or maybe a right-handed bass. We never really had a chance to play under ideal conditions, but I know he dug me; once we were about to jam and I warmed up by playing a rapid major-seventh ascending arpeggio a la Johnny Smith, and I remember Jimi saying, "Yeah."

Jimi's live recording at the Fillmore East, *Band of Gypsies* (with Billy Cox on bass and Buddy Miles on drums), is probably the best record in the history of this kind of music. However, I recall a jam session at the Café Au Go Go where Jimi went onstage and hooked up so intensely with Buddy that it almost revolutionized the world. What was basically a blues-rock jam took on surreal qualities due to Jimi's ability to pull the best out of the players. What I remember most distinctly was that Jimi had his amps under such meticulous sonic control that his distortion took on tonal qualities that later were produced only by synthesizers. His guitar no longer sounded like a guitar, but like some sort of spaceship-engine-rocket-amphetamine-rush matrix. It was louder than just about anything that I had ever heard. And it sounded sweeter than anything I had ever heard. That was the interesting and amazing thing—the volume was never painful or obnoxious. Hendrix's mission seems to have been, in his tragically short life, to bring beauty and innovation to what later became known as the "overdrive" guitar sound.

The only cat I have heard since that night at the Café Au Go Go who was equal to Hendrix's transcendental blues-rock style was Stevie Ray Vaughan. Sadly,

I never heard him live, just on records. Fortunately, my oldest son, Murali, went to several Stevie Ray concerts in New York during Vaughan's heyday, and he brought back glowing reports about how great he was. Some people may remember the interview I conducted with Vaughan for *Musician* magazine where, for the whole time, he thought I was Larry Carlton. I got a kick out of that. It was terrible, though, when I got a call a few months later and learned that Stevie had died in that helicopter accident. Go figure—Stevie had beaten his demons, was on the road to recovery and prosperity, and then that had to happen . . . .

Fast forward to November 27, 2006, a Jimi Hendrix birthday tribute at B.B. King's Blues Club in NYC. The promoter/documentary filmmaker, David Kramer, called on the players who had a relevant connection to Jimi. I was honored to be one of the players David asked to participate. David had visited me earlier that year at a gig I did at the Watercolor Café in Larchmont, New York, to show me some of the interviews he had done. He had included people like Rick Derringer, Cornell Dupree, and Bernard Purdie—players who were there with Hendrix, either playing with him or observing his genius. David also showed up at one of my New York 'Chesky Record' dates in the Spring of 2006. At that session, (the second CD for myself, Victor Bailey, and Lenny White), one of the tunes we did was Hendrix's "Manic Depression." David was blown away by it and asked me to invite Lenny and Victor to play a couple of tunes at the tribute show, which I did.

So November came around, and there we were, hangin' out with Cornell and Chuck Rainey, in Rockland County, where David lives. We came up two days early to prepare. The day we arrived we went out to a little club in Valley Cottage (where my analyst, the late Victor Nielsen, had lived—ironic!) to jam. The whole happening took place around the midnight hour . . . we had to sit through some other bands, including a Hendrix "clone" band from Sweden. While we were sitting there I had the greatest talk with Cornell about the philosophy of music—can't remember the specifics—it was simply a great conversation. My son, Murali, came down from finishing one of his blues gigs and joined us in the late night jam—somebody filmed it—it wasn't bad. At one point we had my wife, Tracey, singing, along with Murali playing and singing, and Chuck and Cornell doing their thing. It was pretty loose, but it got us ready for the big bash at B.B.'s two nights later.

Monday night at B.B. King's was a marathon as well as a tribute. There was a long line of artists, including Jimi's younger brother Leon, Jose Feliciano, and Buddy Miles (Buddy was reverend-like). Man, Buddy has a back-beat so solid you can drive a truck inside it, but the cat who killed me most on guitar was Johnny Winter. A very healthy-looking Johnny came on stage, sat down with what looked like a white flying V solid body with no head stock, sang "Highway Sixty-One Revisited" by Bob Dylan, and played slide guitar like you wouldn't believe. He played basically the same great solo every tune.  Some cats can do that—if it ain't broke, don't fix it!

A few acts after Johnny Winter, Victor, Lenny, and I (joined by Murali) finally went on and played "Manic Depression".  Then Murali sat down and Lenny, Victor, and I (we call ourselves "CBW" for short) did our signature version of Zeppelin's "Black Dog".  Victor and I played tight lines in octaves (à la Jimi and Noel Redding from all those years ago) and then we traded eight bar phrases while Lenny alternately played time or rocketed into his unique style of jazz-influenced rock drumming.  We brought down the house—it was a fitting moment for me, because my respect for Hendrix and influence from him has stayed with me for nearly forty years now.

There is a misconception about Hendrix and me that should be addressed here, just for the record.  This took place in the *Downbeat* interview when I was drunk, and I was quoted as saying that I "hated" Hendrix.  I made that statement with a humorous, lovingly-sarcastic tone, as in a situation where someone will say they "hate" somebody in an admiring way, not unlike when Leonard Bernstein said of Wagner, "I hate him—on my knees."

# *Chapter 20*

*Struggling to find a voice: jazz-rock was a "scary term"*
*back in '66*

Y PROBLEM, MY CHALLENGE, BACK IN 1966–67, was to digest all this loudly amplified pentatonic-scale music coming from the likes of Clapton and Hendrix and somehow combine that with other important influences to create my own style. I wanted to find a concept that would infuse the fresh, contemporary sounds of rock and pop with the jazz tradition.

The first thing I had to do was decide how to incorporate jazz ideas into a blues-rock rhythmic environment. The partial answer for this would come from the avant-garde—players like Albert Ayler and Coltrane's disciples, Pharaoh Sanders and Archie Shepp. Technically speaking, I wanted to make the little finger of the left hand a new feature of lead guitar playing, because I wasn't going to settle for simple variations on the pentatonic. Rather, I would play, over a rock beat, lines that sounded more or less like jazz guitar and implied a more chromatic sound to the phrases.

I wanted this new style to develop naturally. It was my desire to bring together the best of both the rock and jazz worlds as they manifested themselves on the New York scene. I didn't want it to be forced—it needed to generate itself organically, in the same way that bebop came out of swing, or that R&B came out of pure blues. I wanted my style to be natural, but also to be original because I thought it was imperative to find my own voice.

I wanted to improve the intellectual content of the limited phraseology of rock and blues playing and, at the same time, to inject more "down home," blues-based energy into jazz ideas. I'm sure I wasn't the only cat trying to do this, but I was strongly urged by players I respected to avoid simply emulating my jazz heroes. (What's funny is that, early on, my plagiarism was so clumsy I had to get more with "my own thing.")

Today, the approach to developing an instrumental concept in jazz is different from what it was in the mid-'60s. Originality seems to have been crowded out by the desire to plagiarize (albeit plagiarize well) the great improvisers who have gone before. But that's cool with me. There seem to be cycles of creativity in all the arts, and these variations of emphasis take place when they need to, in jazz, painting, poetry, architecture, etc. Down the road, the emphasis may shift towards more originality again. During the "do your own thing" periods, there can be a tendency for some of the more experimental stuff to sound pretty bad—this I know personally! But regardless of which emphasis cycle we're in, I enjoy all the new young players who have emerged—talent is talent.

# *Chapter 21*

## *First recordings as a leader—madman or genius?*

I STARTED MY RECORDING CAREER in New York. I had done the Dynamics and Mahaffay recordings in Seattle; although they were important to me at the time, I count my first East Coast dates as the real beginning of my recording career.

My first record was the one with Chico Hamilton, which was followed by the Free Spirits record and then my first Gary Burton record, *Duster,* which I still like today. After that, I did an avant-garde session with Carla Bley and Michael Mantler called *The Jazz Composers Orchestra.* Bob Thiele also got me a single session on a Chico O'Farrell date where I played a blues (Pat Rebillot was on piano—that was a gas). I was on my way.

After two or three more discs with the GB Quartet, it was time for me to do my own thing. What eventually came to be known as *Lady Coryell* began as a project with an up-and-coming outfit on 10th Street called Apostolic Productions. They had a studio that was built entirely with "hippie labor"—not exactly Columbia Records, but what the hell, they liked me.

I had written some songs with vocals, but I also wanted to do some straight-ahead. I decided I wanted Elvin Jones and Jimmy Garrison—John Coltrane's rhythm section—on the record. We did a complete session with Elvin and Jimmy, but I couldn't handle the pressure of my first date as a leader and most of the music we recorded was not suitable for release. We ended up using only "Stiffneck," a guitar-drums duet with Elvin (done only because Jimmy was late for the session) and a blues, which had a nice feel. I still get comments about that one. For that blues I decided to alter my drug-induced mindset to heroin, so I could play slow and soulful. "Horse" made me irritable and nasty—I didn't like it much, but I continued to dabble in it.

We combined the two usable tracks from those sessions with some selections from the multi-track sessions I had done with just Bob Moses and myself. Producer Danny Weiss had done his best to work with us—I think he dropped some acid along with Mose and me, so he could better understand what we were trying to do. The whole thing was far from perfect, but finally we had something.

The recording quality was terrible (it sounded like it was recorded underwater, according to a letter on Maynard Solomon's wall in his Vanguard office), and some of my singing was pretty "out there." I remember that Eric Clapton liked it, but it was not universally embraced by all who heard it. What the hell, it was what it was—and I had my first record as a leader.

Tom Mathiessen, a photographer I'd known from Seattle who'd moved to the Apple, created the album cover—a connection with "home." It had a small cameo shot of my new wife, just above my head, with a shot of my Super 400 off to the side. Tom came up with the design and took all the photos.

In short order, I made a follow-up album for Vanguard; this time, the emphasis was on rock. We got Chuck Rainey and Bernard Purdy on bass and drums, respectively—they were the top studio funk players—and I rocked out. The album was called, simply, *Coryell*.

I also called Ron Carter to play bass for the session, and, embarrassingly, I had called Chuck for the same day—so I had to ask Ron to come back another day. When he did, he laid down some beautiful electric bass, including a line on a tune called "Ah Wuv Ooh." (My wife was pregnant with our son, Murali, at the time and engaged in a lot of baby talk, which is where that title came from.) I think that Ron's presence helped to attract favorable attention from the critic Ralph Gleason, who wrote a nice review of the record. He hadn't always been so kind—he had panned the Gary Burton Quartet's performance at the Monterey Jazz Festival in 1967. (I met Janis Joplin for the first time at that festival.)

I recall giving a copy of *Coryell* to John McLaughlin shortly after he came over from England. I called him one day, and while we were talking he picked up his guitar and started playing rock licks, as if to mock the way I'd played on the record. I felt funny and decided then and there that my next record would have to have more bebop. And that I'd ask John to play on it.

# *Chapter 22*

*Johnny Mac, the guru, and the* Spaces *sessions—can one be spiritual* and *rich at the same time?*

BEFORE WE GET TO MY NEXT RECORD, a little background: after Tony Williams left the Miles Davis Quintet (which I had seen in concert many times), he called and invited me over to talk about his new group. I was honored and wanted to do it. I was really impressed with the expansive nature of Tony's personality and his musicianship, which seemed very advanced—and not just for a drummer. I could see the incredible power of his association with Miles. The chemistry went both ways between Miles and his players—Tony had this uncanny ability, starting with Miles, to make other players sound good. His innovative use of the cymbals, as well as a different approach to the use of the high-hat and his disguising of the downbeat, helped to bring jazz drums into the psychedelic era.

Eventually, however, I decided to start my own group, and that left the door open for another guitarist to join Tony's group. That guitarist was John McLaughlin, or "Johnny Mac" as he was known in England. So Johnny Mac comes to New York and not only gets the gig with Tony but gets the gig with Miles, too, and makes all those great recordings with Miles in 1969–70, including In a *Silent Way, Bitches Brew,* and *Jack Johnson.*

I was in the process of moving from Manhattan to Rockland County at that time, and I invited John to stay at the apartment on West 73rd Street until he could get settled. This strange generosity came from me chiefly because when I heard John's debut with Tony's group at Count Basie's in Harlem, I saw that this was a seriously different kind of player who had originality plus technique to burn. This was a special dude.

John was into clean living and spirituality, which I wasn't—I touted getting high. John was the opposite. He was through with the drug phase of his life and wanted to seek a more spiritual avenue to get to the best of the music.

In retrospect, I can see that throughout the history of jazz some musicians have taken to spiritual paths in order to be better people and better players. It was obvious that Coltrane had had a spiritual awakening when he made A *Love*

*Supreme.* There have also been musicians who converted to Islam, like Yusef Lateef and Ahmad Jamal. The phenomenon is not unlike the story of Malcolm Little, the Harlem hustler who became Malcolm X. At this time, in 1969, I was about to be given the opportunity for a conversion to purity, but it didn't take right away—for me, it was going to take a long time. No regrets, however, because at least a seed for future spiritual progress had been planted. I have to look at it that way.

I invited John up to my new place in Rockland County, and he went down to a spare bedroom, where I found him sitting in some sort of lotus or meditation position. At that point, I started to think about whether Eastern philosophy might work for me—for my life and for my music.

When we did the Vanguard date for *Spaces*—with John plus Miroslav Vitous on bass, Chick Corea on keyboards, and Billy Cobham on drums—I learned that producer Danny Weiss also had an interest in Eastern philosophy, especially ideas grounded in Indian culture. Danny was going to meet a guru on the evening of the first day of the sessions. The guru's name was Sri Chinmoy, and we all drove up to Connecticut for a meeting; we became disciples that night or soon after. It was a landmark decision for me—opening the door to Indian culture, not only to the religious aspect but to the musical side of this ancient land.

That night, after Guru made his meditative presentation, John asked him, "Can one achieve enlightenment through music?" and Guru immediately recognized John as a special person. John became his number-one disciple.

I tried my best to be a good disciple, but I was blind to some aspects of my spiritual progress, and that got in the way. My pursuit of Guru's goal of realization was hampered by my drug and sex karma. The whole thing among the disciples tended to be competitive, with devotees jockeying for positions close to Guru, or to his "wife," Alo Devi, a Caucasian Canadian. (They may have been legally married, I'm not sure—no disrespect intended.)

Alo once scolded me for being arrogant because I said I was looking forward to receiving my spiritual name. (Gurus choose these names, and Guru eventually gave my first son, born in 1969, his name—Murali. It means "Divine Flute of Lord Krishna.") Guru said I needed to put in more time to prove myself as a good disciple—I think he said a year—before he would give me my name.

Well, I never got it. I left or lost interest or something. At that point, my life's most important goal was to drink beer and get high (besides playing music and supporting my family). I'd be meditating in front of Guru and thinking about smoking a joint. I was usually high anyway. He had told his disciples that drugs were not allowed in our group of devotees, so getting high and trying to meditate were in conflict—and, as usual with me, getting high won out.

It was not a total disaster, though. Being with Guru got me into eating Indian food and listening to Indian devotional music, among other things. On more than one occasion, John and I played Indian music or some original devotional songs based on Guru's poetry. One time it was at a place in the Westport train station called Love and Serve—a restaurant that had been opened by Guru's disciples. In New York, we played at Cami Hall (across from Carnegie Hall) on 57th Street. A lot of fans of John's and my music came to this concert, including the producer Bob Thiele.

All these efforts paid off down the line. I learned a lot about Indian culture through my truncated discipleship, and I turned Carlos Santana on to Guru, which I feel was a good thing for Carlos at the time. A foundation had been laid for me to have experiences with Indian musicians. I could say "gigs," but with Indian musicians it has really been more of an experience, because the music and the presentation of that music are so deeply connected to Indian culture.

For example, I went into a studio in Stuttgart in 1975 or '76 to record a track or two for former Johnny Mac sideman Stu Goldberg. From doing that session, I met Dr. L. Subramaniam, and he and I became playing companions in a musical relationship that has lasted more than 30 years. "Mani" is a great classical violinist, and he and I have done many recordings and concerts—plus he has worked hard to understand the Western system of music, resulting in some exercises in "fusion" that have been rather interesting. Working with Mani has also allowed me to connect with other great Indian players, notably bansuri players like Hari Prasad Chaurasia and Ronu Majumdar. Because of the McLaughlin connection, I also got to sub for John in his Indo-fusion band in 1982 with Zakir Hussain, L. Shankar (Mani's brother, also a killer violinist), and a hell of a percussionist named V.K. ("Viku") Vinayakram. All of these encounters helped to solidify my strong connection with the enormity and breadth that is Indian culture.

So—if it weren't for meeting Guru, back in 1969, I wouldn't have had this "extra" career playing with Indian musicians or going to India and seeing what the country is really like. Anyone for people, lots of people? . . . I mean, in contrast to the West, India is packed with people and animals, has terrible roads clogged with traffic, and has lots of pollution. But the populace is laid-back and peaceful, with all the citizens pretty much getting along with each other. There are exceptions and aberrations, of course, but let's put it this way: when you're in India you truly know you're in a foreign country. They are very polite people, and they have a great deal of humanitarian respect built into their daily lives.

But let's get back to the *Spaces* sessions. The first day was strange because Chick and Billy and John had just come from a *Bitches Brew* session with Miles. They had definitely been taking some different approaches to the music at that session, because when I threw down the first piece, "Tyrone" by Larry Young, the cats did not play it straight. They were all going into outer space. I was trying to stay inside—sticking more to the form and expressing more "literal" ideas—and when I heard them going off into the stratosphere, I just held my ground and stuck to playing the tune in a straight-ahead way. The resulting track didn't end up on *Spaces,* but it was released later on *Planet End.*

Almost nothing we played that first day made the cut; it seems as if we got most of the music that went on the record on the second day. It just took a while to get comfortable with each other and the material. It often happens in recording situations like this that the first day doesn't produce something that sounds like a band—and it has to sound like a band, somehow. Plus, when you have players of the caliber of Chick, John, and Billy, there's going to be kind of a shakeout period in the studio where, as they examine the music we're trying to record, it almost functions as a rehearsal.

Miroslav was very helpful. He and I had become friends through touring on the George Wein circuit, and he was always making useful suggestions—for instance, he played the title tune's melody with the bow, giving our hastily-put-together ensemble an original group sound. Miroslav also got excited about playing Scott LaFaro's "Gloria's Step," from the Bill Evans songbook; bassist Gene Perla had showed me the chart, and I passed it on to Miroslav. We did it as a trio—Miroslav, Billy, and me.

The most memorable track, for many, was the duet I played with John, Django-style, on "Rene's Theme," which was written by the Belgian guitarist Rene Thomas. (Rene later told me we weren't playing his tune exactly right, but that was okay—he still liked it.) John played a Gibson acoustic that had been lent to us (we were told) by John Sebastian of the Lovin' Spoonful. I played my Super 400, unamplified, and the engineer was, thank my lucky stars, David Baker; he not only knew our sounds inside and out but was conceptually in tune with the music. There was some editing of my solo, I believe. I think John's solo is on there pretty much intact; it's a classic, quirky improvisation that reflected his eclectic musical evolution at that time. John was quite adept at going in and out of the harmony, something I loved to do as well.

*Spaces* did not do that great upon initial release, but when Vanguard re-issued it a few years later, it sold 250,000 copies. Not bad for a record that sounded very little like traditional jazz and practically nothing like rock. The underground music press in New York jumped right on it. I recall one review where the writer said—talking about the way John and I related to each other on "Rene's Theme"—that "one of us arrived at our destination by subway and the other by jet plane."

A few years after *Spaces* came out, I was doing a radio show with Buddy Miles and Dr. Billy Taylor. They played the title track and asked Billy what he thought of it. Now, Billy Taylor is the epitome of straight-ahead jazz; in the mid-'60s, I had been grateful to his radio show for keeping me sane amidst the insanity of the Lower East Side. Anyway, Billy listened to the tune "Spaces (Infinite)" and said, "That was some good music." He didn't say "jazz"—I wouldn't have expected him to.

Years later, in 1997 or '98, I did another radio show with the Good Doctor, and this time I got to play with his trio. We played some Wes Montgomery stuff (Billy was very close to Wes), and it was a beautiful experience. During that show, which was recorded at the Kennedy Center recital hall, Billy told me that, as a young man, he had heard Benny Goodman play at the New York World's Fair in 1938 with Lionel Hampton, Teddy Wilson, and—yes—Charlie Christian. Billy said Christian blew everybody off the stage. I never forgot that.

# *Chapter 23*

*Jack Bruce and friends; Coryell and Mandel go to London to have tea with—hey—Mitch and Jack*

I'D BECOME FRIENDLY WITH JACK BRUCE when we had worked opposite each other at the Fillmore West; I was with Gary Burton and he was in Cream. Later, when the GB Quartet was playing in London at Ronnie Scott's, Eric Clapton, Ginger Baker, and Jack all came down to the club, and we hung out. It was nice the way we admired each other's music and supported each other.

Cream broke up in 1969, and I invited Jack to come over to New York and play at Slug's with my band, which had Mike Mandel on organ and Steve Haas on drums—the Seattle contingent. I wanted Jack to become the bassist in the band, but it didn't work out. Mike Mandel tells me that saxophonist Gato Barbieri sat in with us that weekend—I don't remember that, but Mike's memory is pretty good, so it must have happened. I do remember noticing how excited Jack was to be playing in a funky jazz dive on the Lower East Side—at one point he bit his guitar strap as a gesture of enthusiasm. I really don't know how we sounded, but we had a lot of energy, and the people at Slug's were digging that an ex-member of Cream was onstage.

Another thing I remember about that gig is that the Sharon Tate tragedy occurred at that time. We finished playing on Saturday night and drove up Sixth Avenue to the famous newsstand near Eighth Street, where we picked up the early Sunday edition of the Times—and the story of the murders by the Charles Manson "family," in all its horror, was on the front page. I had attended the same high school as Sharon back in Richland, Washington, and delivered her family's newspaper. One night I had gone to collect for the paper and chatted with her for a few minutes. She was a real knockout. What happened to her—that whole Manson thing—was terrible.

In December 1969, Jack called and asked Mike and me to play on the Jack Bruce and Friends tour that was being put together. Mitch Mitchell was going to be the drummer. Mike and I were over the moon. We flew to London (first class on British Airways), moved into the third floor of Jack's house, went to a party at Robert Stigwood's mansion, and rehearsed. Between rehearsals, we talked about our children—my wife and I had just had Murali (who was called "Illya" at the time), and Jack and his wife, Janet, had their boy, Joey. The little boys were about the same age—just a few months old.

Jack's time with Cream had rewarded him well. Stigwood was managing him, he had a good record contact, and he had signed on Bob Adcock as his road manager. His house was really beautiful, and he owned an Island up near Scotland called "Sanda." Jack had a grand piano upstairs where we'd work on music. He played the piano very well, and I could see he was a trained musician. Jack hailed from Glasgow, which had a rep for being a tough Scottish city, but, at the same time, coming from there had given him a good bit of sophistication. The first time Jack sat down at his piano, he played a phrase from Jerome Kern's "Old Man River"—the line that goes: "Here we all work on the Mississippi." That was in response, I think, to a line from my album *Lady Coryell* where I sing: "I used to play downtown with Jack, my Mississippi River boy."

Jack had come to New York to play with me at Slug's, which was "downtown"—so, to complete the poetic connection, he had played the Kern phrase with "Mississippi" in it. Maybe that's not what he meant at all, but if it was, it was a nice gesture. I never asked him about it.

One night when Jack was playing the piano, he played a swift pentatonic scale a half-step above the tonic, which resolved, due to the nature of the scale, a half-step down to the root note. I never forgot that. I loved that phrase, and it showed up in one of my compositions about a year down the road. I used that pentatonic fragment for the beginning and ending of the piece, which ended up being called, surprisingly enough, "Scotland."

Jack, Mike, and I prepared the music for the tour. It was relaxed and exciting at the same time, and there was a lot of British music-press interest to help stimulate things. Our first gig was in London—Jeff Beck showed up, as did Noel Redding, who gave me lessons on how to whack guitar chords like a British rock star.

Then we went to the States and opened at the Fillmore East opposite Mountain with Leslie West on guitar, the late Felix Pappalardi on bass, and Corky Laing on drums. McLaughlin was there. Hendrix was there. My wife and our baby boy, in his crib, were there, too. Hendrix stood over the crib, and the two of them seemed to connect in a mystical way, as if something were being passed from the grown-up genius into the infant. Murali, it turns out, grew up to play blues and sing soul—so judge for yourself.

On opening night we played first, doing music from Jack's solo record *Songs for a Tailor,* including a song that so many people still love to this day, "Theme for an Imaginary Western." They way I remember it, after we played the people didn't want us to leave the stage, and when Mountain came on Felix had to yell at the audience to "shut the fuck up" so they could play. What Mike remembers is completely different. He says that we were not really playing together, and that people in the theater told us so, yelling, "Get it together!" The truth must be somewhere in between.

There is a bootleg from that weekend—the last set of the last night—and when I listened to it years later, it sounded like a jail break. It was poorly recorded (probably from a seat in the audience), and it's hard to hear everything, but I thought that my playing was pretty good. I was bringing a lot of jazz phrasing into the mix, especially on the big hit numbers like "Sunshine of Your Love." Also, to this day, "Theme for an Imaginary Western" holds up well—good melody, good changes, good emotion.

I can't talk about the Fillmore East without adding a word about Bill Graham. The raucous-arty atmosphere of Bill's cutting-edge music palaces was unique, and places like that simply don't exist anymore. Bill was a real piece of work—a German Jew who escaped from the Nazis and came to America, where he brashly achieved mega-success in the music business. Boy, what a foul-mouthed dude he could be—but I have to give him credit for recognizing the new guys and new groups as part of a special movement in music in those days. One of my biggest regrets, early in my career, was that Bill had offered to book the Free Spirits at the Fillmore West in San Francisco right at the moment when I decided to leave the group and join Gary Burton.

With Jack Bruce, I was playing a Fender Strat in addition to my Super 400—and it was fun, regardless of what really happened musically. It's too bad that Strat got stolen out of my van on Tenth Street one day. The same thing happened to Murali many years later; a prize Ovation Adamas guitar that I had given him got nicked out of his car. Rule number one about New York City and guitars: never leave a guitar in a vehicle.

After our Fillmore East debut, Jack Bruce and Friends toured all over the U.S., playing mostly on weekends. We did Philly, Chicago (where we were visited by the notorious Plaster Casters, as well as the James Gang's Joe Walsh), Houston, Detroit (where Mitch played a great drum solo), and San Francisco. We played in New Orleans right at Mardis Gras time, and the opening group there was a band called Zephyr, with the late guitarist Tommy Bolin, who later went on to play with Billy Cobham and Alphonse Mouzon.

One funny thing I remember about being in New Orleans at that time: Julie (who was traveling with the group) and I were on a health kick. Yes, a health kick. This included trying to eat mostly vegetarian and drinking raw juices, for which purpose we carried a juicer—on the road. So we had this big bulky juicer in the hotel room the first night we got to the hotel and we were trying to make juice from strawberries. (That's all we could find in the way of fresh fruit in the Big Easy—things were a bit hectic due to the huge crowds attending Mardi Gras, and as a result it was hard to get around town to shop.) At the same time we were "health-ing" it with the juicer, we were also getting totally blasted with whatever was avail-able—I seem to recall a lot of alcohol going around in addition to the usual staples like grass, etc.

When the junket was over, Jack Bruce and Friends never played together again, but somehow we all remained friends. The tour was marked by tremendous consumption of substances known for stimulating—and numbing—the senses. By the time Julie and I flew to L.A. to recuperate from the tour, my nose was all plugged up. We stayed with Fred and Patricia Tackett, at whose house we had met that fate-ful night in '68. Fred is a great guitarist/musician in his own right and a dear friend, and I always appreciated his hospitality. By this time the Tacketts were living in Topanga Canyon, and the clear, dry air there opened up my sinuses quickly. I did get a chance to play with Jack some years later—in Romania, of all places. He still can bang out a killin' version of "Sunshine of Your Love."

And then, lo and behold, Jack and I ended up playing together again in 1999 on a latter-day version of Hendrix's "Manic Depression," for a project headed by the English drummer Steve Clarke. I think it was called *Highly Committed Media Players*. For my solo on the tune, I didn't use a pick; I just played with my right-hand fingers. Hey, it came out different—and Jack's presence had inspired me to do that.

Jack is one of a kind. He has always wanted to be on the cutting edge of modern music and has never lost his zest for creativity—in his singing and com-posing and, of course, his bass playing. During the course of his long career, he has survived a lot of health-related challenges, including a liver transplant. He's a good guy and a unique musician.

# *Chapter 24*

## *The trio and "Hail to the death of rock & roll"*

I WAS TRYING TO PLAY JAZZ in the early 1970s, but I wanted to have a different-sounding group. I wanted electric bass, not upright, so I tried to get the hottest electric bassist in New York, Jerry Jemmott, to join. Jerry was nice—he couldn't do it, but he recommended a bassist from Philly named Mervin Bronson, whom Jerry described as "treacherous." Little did I know what that meant, but I'd find out soon enough.

Mervin was living in the City, so we got together and played a bit. He said he enjoyed the playing so much it felt like he was getting out of jail. So that was good. On drums, I had been using a youngster from Chattanooga named Harry Wilkinson who played on top of the beat and had a modern style, like Tony Williams. Harry and Mervin might have seemed like a strange combination, but they clicked as a tight rhythm section. Pretty soon, we were onstage at the Village Gate in January 1971, recording a live album that was produced by the ever-present Danny Weiss.

I had done a trio record with Chuck Rainey and Bernard Purdy six months earlier, at the Montreux Jazz Festival in Switzerland, and the new trio was using the same approach, which included some vocals sung by me or, at times, my wife and me. The main instrumental thrust was to play a theme and then improvise on it, using a modal approach, going for variations based more on the rhythm and the melody than the harmony. We did some stuff in unusual time signatures like 5/4 ("After Later") and 7/4 ("Foreplay"), and we also played some Cream/Hendrix-type jams where we stated the melody and then went into open improvisation ("Beyond These Chilling Winds").

All of this was done to varying degrees of success, but overall it was different, original, and at times LOUD. I was playing through Sunn amps; I had gotten them after seeing Hendrix use them—Jimi didn't always use Marshalls.

It was around this time that Jimi died. I was as shocked as anybody—he was only 27. I had written a theme called "The Opening" for the Village Gate gig, and there was a short vocal in front that started with these lyrics: "Hail to the death of rock & roll/Welcome to the birth of music with soul." Well, after the Gate record came out, I got a letter from a Hendrix fan who had misinterpreted that as referring to Jimi's death. He wrote that he hoped Hendrix would come back from the dead and "kick my ass!" He didn't understand that I was referring to my own quest, my own attempt to use rock as part of a new form that mixed styles. What I had in mind was combining supercharged rock elements with jazz and Indian improv concepts to make a new music. Thus the line that followed: "We've thrown all the names and labels away/This is the music that we play today."

As a footnote to that, in the late '90s a British group named Corner Shop, which included Indian immigrants, sampled "The Opening" for a tune called "Candyman." It was a success for them, and I dug that, especially since I had made a concerted attempt to include Indian elements in my music from 1970 onward.

# Chapter 25

## Barefoot Boy, *the Count, and* Electric Ladyland—*plus Eddie Kramer*

With two fusion-type trio albums behind me, I wanted to expand the group to a quartet, so it was time to call on my saxophone-playing friend Steve "The Count" Marcus. Bob Thiele called and said he wanted me to do a record, so I got Mervin, Harry, the Count, and Roy Haynes (from my GB Quartet days), and we went into Electric Ladyland Studios on a cold January evening, about a year after the Village Gate date. What was really cool about this date was the presence of Jimi's old engineer, Eddie Kramer. Here we were in the House That Jimi Built with his engineer, and we were about to play some hard-drivin', rockin' fusion that gave no quarter and made no compromise. It was colder than all get-out outside, but inside the main Ladyland studio we were heating up.

As had been the case with the *Lady Coryell* sessions, the first tune of what became known as *Barefoot Boy* was bass-less. Remember when Jerry Jemmott told me Mervin was "treacherous"? Well, in much the same manner that Jimmy Garrison was late for what became the "Stiffneck" duet with Elvin, Mervin didn't show up on time for the "Gypsy Queen" take. We had to do it without him. That was my bass-player-showing-up-late-for-New-York-sessions karma (although I don't think that ever happened again).

For one of the tunes, I hewed a theme out of a Freddie Hubbard phrase I had heard on the Bill Evans album *Interplay*. I took a four-bar lick from Freddie's solo on "You and the Night and the Music," played it three times, and then added a descending pentatonic line that lasted ten beats. That was misnamed "The Great Escape" on the record. The actual tune called "The Great Escape" was not on *Barefoot Boy*; even though we had recorded it the same night, Thiele nixed it. The titles just got mixed up. The tune I had originally called "The Great Escape" ended up being the title tune of a later Vanguard record, which had to be named *The Real Great Escape*.

After *Barefoot Boy* came out, I ran into the great New Orleans keyboardist-vocalist Mac Rebennack, also known as Dr. John, at the Lenox Hotel in Boston. He had heard the record and made a suggestion about "The Great Escape"—when the improvisation started, he said, we should have stuck to the strict form of the theme for the blowing and included that ten-beat part. He had a point; it would have made the track even more interesting. I appreciated that Mac had taken the time to listen that carefully to my music. He's a dear friend and later on, when I had my Japanese radio show in the 1990s with co-host Jimmy Webb, we did an entire show with Mac. It was one of the best shows that we did.

*Barefoot Boy* also had a long version of a piece entitled "Call to the Higher Consciousness." It took up one side of the vinyl disc. The title came from a phrase spoken by Guru—Sri Chinmoy—during the ceremony where he named our first son, Murali. The harmony includes one particularly dissonant chord—kind of a slash chord (a combination of two chords, like Dm/E♭maj7)—that I had heard on Hugh Masakela's first album, recorded at the Village Gate. In Hughie's version, the pianist, Larry Willis (who later became a great friend), played some chords, including that slash chord, in an upbeat African rhythm. In my composition, that chord was there, but it was played more in the spirit of Coltrane's Tyner-Jones-Garrison rhythm-section feel. Roy Haynes really sounded good on that tune—well, he sounded good on the whole record, but on "Call" in particular.

I recall quite clearly how beautifully Steve Marcus played on that record. It was especially gratifying when we were listening to the playback of the bass-less "Gypsy," and Bob Thiele was rhapsodizing about how great the Count sounded. I thought, Of course the Count sounds great—that's why I called him for the date!

When the record came out, some critics—in England, I believe—didn't like it because of the long tracks, especially "Call to the Higher Consciousness." But one person who really did like it was Carlos Santana—he dug the heck out of our version of "Gypsy." Carlos and I were connected through my original jazz guitar mentor, Gabor Szabo. "Gypsy" was one of Gabor's compositions, and he had recorded it on his record *Spellbinder*. Carlos later recorded it his way in a medley that was a big hit for him in the late '60s. Years later, Carlos and I took turns playing (several years apart) with Alice Coltrane and her family, including son Ravi on tenor, when the biannual Coltrane Gala was presented in Los Angeles.

I decided that my next record was going to be different from *Barefoot Boy*. Rather than choosing the players, deciding on some material, and then going in to record everything without performing any of the music, I made a conscious effort to pick the musicians and develop the material onstage first.

I had hooked up with a West Coast agent named Sandra Getz, and she booked a string of gigs for me in October 1971 in Colorado, Washington State, and California. The band was going to be Mervin, Harry, and me, plus the Count. We loaded up in three cars and headed west. My car was a stodgy Volvo I had purchased with the help of Jimmy Webb out in L.A. (I had met Jimmy through my first wife and her association with Fred and Patricia Tackett; Fred was Jimmy's rhythm guitarist and sort of his right-hand man.)

I picked up Mervin in Harlem, gave him a large wad of cash that he used to buy a shitload of coke to go with his notoriously top-quality weed, and we were off. The first gig, in Colorado, was a week away. On the first day, we rendezvoused with the Count and his wife, Eleanor, plus Harry and his wife, Wendy, somewhere in Ohio. We never saw them again until we got to the Rockies.

Mervin and I got to Colorado in four days, maybe a little less. We never stopped to sleep—we were having too much fun. When I arrived at the motel in Boulder, I sheepishly told the front-desk clerk that we were early and would need our rooms now instead of two days later.

Our first gig was at a club called Tulagi's, just off the campus of the University of Colorado. It was a big room for a college club, and most of the audience was college kids. There was a positive, hungry-for-change vibe on the campus—that's one of the reasons we were playing there, I think—but there was a down side to this scenario, a kind of misguided activist agenda by some of the student groups.

When we were playing the last set of the two-night engagement, Mervin suddenly yelled, "Get off the stage—somebody says there's a bomb!" We stopped playing and got out of the club. The club owner told me that a group of African-American students at the university, the Black Student Caucus or something like that, had threatened to blow up the place because "Larry Coryell is a racist guitarist." It turned out to be a hoax—a college prank type of thing. I guess I will never find out what really happened, but it doesn't matter, because our main focus for being out on the road was to develop the music.

In spite of that bomb-scare aberration, something creative had happened at Tulagi's when I was messing around with the vamp-coda of "Beyond These Chilling Winds" from the *Live at the Village Gate* album. Instead of taking the bass line down, I tried starting the vamp with the bass line going up. The vamp-coda required the sixth string of the guitar to be tuned down to D, and when I reversed the bass line that tuning caused me to stumble into a different time signature, 17/8. The rhythm was now five groups of three followed by one group of two—and we had the makings of a different song.

The song was being transformed (quite by accident) into a new composition, so I took the idea I'd heard Jack Bruce play on the piano in his house in London a year and a half before and expanded on it. That section became the intro and the ending. Then the 17/8 vamp (including the improvisational form) became the primary body of the piece, for which I composed a unison line for guitar and soprano sax. Voila! We had a new tune to play on the road.

This new piece was much more interesting than "Beyond," especially because "Beyond" had a vocal part and Mervin was talking me out of singing—rightly so—at the time. With that as a basis, we began to build a new set of compositions to play. Harry had written a piece called "Offering" that was basically modal, and I had put together "Foreplay" (that pseudo-Latin thing in 7/4), which was a repeated set of changes (two scales could cover the improvisation on that). And Harry had a protégé friend from Tennessee named Doug Davis who contributed two good compositions. We played all this new stuff on the West Coast, and when we finished the tour and got back to New York, we went into the Vanguard studios and added my old friend from Washington State, Mike Mandel, on keyboards.

The result was a pretty good record called *Offering*. One memory that really sticks out about that session was when we were tracking "Scotland," my piece in 17/8. Tony Williams happened to be visiting a friend in the building on that block of 23rd Street on the West Side, and he stuck his head in the control room (which was on the ground floor near the entrance of the building) during a playback. He was really digging it. He told us as much, and that made us feel great—we all loved Tony, who was a true jazz drumming innovator. (The last time I saw Tony was at the memorial service for Wayne Shorter's wife in Santa Monica in 1996. I flew in directly from Pittsburgh, where I was gigging, went to the service, and flew back the same day. Tony was there with his new wife, and he was in a really good space—and for that, for him, I was happy. When he passed away unexpectedly due to complications from surgery shortly afterwards, I was devastated.)

After *Offering* came out, we started adding Mike to the band on a regular basis. He was living in Boston but contemplating a move to New York. The next record for Vanguard was *The Real Great Escape,* and Mike was on that one, too. It was more pop-oriented, and it kind of broke the line of jazz-oriented playing we'd established with *Live at the Village Gate* and *Offering*.

The quartet, minus Mike, was booked to play at the Anderson Theater in late 1972 or early '73, opposite Captain Beefheart. This was to be a fateful gig, because I was about to meet up with a pair of producers who would become my managers. The whole thing eventually ended up in a disaster, but it was what it was—sometimes insane screw-ups have to happen so we will learn needed lessons.

The thing with my managers-to-be began innocently enough with the Anderson Theater event, which was deemed a big success for both the quartet and these young producers. Not long after that, I signed a management deal with these two guys, who will be known henceforth as "Tom and Vince." My lack of business acumen had begun to come rather obviously to the surface, so I approached Tom and Vince and asked for some help with my career—especially since I was a bit too cavalier with money. I signed with them in the spring of 1973.

By that time, I had compiled a small collection of original compositions on my recordings and somehow attracted an efficient publishing administrator named Rahn Eckhart. He had moved into the Connecticut house formerly owned by Andrew Loog Oldham, manager of the Rolling Stones, no less, and he had had some success in collecting composers' royalties on behalf of his rather hip roster of clients—most of them British rockers. Eckhart somehow found me and became extremely helpful in sorting out my publishing situation. He had used his native German know-how coupled with his love of music to help a lot of jazz composers, including Gil Evans, Dexter Gordon, and Cecil Taylor. He knew that rock acts could generate some good income, but that it was also prestigious to have some jazz clients as well—luckily, I made that list.

So—as "helpers" in my career, starting around 1973, I had Tom and Vince, and also Eckhart. Tom and Vince were about as different from Eckhart as one could imagine, but I didn't see the difference. And even if I had, it wouldn't have changed anything. I was still pretty green in the maturity department at this stage of my life. Many, many things would need to happen over the next few years to remove me from the rolls of the clueless. I must say—from this vantage point in 2004, as I write this—that nothing does the job of developing wisdom as well as direct experience. The pain aspect of experience seems to be the most effective way of learning some of the basic rules about life.

We had one more tour with that group, which was known as Foreplay (after the name of my tune and not to be confused with the later group called Fourplay), and it was kind of a disaster. During this time I was living way out in the country near Doylestown, Pennsylvania. I had moved there in 1971, after the lease on our beach house in Connecticut ran out. I retreated deeply into drinking, and it became such a problem that I had to see a therapist. He sent me to group sessions made up of young people intent on staying free of drink and drugs. This was my first brush with an organized therapeutic community, and I didn't get the full message at the time. I committed myself to stopping the drinking, but inwardly I reserved the right to get high now and then. Hey, I couldn't give up everything—that wouldn't be hip! How deluded was that? Well, it was what it was, and at least a seed had been planted regarding an aspect of my life that sooner or later I would have to deal with. But let's get back to the music.

# *Chapter 26*

## *The Eleventh House gets started*

SOMETIME IN EARLY 1973, I had a conversation in New York with Alphonse Mouzon, who had been the original drummer in Weather Report. He and I agreed that we were at a stage in our musical journeys where we wanted to make a creative statement that would include rock and funk ideas (and, for me, some contemporary classical) in a modern/progressive direction. Of course, we were "jazz people": I had worked with Chico Hamilton, Gary Burton, and Herbie Mann; Alphonse with Weather Report and McCoy Tyner, among others. But at this juncture, we wanted to head towards combining the integrity of jazz with some of the glitz and excitement of rock and funk. We felt it was a combination of styles whose time had come.

I networked with Tom and Vince on this, and we put together a band: in addition to Alphonse on drums, we got Randy Brecker on trumpet and Mike Mandel on keyboards. We held auditions for a bass player, and the one guy who could play the hard chart ("Ejercicio") was named Danny Trifan. He'd been playing with singer-songwriter Buzzy Linhart. Danny took the chart home overnight and came back the next day and nailed it, so I guess he cheated a little bit. I had asked some of the other bassists to play it cold, so maybe it wasn't fair—but that's how we got Danny, and, with that, we had a group.

That group was the first incarnation of the Eleventh House. The name came from a suggestion by my wife, who was deep into astrology. The Eleventh House in one's horoscope represents your friends, hopes, and aspirations, so we thought it would be a positive name for the band. Our first record was done at Vanguard Studios on 23rd Street in the fall of 1973. We had a lot of rehearsals for the date, and it was exciting in the sense that we were newly formed and still discovering what we could do.

Mouzon brought in a couple of tunes including "The Funky Waltz." Mandel had some things, including one called "Joy Ride" and another titled "Adam Smasher." I brought in, among other compositions, "Low-Lee-Tah," which had an Arabic ambience to it; initially we tried doing it with Mike doubling the repeated guitar pattern on keyboards, but that didn't work. I ended up playing the doubled pattern myself (on two separate tracks), to make it sound "exotic." Randy's solo on "Low-Lee-Tah" was amazing—so much like Miles, yet so much like himself. I was clean and sober, and it was a good session.

As soon as the record was finished, we went to Europe for our first tour. For several months, from the formation of the group through the recording sessions and the tour, I neither drank nor got high. Things were starting to look good, and I even brought my wife and children along on the tour.

That tour in late '73 took us to Germany, Switzerland, Denmark, Sweden, Holland, and France. The Swiss writers were a bit skeptical. The first thing they asked was, "How are you going to keep stars like Randy Brecker and Alphonse Mouzon in the band?" That's typical of the Swiss—they see things realistically. But Swiss audiences are good listeners, and they're quiet and attentive for the most part. If we played well, they got it—totally, in all the details. When we got to France we laid up in Paris, and I recall saying to my wife, "I think the entire answer to life lies in one's children." This was a rather strange thing for me to say, but I meant it. Murali and Julian were with us, and Julian was just a baby, maybe six months old.

We went to the South of France and gigged in Montpelier; during the show, Tom was blocking an entrance door to prevent freebies from sliding in. At one point, he confronted some gate-crashers with a hearty, American-accented "La porte est fermé!" It was hilarious.

Then we wended our way west to Toulouse, where there were more shenanigans. Mike thinks that he might have insulted the French during a radio interview the night before the concert, but I'm not sure that was the source of the problem. What did happen was an agitated group of students decided that "all music should be free"—that is, they didn't want to pay—so they rioted outside the theater where we were performing, throwing rocks against the second-floor dressing room window. Then they turned over some cars and set fire to trash cans. We were transported in police vans that night, and les gendarmes came in to restore order in violent enough fashion to send some of the rioters to the hospital.

The next day, the promoter took several of the band members, including me, to the hospital, to visit and comfort the injured parties. That gesture seemed to create some harmony out of what was a rather strange and uncomfortable situation.

After we left the hospital, the promoter—a lady named Frederica—took me to a shop and had me buy a rather hip-looking Mickey Mouse shirt and a tight white dress suit, complete with vest. We paired that with a black shirt. Pretty fancy! I had the John Travolta look long before Saturday Night Fever. I'm wearing that suit on the cover of *Level One*, the second Eleventh House record. (I had gotten into wearing "hip threads" before, when I was with the GB Quartet. In London, we went to the famous Carnaby Street, and I spent most of my salary on the latest fashions. I recall a black fur coat I'd purchased that caught Thelonious Monk's eye during the Wein tour of 1967.)

I dug my new threads so much that when we got on the train to go to the next gig, I pulled out my suitcase and threw on the white suit so the cats could check it out. Alphonse was also a spectacular dresser. His nickname was "Funky Snakefoot" (which became one of his album titles), and he wore some serious platform shoes that set him apart as a really outrageous clotheshorse.

As we made our way across Europe, I noticed how intelligent our bassist was. Danny Trifan had been home-schooled, and I knew he was bright, musically, but I saw how that brightness also carried over to his love of history. As we traveled through France and Germany, Danny, who usually sat next to Mike Mandel (they were both Scorpios), would point out various castles. He knew the names of most of them, the era in which they were built, and how they were important in the history of the area. After he left the Eleventh House, Danny went on to become a professor of history at a college in Missouri. He came to a Coryell Family concert in St. Louis in 2001, and we had a great reunion. Danny played some good bass when he was with the House, plus he was an ideal sideman with a great attitude.

After France, we went to Belgium, and—it being autumn and northern Europe being what it is—we all got sick. There was something going around called the "Belgian Grippe," and my wife, my kids, and I all caught it. At the height of the illness, we just lay around our hotel rooms with little or no energy. When we were at the gig, they had cots for us to lie down on. After we played the gig, the Belgian Grippe disappeared—go figure.

When we got back to the States, we kept touring, mostly on the East Coast, including places like Buffalo and Worcester, Massachusetts. We also played at the Academy of Music on 14th Street in New York City—there's a picture of me there, wearing a dark-blue long-sleeved sweater, that was used a lot during that time for publicity. All I recall about that gig is how scared I was—the place was packed and we were on the bill with Return To Forever.

The gig in Worcester was at a place called Sir Morgan's Cove, and I started to drink again that night. That was my first drink after being completely clean for several months. My behavior as a bandleader changed drastically when I drank; I started scolding the musicians onstage and acting bossy and unpleasant. It was the beginning of my slide back into the bottle and the joint. Little did I know, at that point, that my return to substance abuse would practically wipe out all the good fortune I'd had while sober at the beginning of the Eleventh House's history.

Around that time, Danny left the band. I'm not sure why. I know that Alphonse had voiced a strong desire to play with John Lee, a bassist we'd met on the European tour. John and his rhythm section partner, Gerry Brown, were playing with a Dutch flautist-bandleader named Chris Hinze. So we replaced Danny with John Lee—John can play, that's for sure—and then Randy Brecker was lured away by his good friend from Dreams, Billy Cobham (the drummer on *Spaces*).

I was so upset about Randy leaving that I went to his place—a spacious loft in the Bowery—and stood outside the door and tried to talk him into staying in the band. It was nothing more or less than alcoholic dramatic-bullshit behavior. At that time, I had no emotional "muscles" to deal with adversity. I just emoted. But I got over it—by getting more loaded.

# Chapter 27

*Mike Lawrence comes into the House and we hit the French trail again, encountering a riot or two; then beloved Mike makes an exit*

WE REPLACED RANDY WITH MICHAEL LAWRENCE, a trumpeter I'd heard at Slug's during my first few months of living in New York. I clearly recall what happened the first time I saw him: there was a jam-session atmosphere at the club that night, but I was too scared to sit in. Then this tall Jewish kid walks forward and goes up on the bandstand and plays his ass off. I couldn't believe it. When Mike came off, I asked him, "How'd you go up there and play with those cats, cold, like that, with no preparation?" And he said to me, "Confidence, man, confidence." Well, in 1974 that confidence landed him in the House. Mike Lawrence played with all the top people in New York, including Joe Henderson. When I told Randy who we got to replace him, he was over the moon—he said, "Hey, he's better than me!" I don't know about that, but it was a heck of a good endorsement.

With Mike in place and playing beautifully, we went back to France. During that tour, we had a daytime event in Paris, and the equipment didn't show up. "Ah, you know the French," everyone said, "they're kind of irresponsible." (Although that situation could have happened in any country.) But I still had an acoustic guitar—a nice, clean-sounding instrument made by Augie LoPrinzi, who had a shop near my house in Pennsylvania. So I played the gig mostly by myself, on that guitar. Eventually Alphonse came in with light brushes on the snare, the rest of the cats provided some limited support, and voila!—we created a special event out of a disaster. There was a writer from *Melody Maker* there, and he wrote a great review, saying something to the effect that, after having heard me save the gig acoustically, the British "should reconsider the way Larry Coryell is perceived in this country."

The French still made me feel uneasy, mainly because I didn't understand their language, even though most of those who were our fans spoke some English. I was starting to see that if I were to feel more comfortable in their quixotic country, I would need to learn more than just "get-by" French. Besides, I was starting to make friends and acquaintances in France, plus I was starting to dig some French classical music, like Satie, Ravel, and Debussy, as well as some of the French-speaking jazz players, like Martial Solal and the Belgian guitarist Philip Catherine.

I have to admit that the years 1974 to 1977 are kind of a blur to me, as everything positive that I did both professionally and personally kept getting sabotaged by my alcoholism. I know that in mid-1973 we were living in Wilton, Connecticut—we had moved from Pennsylvania—but we moved again a year or so later, after the lease ran out, to New Canaan, a few miles to the west. I think our address was on Hickock Road. I really got into coke at this point and became rather skinny. I know I went to Europe a lot, but I don't remember much except episodes of insanity. And I know I started writing columns for *Guitar Player* magazine in 1977.

We kept returning to France to play because the promoter over there, the aforementioned Frederica, really liked me. She was from Corsica, and Corsicans are kind of wild and crazy. We would get high on coke right at our table in a restaurant in Paris, or in some of the smaller cities that had a nice ambience, like Nancy. One time when we were in a castle-turned-recording-studio, Frederica's boyfriend, a rocker name Felix, climbed up on the dinner table and crawled on his hands and knees the length of the table to pour somebody a glass of Champagne. (I wasn't actually there, but I heard about this.)

I loved all the drinking—it was exotic, somehow, doing it in Europe. Or so I thought. I also thought I was getting into less trouble drinking over there, which was a total misconception. At least I was starting to pick up a little bit of French. I remember the way Felix said "evidence"—it sounded like lay-vee-dahnse, but I recognized the word. Oh, that French accent!

Felix was typical of the music lovers on the Continent at that time. They liked hard-rock and heavy-metal lead guitar (Felix loved Ronnie Montrose), but their European sensibility made them amenable to our jazz-oriented, complex improvisations. The presence of Randy Brecker and then Michael Lawrence in the band, playing jazz trumpet, added to this appeal. We were playing something that was familiar to them—the straight-eighths beat and the blues-rock phrasing—but at the same time we were incorporating a sophistication that fit with their love of culture.

In the summer of 1974 we played the Montreux Jazz Festival opposite Billy Cobham and recorded the concert. It came out later on Vanguard on a record called *The Eleventh House at Montreux*. (It was one of my last releases for Vanguard on that particular contract). We played pretty well and it was a successful gig. After that, we went straight to Lincoln Center to play in Avery Fisher Hall for a George Wein production. We played a short set because that's what George liked at his festivals—get on, play for maybe 30 minutes, get off. Oregon was also on the bill, and I remember Mike Lawrence was raving about them as he stood listening on the side of the stage.

Tom and Vince were trying to get us out of my Vanguard contract and onto the roster of up-and-coming Arista Records. The great Clive Davis, who had started Arista after leaving Columbia, was interested in us. We had to retain a big-time New York lawyer, whose name escapes me now, and go through all kinds of painful legal stuff to break free of the Vanguard contract. I was not emotionally strong during this time, feeling strange about even needing to be in court for something, much less a forceful breakup of a record deal. Knowing that I needed a lawyer for a problem—man, that made me uncomfortable. But we did it, signing with Arista and then starting work on *Level One,* which was to be recorded in good ol' Electric Ladyland .

Alphonse had secured the producer, a California guy named Skip Drinkwater, and we all had high hopes for this next step in the musical journey of the House. John Lee was onboard as our bass player, and he was playing great plus contributing some compositions—he was a brilliant "thinking-man's funk" composer. Mike Lawrence had written an extremely good piece called "The Other Side" that reminded me of Horace Silver. And I had new stuff, including some funky things, some 20th-century classical ("Eyes of Love"), and a down-home blues-type stomper named after the band's coke dealer, Ronny Sunshine. The title of that opus was "Struttin' with Sunshine"—oh, what a fucked-up life!

At that time, my progression was one of achievement, self-imposed setback, achievement, setback—forward and backward, ad nauseum. And, of course, there was an unofficial provision in the recording budget for mood-changing chemicals. It's a miracle that those of us who were using got any decent music together at all. But when you combine the self-will of an addict with the availability of nearly unlimited takes in a recording session, you can, with decent production, create some music that makes a rather strong impact. That's what *Level One* did. It had a lot of high-energy overdrive guitar (Steve Khan lent me a couple of axes—thanks, brother, you always did have great equipment) plus some clean electric guitar and (on "Eyes") some steel-string solo acoustic. In spite of all the negative influences that were trying to destroy me and everyone around me, having compositions from the band members brought out the originality in the music, and we made a good record.

Shortly after that, we toured again, hit Europe, had parties, had fights, met new friends, ate good food, and generally lived the kind of life musicians dream about. But after about a year, Mike Lawrence started to feel unwell. Eventually he was diagnosed with stomach cancer and admitted to Sloan-Kettering Hospital in

New York. One thing I remember about his hospitalization was Julie's concern for Mike—she went to visit him in the hospital almost every day. Unfortunately, his life was cut short by that terrible disease. We had a beautiful memorial service for him. As you walked into the funeral home you could hear his music playing over the sound system—it sounded great. The whole band was there, as well as his family. We all made the best of it, if it's possible to say that. The memorial service was followed by an immediate burial, and the rabbi spoke about "ashes to ashes and dust to dust" as we laid Mike to rest in a cemetery near Newark. It was a somber coda for a first-class player. I guess it was time for him to move on.

Mike Lawrence, the hot trumpet player who, as fate would have it, came into my band and did such a great job, was a dignified and noble person. He was a complete musician—a deep jazz talent—and he left us in the prime of his life. To this day, I miss him. As the saying goes, "Only the good die young." After a bad thing like that happens, something good usually follows—and what followed was that Mike's widow, Roberta Lawrence, took some of his uncompleted tracks, added great soloists including Herbie Hancock and Mike Brecker and put out a beautiful Mike Lawrence record posthumously, titled *Nightwind*. It was a shining example of quality fusion.

We had to find someone to replace Mike on trumpet, and—thanks to John Lee—we were able to hook up with Japan's answer to Miles Davis: the inimitable Terumasa Hino. With Terumasa in the band, we got right to work on *Aspects,* our second Arista album. Randy Brecker was the producer, and we had guitarist-composer Danny Toan, percussionist Mtume, guitarist Steve Khan, and saxophonists Mike Brecker and David Sanborn as guests. Plus Randy came out of the console room for a minute to write some horn arrangements and play a bit. But Hino was the killer soloist on this outing. He had incredible stamina and energy and great chops—listen to the trumpet on "Kowloon Jag." He had a crazy fire coming out of the depths of his life and through his horn. He was like a fighting samurai!

There was another important personnel change, on drums. Alphonse had elected to move to California and go out on his own, so John Lee's old battery mate, Gerry Brown, took his place. (Flash forward to 2000: I played a special event at Mars Music in Fort Lauderdale, Florida, with Bill Dickens on bass and Gerry on drums. We'd never played as a trio before, and Gerry played what was, for me, the most perfect set a jazz-fusion drummer could play. It was stupendous.)

With Gerry onboard, the House got to work, noses to the grindstone, on composing and arranging. Mike Mandel had a composition called "Pyramids"; Danny Toan contributed "Titus"—very funky; John Lee and Gerry Brown co-wrote one of those "thinking-man's funk" tunes, "Yin Yang"; John also brought in a tune of his called "Ain't It Is." I contributed, in addition to "Kowloon Jag," the title tune, "Aspects," and "Rodrigo Reflections" (played with Khan in a guitar duo). After the record came out, *Downbeat* magazine played "Kowloon Jag" for Pat Martino in a blindfold test. On that track I used a lot of special effects made by Dan Armstrong—Dan had devised a way to eliminate the need for pedals and have the effects piggyback on top of each other into the guitar's input jack. I had an overdrive sound plus a ring modulator blended into my normal medium-loud fusion volume. I thought the solo was interesting, but Pat didn't like it—at least that's what he said in *Downbeat*. I still think it's a good solo, for what it is, and I think *Aspects* is a good record overall.

Be that as it may, we went on the road with Gerry Brown and Terumasa Hino and played some interesting gigs, most notably a huge festival at a racetrack in southern France. We flew into Marseilles and were driven to the site. There's a video of our performance somewhere—maybe in the vault of producer Michael Lang. I was still wearing that white suit-with-white-vest outfit from Toulouse, believe it or not. I clearly remember one tune from that performance, "Cover Girl" by Alphonse, a progressive-fusion piece that has several sections with different time signatures. We burned on that—I'd love to get the video and check it out. The audience was estimated in the hundreds of thousands, and I'd have to say that gig was the high point of the Golden Age of Fusion. From that point onward, at least for me, the fusion thing started to lose its luster.

# *Chapter 28*

**Twin House;** *meeting Philip Catherine, who leads me to* *Grappelli and a turn toward the acoustic guitar*

I WAS GROWING WEARY OF PLAYING LOUD MUSIC and wanted to focus more on the acoustic guitar. I also wanted to play with other people, notably my fellow guitarist Philip Catherine. We seemed to have a good rapport and shared some of the same influences, like Miles and Joe Pass, but he was also strongly influenced by Django Reinhardt. I had always dug Django, but Philip was an authority on the legendary gypsy guitarist—he knew everything about him and could play most of his music, many selections note-for-note. You could say he was into Django like I was into Wes.

My first encounter with Philip was at Montreux—I'm not sure of the year, but it was in the early 1970s, the same year when I recorded a solo album there, *European Impressions.* John Lee had given me a Philip Catherine album with a tune called "September Man," one of Philip's compositions. That tune struck me because Philip's lead line reminded me of a McCoy Tyner solo. At that point in my musical journey, I hadn't heard a whole lot of guitarists who were emulating McCoy's phrasing, so I took notice. The fingering of the line was quite difficult for me, so I asked Philip how he did it. His approach was a surprise—he would make large interval jumps on the same string, in a way I'd never seen before.

I played "September Man" (with my own fingering) for Philip, to show my respect for his music. Then we got together and started exchanging ideas. At some point early in that process, he showed me Django's "Nuages." It's a tune that's been done to death by guitarists, but it has a truly romantic melody and beautiful changes—if you're a jazz guitarist, you pretty much have to play "Nuages" at some point. We ended up recording it in London for a record called *Twin House* (so named to keep a connection to the Eleventh House). The record was enough of a success in both the U.S. and Europe that we were able to do a nice series of tours together.

Philip and I had struck a deal with producer Siggie Loch in a funky little jazz club in Hamburg, and the recording session took place in the same London studio (or so they told us) where the Rolling Stones had cut "(I Can't Get No) Satisfaction."

We got a cassette the day after the session and took it with us on a train to a gig somewhere in the English countryside. As we were trying to play it, a grouchy old lady sitting near us complained that we shouldn't be running a cassette player on the train. She implied that we were ill-mannered. I interpreted this as disrespecting the music—after all, we musicians are hearing music, recorded or live or in our heads, nearly all the time. I wanted to say, "Lady, you mean you can't dig somethin' this swingin'? These sounds are designed to bring happiness to your mind and peace to your heart."

We couldn't please her, but we were able to please a large number of the jazz lovers who heard *Twin House,* and a Belgian artist (a friend of Philip's whose son, Nicola Fiszman, is an excellent bassist) even made a beautiful wood-and-metal sculpture in honor of the record. At the end of the year, we were selected as Duo Artists of the Year in Germany. Too bad that little old lady on the train couldn't enjoy the first public playback of *Twin House.* The moral of this story is that just because some people don't like what you do, it doesn't mean that they represent the majority of listeners—and don't forget that.

Philip and I went on to make several more recordings together, including a thing we did in Germany called *Young Django,* with the legendary violinist Stephane Grappelli and the incomparable NHØP (that's Niels-Henning Ørsted Pedersen for you squares) on bass. Near the end of that session, I took a Charlie Christian phrase I'd heard years before and composed a blues tune around it, calling it "Blues for Django and Stephane." To my surprise, that simple blues went on to become a rather popular opus. It's been recorded by many other guitar-and-violin duos over the years.

I was gratified by Grappelli's fondness for my playing. In spite of my idiosyncrasies—like having cognac and beer for breakfast (with Stephane and Philip in attendance, shaking their heads)—Stephane said that I had, in his words, "something special." We ended up doing a beautiful tour of Europe to support the release, going to Scandinavia, Germany, and Austria. All of the players on the album, including NHØP, were on the tour.

Philip and I had a strong, high-quality duo, but on the tour we were mightily overshadowed by Grappelli's virtuosity. We were two orbiting moons to his Sun. It struck me that way because, among other reasons, Stephane could so strongly carry the vedette (as they say in French). For example, he could take an intro and carry it along for several minutes, making it sound like a Bach partita. And the sheer power of his violin's sound was a dominating force.

Stephane could also think on his feet. There was an incident in Stockholm where he was in the middle of playing a cadenza and an audience member (probably gay, like Stephane) shouted out, "Mon petit poulet!" during a particularly delicate and complex passage. Grappelli was not pleased, and without skipping a bow-stroke he shouted back in English "Shut up!" and continued with the cadenza. We all cracked up.

Grappelli was in his seventies when I started playing with him, and he knew many, many tunes. He knew most of the lyrics to the tunes that had words, and that aided him in his interpretations. Stephane could also play killer piano, in a kind of stride style with lots of chops; he'd often play the penultimate number of the concert on solo piano. He was a true melodist and a preserver of the best style of European swing jazz from the 20th century. And it was amazing to hear him with an orchestra—he soared right over it without amplification. Being around Stephane in his golden years showed me that you can go on practically forever with music; your skills are simply honed finer and richer.

Stephane had bypass surgery during one mini-tour we did, and I think I played with him only one more time after that operation. The last time I saw him perform, somewhere in Europe in the 1990s, the audience wouldn't let him off the stage—I think he did at least five curtain calls. He continued to perform with strength, even though his body was slowly giving way, to the very end. I was very lucky to know and work with Stephane Grappelli, and I have Philip to thank for that. Merci beaucoup, Philip.

# Chapter 29

*The* Guitar Player *columns—this could be the start of . . . well, it sort of was*

Around this time—I believe it was in 1976—I was asked by *Guitar Player* magazine to write a monthly instructional column, along the lines of the "contemporary guitar" concept. In my inaugural column, I wrote about an experience I had had with Dizzy Gillespie. If I'm not mistaken, the Eleventh House (the version with Hino on trumpet and John and Gerry as the rhythm section) had just finished the tour that began with that big shindig at the racetrack in France. We had been in London, to play on an important BBC television music show from that time period, "The Old Grey Whistle Test." I think Philip appeared with the band on that show, at least for some of the numbers.

After the show, I got word that Dizzy was at jazz singer Annie Ross's pad, playing cards. I went over there, and Dizzy and Annie gave me a gracious welcome. Somehow the conversation shifted from cards to music, and I ended up talking about the evening's most significant musical point in that *Guitar Player* column, which was called "Learning from Other Instruments." I wrote:

[Dizzy] showed me a thing he wrote which sounded similar to "Honky Tonk" except he turned the beat around. Instead of the obvious sounding and-ONE, and-TWO, and-THREE, and-FOUR, etc., he switched it to one-AND, two-and, three-AND, four-AND, one-AND, two-and, three-AND, four-AND, etc. Furthermore, Dizzy's line, instead of having the straight 4/4 shuffle pulse, was played over a triplet rhythm with three beats for every quarter-note—in other words, 12/8.

**Dizzy's Line**

Dizzy also played some piano the same night that he "turned the beat around," as it were, and showed me how he was influenced by Duke Ellington's "The Mooch" in utilizing a chord progression for Dizzy's own "Birk's Works." As I watched Dizzy playing the piano, I came to see the great disparity between guitar players' changes and piano players' changes, with the latter usually being hipper, because pianists have more notes at their disposal plus more opportunities for closely voiced chord clusters.

I'm so glad I documented that lesson with Dizzy back in 1976—not simply because it gave me material for my column but because the principles he demonstrated still very much apply.

That first column was also autobiographical, and I wrote about my early days as a jazz musician:

I moved to Seattle, Washington, in 1961 to study journalism and ended up a "college dropout" who opted for music. As I drifted away from my formal studies I became deeply interested in every aspect of that music called "jazz."

The first interesting discovery I made was that I had no kind of "time feeling" for jazz. My "rock" time feeling was rock-steady, however, so I figured I needed to learn the more sophisticated rhythmic concept of "bebop" as created by innovators like alto sax man Charlie Parker and trumpeter Dizzy Gillespie. This was a difficult task requiring a lot of new learning, so I set out to conquer my rushing (which was my main problem) and my tendency to play too many notes (another problem I'm still trying to solve).

In order to do this I stopped trying to play fast and tried to intuit purely "musical" phrases, using technique only when it was "musical" to do so. A lot of slow and soulful phrasing interspersed with speed makes for a better solo. After examining some of Wes Montgomery's recorded solos, I began to get the message: augment your guitaristics with non-guitar sources. In addition to studying the records of Parker and Gillespie, I listened to trumpeters like Lee Morgan and Miles Davis, saxophonists John Coltrane and Wayne Shorter, pianists McCoy Tyner and Thelonious Monk, and drummer Art Blakey, as well as guitarists like Kenny Burrell and Grant Green, who played more "horn-like." By absorbing the musical attitudes of these horn players and horn-influenced instrumentalists, I came back to my guitar with some different viewpoints— viewpoints designed to develop all the qualities that a good player (not just guitar player) possesses.

I've heard it said that "the teacher learns more than the student." This definitely applies to one-on-one guitar lessons, and it also applied to my *GP* columns. Writing a one-page instructional column forced me to make sure I knew what I was talking about, limited though my knowledge was at the time. Sometimes I edged out towards the frontiers of jive, but my *GP* editors pulled me back from that brink.

I had to be sure I knew what I was talking about, which is why I drew from direct experience so many times. To go back to that first column again, here's what I wrote about developing solid time:

> I have discovered in playing one-on-one with other musicians (horns or pianos) the dying art of rhythm guitar playing and the beautiful, delicate thing called "comping," which means, to me, sympathetic accompaniment.
>
> I developed through comping a sure-footed time feeling and an ability to listen on a higher level, because the object was to make the other guy (the soloist) sound as good as possible. Through learning standards (tunes like "Stella by Starlight" and "On Green Dolphin Street"), comping 80% of the time and soloing 20%, I established a foundation for improvising. By playing the non-soloist's part and really listening to the interaction between the comper and the soloist, one begins to learn about a solo.
>
> It was my experience with bassists which made me aware of the contrapuntal nature of improvising. With a bass line underneath, a qualified improviser can create beautiful solos out of his knowledge of the melody and chords and how they relate to the bass line in an automatic, almost doing-it-without-thinking-about-it counterpoint."

I called on my direct experience in another column that I wrote about going back to acoustic after playing electric for a long time. I couldn't get the right touch on the acoustic, and other guitarists were telling me I was hitting the strings like a hockey player taking a slap shot. Here's how I documented it in a column from October 1977:

> I still have a tendency to play too hard on the acoustic. I'm working on a right-handed picking attack that will reduce unwanted noise to a minimum and accentuate and creatively utilize those noises that "cannot be helped." [My point was that some noise when playing the acoustic was not harmful; nay, it was good—it filled out the full story of the guitar's natural sound.]

All in all, I find switching from the electric to the acoustic is a purifying experience, inasmuch as it renders fresh previously bromided electric pieces. It also encourages the player to really dig into his most soulful creative aspect to make funky phrases and bends project as well as they might on the electric.

Furthermore, when returning to electric after a long sojourn on acoustic, the electric idiom feels less jaded and more spontaneous, because you've been away from that sometimes uncontrollable monster, the amplifier.

I've been fortunate to accumulate experience on both acoustic and electric guitars. Today, in these technologically advanced times, you can amplify the acoustic guitar in such a way that it's loud enough to be heard in almost any setting without sounding harsh. And when you throw in a bit of reverb to get that "dryness" out of the sound and combine that with a subtle, slow chorus, you can play solo in front of a large audience and sound like a small orchestra. The acoustic guitar also, for me at least, pushes the music in a slightly different direction—that is to say, it tends to have more characteristics of classical guitar.

On the other hand, I rarely play electric guitar with distortion anymore; I like to go with a pure sound with maybe, when appropriate, chorus and reverb (and sometimes digital delay)—but that's it. More and more, I see that the sound of any player's instrument is really in his two bare hands.

As I review my *GP* columns from the distance of 25 years, I can see that I didn't always hit the mark. Some of the stuff is rather embarrassing when compared to what I know now. I was trying to demonstrate subtle points that could improve someone's playing—but, as I've revisited these "fine points" again and again, I have often found simpler, less intellectual ways to communicate the essential information. (You'll find a selection of some of my favorite columns, along with present-day commentary, in the back of this book.)

Writing the *GP* column gave me a regular and steady way to communicate with my fans, my fellow guitarists, and other musicians. I got (mostly) good feedback about the columns, and readers appreciated the way they were like a monthly letter from me, talking about my gigs, the people I was playing with, and so on.

Quite often, I would write a column in response to someone or something I came across in my travels. For example, one time I was on tour in Germany, and due to excess imbibing of a certain Saxon brewed liquid refreshment I caught my hand in the electronic door between the train cars. It got bent backward quite a bit, and it was a real struggle to play—but I wanted to keep doing the gigs. So I wrote a column about strengthening the injured muscles of the left hand; it was an exercise involving whole-tone and diminished intervals. I wrote: "At first my muscles were quite weak, but after regularly practicing these whole-tone and diminished exercises, I discovered that my left hand was beginning to respond. It is now slowly returning to normal. I look back on the accident as a blessing in disguise—a message from that Great Guitar Player in the Sky to stop resting on my laurels and get back to the kind of work (and I do mean work) that got me where I am today."

That was fine and dandy, and I got some sympathy from my readers—which I appreciated. However, that accident was really a result of my clumsiness from being overly sloshed, and I remember overhearing my rhythm section, John Lee and Gerry Brown, telling someone on the train (when they thought I was out of earshot), "Don't give Larry anything to drink—please."

# Chapter 30

## *The record with Miles that never happened*

ONE OF THE SIGNIFICANT THINGS that happened to me in 1978 was a record date with Miles Davis. Miles knew Elena Steinberg, a friend of my wife who was living with Jimmy Cobb, one of Miles's former drummers. Elena had access to a place near the Norwalk-Westport line in Connecticut, not far from where we were living in Fairfield County. Miles had had hip surgery and was suffering from a lot of pain while trying to recover, so he came up to Elena's place in Connecticut to convalesce.

Miles being Miles, there were always fans and other interested parties hanging around—because with Miles there was never a dull moment. He was always thinking about music, too, even when he was not feeling well or was pursuing his other interests, like boxing or cooking. I learned about his interest in boxing the first time I visited him at Elena's little house. Without warning, Miles walked up to me and punched me in the stomach—hard. My midsection hurt for nearly a week. Miles thought it was funny. Another time when I was hanging out at Elena's house, I noticed that Miles kept some of his beers on the porch. (It was February, I think, so it was cold outside). He stepped out onto the porch, grabbed a Heineken, drank most of it, walked into the house, and handed me the nearly empty bottle, which I proceeded to finish off. Miles looked at me and said, "Once an alcoholic, always an alcoholic." He had me pegged.

Miles said a lot of ridiculous shit, especially about women—he made a lot of risqué sexual comments. Plus he carried himself with almost an air of entitlement—which was okay as far as I was concerned—and was kind of short, bordering on rude, with the women around him. I think some of that was due to his upbringing; he had become habitualized to a certain kind of macho behavior. On the other hand, Miles was mentally sharp and well-informed about things like African-American history. He could keep you on your toes with his incisive comments. One time, when he knew that my wife and I were going through a rough patch, he said, "I'm not a parent." By that, he meant that he was aware of the problem but wasn't going to make any value judgments. I also remember Miles telling me that sex was "a very small part" of a marriage, by which he was implying that every aspect of my relationship with my wife, Julie, that he could observe was terrible. I never forgot that—and I knew he was right.

I kept going over to see Miles every chance we had during his stay in Connecticut, and eventually Miles wanted to talk about music. There was a piano there, and I would bring my guitar over. One afternoon, Miles grabbed my guitar and started playing a funky James Brown–type chord pattern in a "Charleston" rhythm. Then he went over to the piano and played some strange chords. He messed around with that strange chord thing for a few days running, and that little stretch of composition was referred to as "the adagio." I think he had me write it down; in any case, I learned it. All I recall about that was that Miles turned to me and said, "Man, you're quick to learn." That made me feel good—up to that point, I didn't know how Miles felt about me. He tended to speak in riddles, and, because of a previous medical problem involving his vocal cords, he barely had a voice. He always spoke in kind of a raspy whisper.

After a few more days of hanging out and working on his strange adagio, Miles called someone at Columbia Records to set up a record date. He invited drummer Al Foster, a really good local keyboard player named George Pavlis, bassist T. M. Stevens, and me. We went to Columbia studios to record . . . what? We really didn't know. Someone brought Miles's trumpet, and I was nominated to take the horn into the booth where Miles was talking with producer Teo Macero to suggest to Miles that he play it. Miles refused, saying, "My chops are fucked up." He had been doing a lot of cocaine, and that's never good for a horn player, especially a brass man. At the time, I was having a love-hate affair with that terrible drug myself. I think I stayed off it during this session—or, more honestly, I couldn't get any. Maybe Miles kept it all for himself—or maybe we all stayed straight for the gig and got blasted afterwards.

Because Miles didn't want to play trumpet, they put a synthesizer in the center of the studio for him to play. We set up and plugged in—Miles asked me to play with a wah-wah pedal. Despite all the preparation we had done up in Connecticut with his adagio, Miles started us into a mildly uptempo 12/8 kind of jungle shuffle.

I screwed up my courage and approached Miles inquisitively, saying, "Miles, what about the adagio?"

Miles looked at me at said, "Fuck the adagio."

He had changed his mind. We still used some of the chord passages and harmonic ideas from the adagio, but the session consisted of two takes of about seven minutes each of this upbeat shuffle with pseudo-atonal ideas improvised on top. Miles would feed me a fragment and I'd respond; it was a novel way to witness the formation a composition and an unusual way to conduct a record date.

After we finished, Miles got a cassette. He took it back to Connecticut and played it over and over again. He'd call friends long distance and play it for them over the phone. He told me the work was "mine"—he was giving it to me—and that he wanted it to be the first tune for a project with Columbia Records, built around me. I was flattered and flabbergasted. Miles was trying to help my career—wow!

Miles later called and asked me to join his band. To this day I'll never know why I refused. I think I told people that I said no because the pay was low and I had a lot of duo work scheduled with Philip Catherine. I got cold feet. I guess I should regret it because I'll never know what I could have played in Miles's band, but at the same time I can't regret it because Miles ended up playing with some of my favorite contemporaries, like Joe Beck, Mike Stern, John Scofield, and Robben Ford. They all distinguished themselves with Miles. I guess I had my own musical mission to follow. It just wasn't to be for Miles and me—and that recording was never released. End of contemplation on that subject!

A conversation with Dizzy Gillespie.

Larry, 1982, at the
Bach Dancing and Dynamite Society,
Half Moon Bay, California.

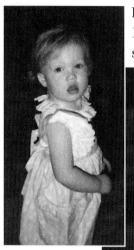

Daughter Allegra, born in 1988, at age one and at age seventeen.

Larry jams with daughter Annie while grandson Zach "stands in."

Grandsons Charlie (left) and Jackson (right)— the sons of Murali and his wife, Mary.

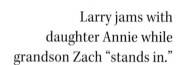

Larry with sons Murali (left) and Julian (right).

Larry shaking hands with SGI President Ikeda in Fukuoka, Japan, in 1987. Also pictured is, left to right, Herbie Hancock, Wayne Shorter, and Ronald Shannon Jackson at a very important Buddhist event.

Larry with Marcel Dadi during an in-store appearance in France when they toured together in 1991. Marcel was an outspoken champion of the Chet Atkins' finger-style of playing, and founder of a society dedicated to "pickin'." The society hosted Chet in France every year, and Larry was pleased to be invited one year.

John McLaughlin, Richie Okon, and Larry, at the Blue Note in New York.

Larry (left), Joe Beck (center), and Chico Hamilton (right) at Lincoln Center for Chico's 80th-birthday celebration on August 17, 1991.

Phillip Catherine with Larry in Brussels, 2004.

Larry with George Brooks on saxophone at LeClub in Moscow, 2004.

Joe DiOrio and Larry at Birdland, 2004.

Recording session for *Spaces Revisited* (February 1996). Left to right are Bireli Lagrene, Richard Bona, Larry, and Billy Cobham.

Larry with Max Roach in Israel.

Tracey in Riverton Park,
New Jersey, 2004.

Larry and Tracey, 2006, at
SGI Santa Monica, taken by
good friend Edward Clark.

Larry and Tracey at the Bach Dancing and Dynamite Society,
Half Moon Bay, California, September 2006.

Larry and Tracey at the Tin Angel Acoustic Café, Philadelphia, January 2005.

Larry with his first jazz guitar teacher, John LaChapelle, in Larry's hometown of Richland, Washington, September 2006.

Larry on tour with "Bombay Jazz," his Indian fusion band.

# *Chapter 31*

*1978 to 1981: Things get* **really** *ugly with the drinking and drugging, but there's a rainbow to safety waiting in New Jersey*

**M**Y CAREER WAS GOING WELL, despite what happened with Miles, and then things got even better: I got a great offer to tour Europe with Paco de Lucia and John McLaughlin. I was their second choice—John's manager had thought of getting Leo Kottke, but that didn't work out. So off I went to Paris in 1979 with Paco and John.

At that time, the whole thing with the Ayatollah Khomeni was breaking loose. Khomeni was living in exile in France, getting ready to go back to Iran to start the Islamic revolution. The French papers were full of stories about this. I was staying at the Hotel L'Univers on Rue Gregoire du Tours—kind of a dump, but what the hell, it wasn't far from John's apartment near the Pont Neuf. The three of us rehearsed for hours every day for about a week.

John and I found that we had to adjust to Paco. Paco didn't read much and wasn't a jazz player, but he was hip—really hip. He kept asking me what scales went with the chords in the songs we had selected, and I started to see that there were connections between jazz/fusion improvisation and flamenco. I'm sure John saw this as well. So Paco learned some scales from us, but we learned some scales from him, too. One was this flamenco scale that turned out to be the descending version of what I call the "jazz minor" scale; I wrote a *Guitar Player* column about that. On another day, Paco started playing this tasty fingerstyle fragment he'd composed that later on became the nucleus of "Tres Hermanos (Three Brothers)."

The thing about Paco's genius was that his playing—especially alone—transcended the "gypsy sound" associated with traditional flamenco. His exceptional technique and finesse made him sound like a jazz/classical virtuoso. He had timing, taste, and fire—and John and I ate it up. For "Tres Hermanos," John wrote a bridge with some nice chords, and I contributed a rising, rousing arpeggiated phrase to top off each "A" section. And if that wasn't enough to forge our "macho-music" unity, all three of us were into playing cards and those little handheld electronic games. "American Football" was one of our favorites on the road. John and Paco were much faster at it than me; they would always end up in a fierce competition for who was champion long after I had dropped out. Playing those games kept our competitive juices flowing, and it spilled over into the way each of us played. The games required—guess what?—quick hands, not unlike what we were doing on the stage. I had never had to play quite that fast before, and before long I opted for slower phrasing rather than just running up and down the scales as fast as I could, because John and Paco could do that to the max all night.

The tour started in Germany, and the response was incredible—despite my continued dependence on the bottle and the problems that was causing. We're playing to sold-out houses, and after the concerts I'm sneaking downstairs to drink some more. And then I started having problems with blackouts during the performances. I'd come off the stage, wondering what had happened. One time John was furious with me: he said I cut him off—aaargh!

I didn't realize it yet, but this was the beginning of the end. I will spare you the morbid details of my decline and just say that some of the things that happened on that tour were funny, like when I danced faux-flamenco between solos in Yugoslavia, and some were profound, like when we played Madrid and they said we were the greatest act to hit Spain since the Rolling Stones, but all of it was the truth.

That first successful tour was followed by another, this time including the Albert Hall in London. Before that gig, we played Barcelona and somebody gave me a pill—I don't know exactly what it was—but it kept me up all night. So we had to fly to London and I was hurting! When we got to the Albert Hall, it was freezing—and the British public was cold and reserved compared to the hot responses we'd gotten on the Continent. I decided I need some blow, but I couldn't get any. Tragedy! I had to play with a terrible hangover, with such a bad physical feeling. I can't describe how it felt, except to say it was like being sick, but sick from my own hand—that's the rub.

Somehow I got through the Albert Hall concert. It was filmed, and it came out on TV and then was made into a DVD. But I've never watched it. You see, alcoholics can't stand success, and at that time I was doing everything I could to sabotage things with my drinking. So I can't watch that performance—all these years later, I'm still disgusted with the shape I was in that night.

It would get worse. As I hurtled toward my final decision between life and death (it came down to that choice—I'm not being dramatic), I would try to tour Europe in the summer of 1981. It was looking good—I was booked for the North Sea

Jazz Festival, going to play opposite Chick Corea, doing a show with McCoy Tyner, and then heading to Italy with the Count Basie band.

What happened was that I got hung up in Holland, missed the flight to Switzerland, and missed my gig on a boat in Lake Geneva in Montreux. That was the first fuck-up. Then I got plastered during this big guitar extravaganza with Philip and Bireli and who knows what other players, and it was a disaster—the promoter, Claude Nobs, looked on in horror. At North Sea, George Wein wouldn't pay me because I was smashed.

The disaster reached its peak—or nadir—at Nice, when I somehow ended up on Marseilles heroin. Jimmy Raney was there, sober, giving me encouragement. Tal Farlow was there, tolerating this fiasco because he knew how much I respected him. The final nail came when I was brawling loudly with some North Africans late at night in my hotel room, which happened to be next to the room of Elvin Jones and his wife, Keiko. Keiko came in, grabbed me, kicked out the North Africans, and hustled me into their room. She threw me into their bed, and they slept on the floor while I slept it off.

The next morning, I called room service and ordered six Heinekens for breakfast. That's when Elvin gave me the business. He looked me straight in the eye and said, "You should be in a hospital." I knew he was right.

Elvin passed in 2004, and of course we remember him for his drumming genius, especially when he was the driving rhythmic force of John Coltrane's famous quartet. But I will always cherish Elvin for his humanity and for the compassion that he and his wife demonstrated in my dire hour of need in that bleak summer of 1981.

There were a couple more performance disasters that summer, the first involving the Count Basie band in Italy and then opposite Chuck Berry in Munich, before it all came, mercifully, to a screeching halt. In Munich, I came across some really strong local beer. After two or three bottles, I was three sheets to the wind. Dexter Gordon was going through something similar at that time. He was messed up and I was messed up, but somehow we had a nice conversation backstage in Munich before returning to our respective self-destruction. Mine was manifested by trying to play some blues (with whom I could not tell you) on a Hagstrom solidbody guitar, but being horribly out of tune. Yeeeeech! It all ended at the airport as I prepared to slink back to New York, the Count Basie guys looking at me like I was a leper or something. Oh, those looks—to this day I still remember their disdain and pity.

I crawled back to Connecticut and did some more stupid stuff, luckily not killing myself in the process, and then waited to be driven to Fair Oaks Hospital in Summit, New Jersey. On September 10, 1981, I snorted my last bit of coke before getting into the hired car. That was the last time I would have a drink or a drug—at least up until today, as I'm writing this. I was about to make a life change that was long, long overdue. I didn't realize it at the time, but I was ready to get rid of my adolescent mindset about drinking and smoking and snorting and popping. The thrill was gone.

They meant business at Fair Oaks. On the first day they threw me in with the rest of the patients, all of whom were as sick or sicker than I was with alcoholism and drug addiction. I sat in on a session where the counselors were grilling this guy about his drinking and the trouble it had caused, and they were not being gentle. They were nailing this guy with the truth. All of us had an illness that we didn't really understand, but the counselors—all recovered addicts and alcoholics—did understand, and they were letting us know in no uncertain terms how serious our situation was.

I walked out of that first session more than impressed with how serious this place was. Hell, I was more than impressed—I was shocked. This was the real thing. The buck was stopping right here. We had to do what we were told, or it would be check-out time—and I mean the ultimate check-out!

When I finally came down after 17 years of putting poison in my system, I became seriously afraid of getting intoxicated again. It became abundantly clear that I needed to clean up my act—100 percent. They even made us drink decaffeinated coffee, so we wouldn't get wired.

An adjustment as drastic as total abstinence was going to require help. I was encouraged to get help from the other patients, and at first I thought this was kind of ineffective—but then I started to see that you can't lie to someone who's also a liar. We couldn't manipulate each other because we knew each other's games.

It was rough. At first, my family and friends didn't come to visit because New Jersey was so far from Connecticut. When they did come—Julie, a friend, John Leahy from Westport, Murali and Julian, who were 12 and 8 at the time—boy, it was sad when I was locked back in my wing as they trudged back to the car. That was painful. As I fell into my bunk for the night, all alone, I said to myself, "Okay, Larry, this is it—you have to make this change in your life or there will be no life to have, not to mention any music to play."

With lots of support, I became willing to make this change. Slowly, I put together a clean life, at first in that hospital and then when I got back home. Getting clean became the number one priority—and staying clean and sober is still the most important thing for me. Without a clear head, I can't do my thing. I have come to understand that life is complicated and not always a bed of roses, but compared to being zoned out, drunk and senseless, going through pain when you're sober compares favorably. And I have a sneaking suspicion that problems are good for us in the sense that if we've got the right attitude, we can grow from the setbacks and obstacles we encounter.

# Chapter 32

## *Fall 1981: Recovery!*

I LEFT THE HOSPITAL AFTER 12 WEEKS and went back to Westport, and life kept coming at me. Fortunately, I had a gig lined up with Kazumi Watanabe in Japan, so by December I was in Tokyo and doing my thing without the hindrance of mood-altering substances.

I discovered that I couldn't really play my guitar sober. I would try and hardly anything would come out, so I had to start learning how to play all over again. Back to the basics: scales, chords, arpeggios, practicing everything slowly and rhythmically. I recall trying to play a Bach bourrée that I'd learned during my days on the Lower East Side. I couldn't get through it. I had to slow it down and relearn how to finger the phrases and solidify the timing.

I also discovered that it was physically painful to play the instrument—I must have really screwed up my body when I was bombarding myself with poison. Because of this, I took up something I thought I'd never do: jogging. Yes, jogging, that slow, shuffling run that's done by suburbanites. I jogged two miles a day—no more, no less. Never thought I would join that crowd, but what the hell—it worked. I found that the running actually gave me a free "high"—the oxygen went to my brain, and my mind worked better.

During the early months of my recovery, I began to work with a guitarist friend in Connecticut named Brian Keane, who was also cleaning up his act. We had been playing together as a duo on and off locally, and it worked out that we could go out and play some duo gigs in the Northeast. We played in Washington, D.C., one night, and I recall seeing an old friend snorting coke in the dressing room at that gig—I think it was at the Cellar Door. Seeing that didn't bother me, so I felt good—this new life was working. I didn't feel tempted or repulsed; I was just neutral. I was more interested in the music I had to play and doing the gigs I had, because I felt grateful to have them.

When we finished that gig, we had to drive back to Connecticut. In the old days, we'd have scored some blow and reefer and partied our way up Interstate 95. Not this time! Without the aid of drugs, we had to stop every few miles to change drivers and guzzle coffee. Welcome to reality, Coryell—that drive showed me how much my physical condition had been weakened by my addictions. There was going to have to be an overhaul in the personal-health department so I could develop the strength I needed in my body as well as my mind and soul for the long road ahead as a straight-shooter.

Brian and I did another gig in upstate New York at St. Lawrence University. It's way up north, near the Canadian border, and I don't think they get a lot of players from New York City up there—so when we did our little two-guitar act, they went crazy. I mean, absolutely crazy—after just one tune! That was encouraging.

Brian went on to become a successful composer for film and television—recovery was good for him, too. It's always fun to be watching some interesting show and say to myself, when I hear the music, "Hey, I think that's Brian—I know that sound!" And it usually is—he's done a ton of stuff, and he's good at what he does. I really appreciated the time we spent together at the end of 1981 and the beginning of '82. It was good to have a like-minded friend at such a crucial time in my life.

Another good thing that happened to me during my first year of recovery was that I stopped smoking. Because of all the coke I had snorted, my nasal passages were in rough shape, so I went to a doctor. He scheduled an operation to fix the damage. A friend of mine—I think his name was Robert—had the temerity to suggest that I use this operation as an opportunity to stop smoking. I'd been smoking more than ever since becoming clean—I needed a substitute, I guess. I told my friend that he had no right to tell me what to do. The nerve! Well, it turned out that after I had that operation, I never smoked another cigarette. It just worked out that way. So thank you, Robert.

Years later I was performing at the 1996 North Sea Jazz Festival with Trilok Gurtu and Andy Summers. We had an afternoon concert that was videotaped by Dutch television. When I went back to my hotel that evening, they were airing our performance plus the performances of two (quite famous) friends of mine, who are also in recovery. I had a moment of tremendous gratitude as I watched our respective artistry manifesting itself without the aid of a single drink or drug! I couldn't have imagined back in the early 1980s, when I was just getting on my feet, that I would receive such a wonderful benefit 15 years down the road. Furthermore, the highlight of the Coryell/Summers/Gurtu set was a composition called "The Three Marias," written by my dear friend Wayne Shorter—I'll speak about Wayne's positive influence on my recovery in a later chapter. Ironically though, July of 1996 was when Wayne's wife Anna Maria perished in the infamous TWA Flight 800 disaster, as well as a dear friend of mine, French guitarist Marcel Dadi.

# *Chapter 33*

## *Diving into reality*

OKAY—I WAS FINALLY ADJUSTING to a drug-free and alcohol-free life. And I quickly learned that many people didn't really care whether I was sober or drunk. They had their own problems. A major change had taken place in my inner life, in my attitude, but reality was still out there—and one hard-hitting aspect of reality was waking up to the fact that being a jazz player was very much a business.

It was time to take care of business and rebuild my professional life from this new, clean foundation. And that involved taking a more serious approach to playing: playing was a way to support my family, not just a big party. So I began to pick up my music contacts from where I had left off before I went to Fair Oaks. One contact with whom I reconnected was the producer Teo Macero.

Before I went into rehab, I had done a horrendous project involving Ravel's "Bolero" for Teo—it was one of the worst recordings I ever made. Somehow, though, Teo still believed in me, and he called to propose a solo project doing Rimsky-Korsakov's "Scheherazade." This turned out to be a good thing: I got engaged in something difficult and interesting, plus I was able to make up for that "Bolero" disaster. I worked my ass off on that project, and as I listened to the playbacks in the Columbia Records studio I realized how fortunate I was to be "back on the scene and clean." My playing was far from perfect, but at least there was a clarity to it that had been missing.

After that, I got the opportunity to tackle an even more ambitious classical project—once again, under the direction of Teo. It was three ballets by Stravinsky. My friends at Philips Phonogram in Japan felt I would be the right person to record guitar versions of "The Firebird Suite," "Petrouchka," and "The Rite of Spring." I was petrified—but hey, I needed the gig. What followed was some of the most intense music study and practicing of my life.

The first thing I had to do was get the sheet music. There were no solo versions, but there was, I think, some two-piano music for "Petrouchka" and "The Rite of Spring." For "Firebird," I had to work with sheet music that had the full orchestra for part of the piece and a piano reduction for the rest. I also listened to some recordings.

Philips Phonogram wanted me to play everything on solo guitar, but I convinced them that "Petrouchka" would be better if I could record it with two guitars, playing one part and then overdubbing the other. It was a big job to go through the original scores and arrive at lines and voicings that would faithfully reproduce Stravinsky's intent. This was my constant assignment, and it became enjoyable because I found that I was getting involved in Stravinsky's creative process. I had to make decisions about the music, just as he had. Then, once the note, chord, and voicing decisions were made, I had to see if I could actually play what I had "reduced" from Stravinsky's score. This process took a long time—months—but it was a good way to keep myself occupied. Being so totally focused on something that difficult was the best thing that could have happened to me at that time.

When we were ready to record, it was a two- or three-day session with Teo, an engineer, and a Japanese co-producer. I just went in by myself and did it. I was still 39 years old, just shy of my 40th birthday in 1983. "Petrouchka" came out especially well, I think, because I was able to overdub the second guitar part and make corrections. "The Rite of Spring" was nerve-wracking because the second half is so complex and has so many odd time signatures. It was far from perfect, but we accepted it. I did some fusion-type improv in places, which for the most part I regret—not that it wasn't a good idea to improvise, but if I had to do it over again I would take more care with those sections.

Soon after the Stravinsky came out, there was a cover story about me in *Downbeat,* written by Bill Milkowski, and I was hopeful that it would be a successful project. In reality, though, it flopped at the box office, so to speak—no one reviewed it that I know of, and nothing came of it. Who knows—maybe in a few years it will turn up on classical radio stations as an interesting artifact of the musical experimentation that took place at the end of the twentieth century.

# *Chapter 34*

## *Buddhism: Coryell begins chanting and life changes*

A S I CONTINUED MY DIVE INTO REALITY, I became convinced that although I was doing all right with drugs and alcohol (or, more precisely, without them), I needed some sort of philosophy to give me added strength to deal with life. I saw that I needed to be a less neurotic and controlling person; in other words, I needed to take my innate willpower and focus it, or align it, with a view that was value-creating.

When I was really out of it in the 1970s, several players whom I respected wanted to get me to chant Nam-Myoho-Renge-Kyo. The cats who were on my case—Wayne Shorter, Buster Williams, and Herbie Hancock—had already been chanting for quite a few years. I recall one day during a trip to Israel in the early 1980s when Herbie and I were hanging out in Tel Aviv, and he gently but assertively explained to me the benefits of this chanting Buddhism. This wasn't the first time he had tried to nudge me in that direction. He knew I needed it—he could see I was destroying myself.

A few years before, Wayne Shorter had given me what's called a "Gongyo book"—a series of prayers, a liturgy, for this chanting practice. Both Wayne and Herbie told me that the most important part of the practice was the repeating of Nam-Myoho-Renge-Kyo. They told me about people who had experienced great benefits from chanting, but in most of those cases the individuals had been chanting for quite a long time—several hours at one stretch. I thought this sounded like an admirable discipline, and I tried chanting one time in France, even though I was not in great shape. After what I thought had been at least 45 minutes, I looked at my watch and saw that only seven minutes had passed. Whoa! This chanting thing was going to be deeper than I thought.

On that day in Tel Aviv, Herbie and I were sitting outside with the sun streaming down, and I looked carefully at him. I could see the positive impact of this practice. He had a look of confidence combined with a kind of transcendence. Now, I had tried the Yoga practice with Sri Chinmoy and not done too well with that, but once again I felt drawn to what I was hearing. Herbie had always been a nice guy, but I could really see a change in him, so I thought I should consider trying this chanting thing. I had seen positive changes in Wayne and Buster, too. So, now that I had that horrible drug and alcohol thing off my back, I felt that this would be something worthwhile for me to try. It looked to be the kind of thing that was demanding, but if you did it well, there would be a positive spiritual payoff.

Then I met another musician who pushed me in that direction. Bunny Brunel, a bassist, had been chanting for a while, and he came on the road with Alphonse Mouzon and me—we had a trio—in the spring of 1984. Bunny noticed that I had a Gongyo book, and the next thing I knew he was in my hotel room early each morning, taking me through that book. Pretty soon, we'd chanted through that Gongyo book at a record-setting pace—we'd always be a bit short on time, being on the road—and I was starting to get into a rhythm.

At the end of the tour, Bunny told me that I should join the organization known as the Soka Gakkai (Value Creation Society). There was a branch in New York, and on the evening of April 24, 1984, I went to the temple in Queens and received the object of devotion, a scroll called the Gohonzon. I've chanted every day since then. It gets me in rhythm with the universe.

If you were somehow able to turn up the volume of the cosmos, the sound would be: Nam-Myoho-Renge-Kyo. That's the basis of this practice, which is based on the life story and writings of the man we consider to be the True Buddha of the Latter Day of the Law, Nichiren Daishonin, who was persecuted for establishing this practice in 13th century Japan. In the late 1920s and early 1930s, Nichiren's Buddhism was revived in Japan by a group of educators, and after World War II the organization solidified under the leadership of Josei Toda and his young disciple, Daisaku Ikeda. It is Mr. Ikeda—Sensei to me—who is my spiritual teacher and who has taught me, among other things, the real value of education.

A little while later, in the early 1990s, I made *Equipoise* for Joe Fields's Muse label, playing with a straight-ahead quartet that included bassist Buster Williams— my fellow jazz chanter—and pianist Stanley Cowell, who composed the title tune. Stanley would later would become a member of our chanting group, thanks to Buster's patient but persistent encouragement.

In the mid 1980s, other things were developing in my life, too, both musical and personal. I was swinging back to more straight-ahead jazz—and I was growing apart from Julie. By 1985, I decided I had to take a hard look at my marriage and weigh all the elements, including my two sons, Murali and Julian, whom I loved dearly, to see whether I could continue to be with their mother. It was not fun, but I believed it was necessary. I didn't want my happiness to come at the expense of other people, but at the same time I needed to be honest about my life. In early 1985, I filed for divorce.

That's also when I met Emily Remler, a young jazz guitarist who was getting some well-deserved critical attention at the time. I heard one of her records—a trio setting with my old friends Bob Moses and Eddie Gomez on drums and bass—and was impressed. Emily was creative, smart, swung like crazy, and had a time feel that was just about the best I had ever heard from any guitarist, male or female.

Emily and I started playing together as a duo. We toured the United States and Europe off and on for about a year and were briefly involved romantically, until I realized that we had very little in common. We made a duet record for Concord Records, *Together,* which still stands up today, I think, especially as a testament to Emily's genius. When the record was released there was lot of reaction from the jazz guitar community. One publication, *The Texas Monthly,* had a long article analyzing the different soloing approaches we had. They surmised that Neal Tesser, who wrote the liner notes, had confused my playing with Emily's and Emily's playing with mine! I thought that was kinda funny because ever since I started doing two-guitar things, even musicians who knew both of us sometimes couldn't tell us apart. The first example of this I recall came from Jack Bruce, who also said he couldn't tell me from John McLaughlin when he first heard "Spaces." But where McLaughlin came off sounding like a high-flying rocket, Emily was like a poet when she played. I recall one bizarre incident on tour in Germany when we were in a doctor's office. The doctor had a guitar there, an entry-level solid-body, with a small amp. Emily picked it up and plugged in and started playing just with her fingers—no pick. We were all mesmerized by what she was doing: chords, timing, feel, counterpoint, and spontaneity.

Emily died an untimely and all-too-early death in 1990 at the age of 32. Monty Alexander, her ex-husband, said it best: "She's out of town." She'll be back—I believe that—the music was just too good.

Around that time, I also continued a collaboration with classical guitarist Sharon Isbin and Brazilian guitarist Laurindo Almeida called "Guitarjam"—one of the many three-guitar projects I've done. For some reason, I end up getting into multiple-guitar groups; sometimes it's just a duet, sometimes three, and one time, under the auspices of Sue Mingus, there was a "Mingus Guitars" group that had five or six guitarists with a rhythm section.

I had another kind of collaboration in my personal life. Over the years, I had consulted with an astrologer who predicted, either directly or by inference, many important events. For example, right around the time I hit bottom with drugs and alcohol, she told me to take care of my health. In 1981, she said that she saw in my chart a "period of incarceration"—that turned out to be my time in rehab. And she also predicted that I would meet a woman who would be my wife and the mother of my daughter. As it turned out, she was right.

In February 1986, I was living alone near Westport, Connecticut, when I met my second wife, Molly, who was 29 at the time. We got married September 3, 1987. Seventeen years later we ended up getting divorced. In retrospect I did give her my best self for many years. I see now why she came into my life when she did. I needed the stability, someone who was my opposite to counteract me. It worked for a long time. After having grown more emotionally I discovered I was evolving toward another type of relationship. I would start a new life in 2005 with my third wife-to-be, Tracey (I will speak more about her in the Epilogue). These transitions involving life issues are very heavy and involve a lot of insanity, but I knew with full confidence that I had to make the change, and I have no regrets.

After my first divorce became final in the fall of '86, Molly and I rented a house in Westport. Murali moved in with us, as his mother had moved to New York State with our other son, Julian. I felt guilty about not being with both my boys, but I knew that if I wanted to stay sober I had to restructure my life. I wanted to stabilize things at home, build a solid foundation for my boys, and then get back to my music.

This whole process was difficult and painful, as any family that has gone through a divorce knows. For me, the discomfort almost bordered on insanity as I endeavored to stay involved with my boys in a meaningful way through all the changes in my personal life. My goal was to move forward in a positive way, to work my way to a healthy personal life. Murali was going through his own problems as the 18-year-old son of dysfunctional parents, and Julian, four years younger, was coping in his own brave way. This period of 1986–87 into 1988 was a rough time of adjustment for all of us.

It was during this time that I got a call from an old friend, a producer named Jack Lewis. He was very hip, had worked with the Lovin' Spoonful in the '60s, and had recently overcome cancer. He had a project that had been funded by Desilu out on the West Coast: he asked me to get some guitar players together for a concert to collaborate with and honor Tal Farlow. I managed to round up John Scofield and John Abercrombie, and the producer grabbed Larry Carlton out of L.A. John Pattitucci agreed to play bass, and I called Billy Hart to play drums. The concert went pretty well, and it came out on a record called *All Strings Attached*.

I have to say that Larry Carlton stole the show. As good as the other guitarists were—Abercrombie did a lovely duet with Tal on "Beautiful Love," and Sco was his usual exalted self—Carlton, with his solidbody Valley Arts guitar, his pedals, and his pure heart and soul, tore through "All Blues" like I had never heard it. Check out the video; it's all there. And the bread was pretty good—thanks, Desilu; I always knew Lucy and Ricky were hip!

Allegra was born on January 17, 1988, when I was on tour in Japan. I remember being in the hotel room in Tokyo when the doctor called in the middle of the night to tell me. I was relieved, floored, floating on air—all of that and more. I had been over the moon for the births of Murali and Julian, and Allegra was no exception. These events are marked indelibly in every father's life—they go way beyond the music. Allegra is now a beautiful grown woman of 18 years, studying at Marymount Manhattan College in New York City. She's also been dancing, mostly ballet, for nearly all her life, and she's a helluva hoofer.

Eventually, when Molly and little baby Allegra were ready, they came over and joined me for part of that tour, which was with a Japanese pop star named Yosui Inoue. On the gig the music was strange, but the bread was good and I used the time (several months) to learn some Japanese and get deeper into Asian culture.

Later in 1988, while I was touring Europe with Billy Hart, Buster Williams, and Stanley Cowell, we recorded a good live album called *Air Dancing* at the Magnetic Terrace in Paris. One fond memory I have of that tour is of Buster staying in the hotel to babysit little Allegra. Buster is a phenomenal bassist but also a great human being—even before we started chanting together I felt like Buster and I had been brothers in an earlier existence.

*Air Dancing* captured the Cowell-Coryell-Hart-Williams quartet at its peak; we had a great rapport, and Billy and Buster were as tight a rhythm section as you could want. Branford Marsalis happened to be in Paris playing with Sting, and after his gig he came down to the club and sat in—while we were recording. However, there was no microphone set up for the saxophone, so when Branford played his solo on "Impressions," you couldn't hear him on the recording. As a result, we edited out his solo. My solo followed Branford's, and when you hear the record, there's a big applause as I begin my solo—that huge hand was for Branford! He's a great player; he's got a great sound, his quality of improvisation is brilliant, and he's as soulful as they come. It was an honor to have him on the bandstand that night.

One other thing that came out of that recording/gig was a bootleg—seems French radio was taping it for broadcast and apparently some fan recorded the show, then provided what he thought were the titles. A friend told me he had this record of us in Paris; he showed me the CD and I was flabbergasted. The CD said it was recorded in a fictitious place; also, "Stella by Starlight" was listed on the CD, but we didn't play it—the guy just thought it was "Stella." I tried to pursue legal action on the bootleg but soon came to understand it was fruitless. *Domage.*

# *Chapter 35*

*The radio show—oh boy—well, live and learn . . .*

WHILE I WAS IN JAPAN, the promoter who had connected me with Yosui, a man named Araya, helped me land a radio show with a new FM station in Tokyo. It was to be called "Pazz and Jops from New York" and would feature on-air banter and playing by members of the jazz and pop entertainment firmament.

Little did I realize how many painful personal and professional lessons were going to be learned from this more-or-less total fiasco. I think the reason the Universe gave me this show at this time in my life was to help pay for my costly divorce. We had an acceptable arrangement for me to see the boys, but, as I said, it was a difficult time. I got through them, thanks in part to the extra money coming in from that radio show.

The biggest problem with the show, which was broadcast five days a week, was that I couldn't do the whole show myself and be on the road doing gigs and recording—so I had to delegate. Unfortunately, the people I worked with didn't quite have it together as "radio people," so the Tokyo powers-that-be, not liking our early efforts, assigned a production company in New York called Broadcast Architecture to be the "mother ship" for the show.

These guys had a studio in Midtown and were nice enough, but I got the feeling from the get-go that they wouldn't feel bad if my people were out of the picture so they could have the whole thing to themselves. And that's eventually what happened. I had brought in my old friend Jimmy Webb to be my co-host and help me get some pop-oriented artists on the show, but the Broadcast Architecture people didn't get along too well with Jimmy, and it just didn't work out.

I think we were on the air a little more than a year. This Tokyo FM station was very slick—they had learned their on-air style from American radio but actually were more hip than any American radio at the time—and because they were laying out some serious bread on this project, they wanted killer shows. Sometimes we could deliver what they liked—most notably a show with Art Garfunkel, who was Jimmy's friend. And another one with George Benson, who was a great guest and wanted to sing Jimmy's classic "Wichita Lineman." They also seemed to like the show we did with Chet Atkins—Jimmy and I flew down to Nashville for that one. We recorded it in Chet's home studio, and Chet even sang on that show.

But then we gave them a show featuring John Denver, may he rest in peace. John had recently worked with Jimmy, so we flew out to John's place in Aspen and did a pretty nice show, with John singing one of Jimmy's tunes. But the hipsters at FM Japan in Tokyo felt rather strongly that John Denver was not hip . . . uh oh.

That was the coup de grace. We got cancelled. I happened to be in Tokyo for some gigs at the time, so—in typically polite Japanese fashion—FM Japan invited me to have a nice farewell dinner with them. They gave Jimmy and me a fabulous meal, and then they gave us the boot, gentlemanly and decently. As far as I know, "Pazz and Jops from New York" is still a weeknight fixture on that station.

I still have DATs of some of the shows, although the one with Dr. John was lost, unfortunately. There were shows with Herbie Hancock, Wayne Shorter, Carmen McRae, Manhattan Transfer—probably too many shows that featured jazz and not enough that featured pop, but what the hell, I had to go with people I knew and people who were great players/singers/improvisers. That's still my life in music. And I'll bet there were some listeners in Japan who might have thought, Hey, this show from Coryell and Webb is kind of nice—they're bringing in some good people. So that's the way it was, and I have no regrets.

The radio-show adventure did, unfortunately, lead to a falling out between Jimmy and me, and I felt terrible about all that—but a few years back I called Jimmy and we re-established contact. My new relationship with Jimmy isn't like our old way of hanging out and carrying on, but I keep a book of his songs on the piano and go through them from time to time. Jimmy Webb has written some great pop songs. He's a genius at pulling the emotion out of your life with the simple tools of words and music.

As a musician/bandleader/session leader, Jimmy was a strict taskmaster. I remember one time in L.A. in the 1970s when he was recording a solo album and there was an introduction he was trying to get on tape—just his voice and the piano. He must have done more than 100 takes of that intro! It was during the recording of that project that I met Randy Newman. Jimmy had retained Randy to conduct the orchestra on one of his compositions; as I recall, Jimmy was to play and/or sing on that song along with the orchestra, so he couldn't conduct it himself. It was nice to meet the great Randy Newman, even though he didn't know who the hell I was.

There was another session in L.A. with Jimmy during that time with the singer-songwriters Harry Nilsson and Van Dyke Parks, and we all got really drunk.

It was ridiculous. After a few hours of conscious insanity I went into a blackout, and I had to be told the next day what had transpired in the studio. It was not pretty—something about smashing empty vodka bottles against the wall.

In spite of all this craziness, Jimmy was successful—his capacity for turning out tunes that connected with the soul of the populace was uncanny. Another thing about Jimmy's talent was that he was prolific; he wrote one song after another. He could really churn them out, and they were all good songs—he read a lot and listened to pop and classical music, plus he was naturally intelligent, and his piano playing was original. In his honor, I wrote a piece called "Song for Jim Webb" on the piano. I recorded it, overdubbing guitar with the piano part, during the *Restful Mind* sessions for Vanguard.

I've seen Jimmy on TV from time to time, and my son Julian has worked with his sons in the Webb Brothers. I wish him well and will always appreciate his kindness and generosity. Plus I thank him for what I learned from him musically—he may not be a jazz musician, but a good musician is a good musician, and the world of jazz always nods its head with a hearty "Amen!" in praise of that.

# *Chapter 36*

## *Guitar legends in Spain, then it's off to Brazil*

A S THE 1990S BEGAN, I kept busy with a wide variety of gigs, including a couple of interesting overseas projects that came from my agent, Ted Kurland. One involved going to Brazil as part of a Creed Taylor production; the other was this big thing in Seville, Spain, called "Guitar Legends," where I worked with a host of other guitarists. Both events were televised and/or filmed.

For "Guitar Legends," I played with the bassist Stanley Clarke and also worked with Rickie Lee Jones. Because this was such a big production, we got the ball rolling by going out to Los Angeles for rehearsals with Rickie Lee. It turned out that Rickie Lee is from Olympia, Washington—as a former Washingtonian, I felt that was a good sign. It was, because we hit it off well.

Rickie Lee was a bit quirky at the rehearsals—singers tend to be sensitive to just about everything—but we had a good rapport. We worked on a Bobby Timmons piece that she liked, "Dat Dere," one of the crop of soul-oriented jazz compositions that came out of the '60s.

After the rehearsals, it was off to Spain for the big guitar event. There were blues and rock players—I think Bob Dylan was there at one point—and we had our own jazz-and-fusion night. Miles Davis had just died, so our musical director, George Duke, suggested that we play some of Miles's music. George played "All Blues," John McLaughlin played "In a Silent Way," and I played "So What." I also played my offbeat version of Ravel's "Bolero" as a solo piece on my Ovation 12-string. With that plus the tunes I did with Rickie Lee in her segment, I was a pretty busy guitarist on that night in Seville. One crazy memory: right in the middle of performing one of her numbers, Rickie Lee turned around and spat one of the biggest wads of salivary effluvia I've ever seen—right on the stage floor. Singers will do whatever they can to clear the pipes, I guess. I got a kick out of that.

Before we played, I checked out the blues guys. I thought Robert Cray was a good second-generation blues player, and he came off as quite the artist in his set. But what really killed me was Bo Diddley. He was as he had always been during his long career—primitive. The climax of one of his tunes was unforgettable: he was playing in the key of E—the kind of E tonal color that's defined by the dominant 7th sound. This means it's not really kosher to play any D♯s in your solo lines over that dominant 7th chord. To hell with that, said Bo—and this is what makes the blues so great. Bo was playing D♯s all over an E dominant 7th chord. He made it work—and work well! (I have to thank the late great Stevie Ray Vaughan for helping me to truly appreciate Bo Diddley.)

In our segment, John had his Indian-influenced band with the brilliant tabla player/percussionist Trilok Gurtu. They were quite good. Then John played a duet with Paco de Lucia—and, lucky me, I got to introduce Paco to the audience. I simply declared (in Spanish): "Now welcome the Soul of Spain (El Alma de Espana), Paco de Lucia!"

For the finale, all of us guitarists came out onstage to play together—but there was no way for Paco to be heard. Paco, the master of all flamenco masters, plays totally acoustically, and there was no mike set up for him. What a bummer—that was the only real boo-boo in an otherwise rather well-run project.

On the morning after the show, I was on the same flight as Ken Fritz, George Benson's manager. I read Ken some of the reviews, as I had studied Spanish in high school and can read and speak the language somewhat. Ken was relieved that George had escaped any criticism. Most of the praise was for John—they said he was the ultimate fusion guy or something to that effect. John did play well that night, but what I remembered most was what George Benson said after hearing me play "Bolero." He said he loved it—that was enough review for me.

Shortly after I got back to Connecticut, I got a call from Ted Kurland, saying I had to get myself together to go to Brazil for this new Creed Taylor project. What I had to do, in addition to the passport folderol, was meet with Creed in his New York office, so as to be philosophically prepared for the project. Years before, when I was working with my first Apostolic producer, Danny Weiss, we had pitched *Lady Coryell* to Creed, who at that time was on top of the jazz world in terms of recording success, having produced big hits by Deodato and George Benson. Creed turned us down, and we eventually ended up going with Vanguard.

Creed apparently remembered me, though, and a few years later he called me to do some fusion-type dates for several of his projects—all of which were recorded at Rudy Van Gelder's studio, across the river in Englewood, New Jersey. Some of that music was pretty good, and I came away with a feeling that I could work well with Creed. He was a producer who was also a musician, plus he had a grasp of the realities (read: the money side) of the recording industry. And—and this was a big "and"—he had a rather strong track record of success.

So there I was, back in Creed Taylor's office, and this time we weren't talking about music but about the philosophies and religions of Brazil. These were subjects known as "Condomble'" and "Afoche," and the various gods and goddesses of the Yoruba tribe of Nigeria, from which had flowed a lot of the belief system that was to go into the project we were about to do. The players would include Romero Lubambo, one of the best Brazilian jazz guitarists in New York, plus some of the best players from down there, as well as Donald Harrison and my old friend Billy Cobham. Some of the music we would be playing was from someone I didn't know about, singer-composer-guitarist Dori Caymmi. Creed gave me some recordings of Dori's music, and I really dug it. Creed had been the person who opened up the Brazilian thing in the States in the 1960s with the "Girl from Ipanema" mega-hit from Getz and Gilberto, and he had also done the first Stan Getz-Charlie Byrd collaboration—so, based on that, I felt I should pay attention to what Creed was saying and try to go in the suggested direction 100 percent.

I responded by writing two Brazilian-style tunes, which was part of the deal, and then we got our tickets and flew off to the beautiful State of Bahia in northeastern Brazil. What an adventure! We recorded the performances near the harbor in the town of Salvador of Bahia, using rented, poor-quality recording equipment. We learned all the tunes right there in the plaza next to the stage—not much rehearsing—and we recorded and filmed at the same time. It was kind of crazy, but I now see that was part of Creed's plan. He wanted a certain level of spontaneity and, for want of a better word, unpreparedness.

When we got back to New York, we found that the tapes were a mess. The sound had deteriorated to the point where the only thing we could keep were a few solos and Billy's kick drum. Everything else had to be replaced. Rudy Van Gelder couldn't believe it, but he agreed to tackle this engineering challenge.

It was fascinating to watch how Creed would build a performance nearly from scratch. First the percussionists came in for their overdubs. Then, after all the percussion had been replaced, we started replacing the other parts that had gone by the wayside. I did a lot of correcting, so to speak, of the guitar parts. Dori's vocals had to be run through a harmonizer, because he had had a cold during the recording on the plaza there in Bahia.

We spent weeks fixing—maybe "rebuilding" would be a better word—what was to be *Live from Bahia*. When it was all through, a lot of what I had re-recorded on guitar no longer matched what I had played on the film. No matter, Creed said, we'll edit the film to pull the camera away from your hands at the crucial moments. Well—that's one way to deal with that kind of stuff, I guess. It was Creed's baby, so I wasn't going to get it in the middle of a technical process about which I knew very little.

Finally, after many weeks at Rudy's, we brought Romero in to do his solo overdubs on the Milton Nascimento tune "Vera Cruz," and we had a record. To me, the results were mixed, but I have to say that the good tracks, like Dori's "Harbor" and Donald's "Oladun," were really good. So was Billy's "Panama." All that effort—what a studio bill Creed must have run up—well, what can I say? At least I was there to see it happen. The record came out in 1992, and after an initial bit of excitement in the marketplace it faded into obscurity and remains an overlooked, flawed-masterpiece type of classic. I'm sure Brazilian music purists wish I'd done things differently—without so much of Creed's direction—but, hey, my ex-wife Molly played the CD a lot at home because the melodies appealed to her, and it still sounds pretty good today.

# *Chapter 37*

*Coryell gets "commercial"—O, trangression,*
*thy name is airplay!*

T HE NEXT RECORD I DID WITH CREED was something that eventually
came to be called *Fallen Angel*. For this one, Creed brought in my old
friend Don Sebesky to oversee the project. Don was great—we had done that thing
on the Beatles' "The Word" back in 1967, on the date where I first met Eric Gale. We
started this project by having meetings in Creed's office, not unlike the time I had
met with Creed to learn about Brazilian beliefs for the *Live from Bahia* project.

This time, there was a somewhat controversial subject on the table. Creed and
Don wanted me to do a "digital duet" with Wes Montgomery's "Bumpin' on Sunset."
Creed apparently still owned the master to that track, and the original had been on
his CTI label when it was a hit in the '60s. Initially, I did not want to do this, thinking
it would be sacrilegious to mess with anything done by anybody else, much less by a
respected master like Wes—although there had recently been a big hit of this type,
where Natalie Cole sang with recordings by her late father, Nat "King" Cole.

As I thought about the concept of "Wes the father" or, to put it another way,
"Wes the mentor," with me as the "son" or "disciple," it started to make more sense.
Lee Ritenour was doing a Wes tribute CD at around the same time—which I liked
very much, by the way—so I didn't want to miss out on my opportunity to show my
respect for Wes.

When *Fallen Angel* was released, it included the Wes thing, which was called
"Angel on Sunset." The reaction was interesting. The album got a lot of airplay, at
first because of "Fallen," the vocal tune (with very little guitar) that was the theme
from the movie Pretty Woman. Then the stations started playing "Angel"—the Wes
thing—by itself, and the smooth-jazz stations are still playing that track.

All I can say about this strange phenomenon is that it was a good thing
for keeping my name out there, although there was a backlash among purists who
didn't like Larry Coryell moving out of the category of being an "underground"
player. This happens a lot in jazz—I know it happened to Herbie Mann when he
started crossing over into popular music mixed with jazz, as on his hit album

*Memphis Underground,* where the title track was no more than a vamp, and he played other non-bebop stuff like "Battle Hymn of the Republic." Thanks to Herbie's example of not reacting to this kind of negativity, I took the reaction to "Angel" with a grain of salt.

The worst fallout was from Pat Metheny, who really slammed me for doing the Wes thing. I was thrown by Pat's comments, and, of course, many of my friends read what he said and sent me messages like "Ouch!" or "Did you see this?" It was hurtful initially, but in this case the pain was short-lived because the track was so successful and had such longevity. I put it into perspective and moved on. I really don't give a damn what any musician or critic thinks of me—I have my own standards. The only thing that really matters is if you can live with what you've done artistically. Sometimes we make errors in judgment, sure, but if we're cool with it, then we can learn from it and go on to the next thing.

I was glad that I didn't overreact to Pat's remarks, because Pat and I got together at the Newport Jazz Festival in August 2005, and it was a great experience. He was there playing on a Roy Haynes tribute, and we hung out backstage. Pat told me that my solo on "Walter L" from the GB Quartet's *In Concert* from 1968 was one of the best things he'd ever heard. So what the heck—I guess guitar players are human and a little bit crazy. All is forgiven.

The next thing Creed Taylor had for me was something even more "commercial" than *Fallen Angel.* He went so far as to enlist the obviously non-jazz but talented Peabo Bryson to sing a tune chosen by Chuck Loeb (whom Creed brought in to help with production) that was written by Steve Lukather of Toto. It was called "I'll Be Over You," and the production was lengthy and expensive. This was where Creed's "dark side" started to manifest itself—little did I know that he never intended to pay any of the studio bills for this boondoggle, and that eventually I would be summoned to court to deal with Creed's indiscretions. But that would come later. At the time, I cooperated with Creed in a sincere attempt at trying to understand how to craft a pop record. This meant a lot of careful manipulation in the studio, dealing with something in the tune called a "hook"—the catchiest phrase—and then assembling everything sonically into some sort of combination artwork/product.

I ended up not playing much on the track, but the minute it came out—I think it was in December 1995—the number one smooth jazz station in New York was playing it. I heard it as I was driving across the Tappan Zee Bridge. As I was rolling along and listening to this tune over which I had labored for weeks and weeks, I thought to myself, okay—this is not the normal jazz process, but for what we wanted: mission accomplished.

# *Chapter 38*

## *Getting back to a more pure-and-simple approach*

AFTER ALL THE CREED TAYLOR MACHINATIONS, I decided to get back to the "normal jazz process," and I found that the more simple and direct approach involved in playing straight-ahead jazz was quite refreshing. This was the thing about the music that got me excited in the first place—just playing good tunes, some standards and maybe an original or two, with a good rhythm section. So I signed on with Joe Fields over at Muse Records (which later was changed to High Note) in 1984 and started to do record dates at Rudy Van Gelder's studio again. These sessions were short and sweet compared to the grandiosity and days-into-weeks of the Creed productions.

One of the dates was with bassist Buster Williams and drummer Smitty Smith and—at Joe Fields's suggestion—Kenny Barron on piano. The record was called *Shining Hour*. That was a fantastic session. We did the Jerome Kern tune "Yesterdays," and when I was choosing the take to use on the record, I was astonished at how Kenny had played an incredible solo on every take. This was especially true on the section of the tune where there's a progression of fifths (A7 to D7 to G7 to C7); Kenny used altered scales to the max in that part. The result was modern, refreshing, different, and totally imaginative playing. I wish I could have included all of his solos from all the takes we did on "Yesterdays"—that's how much he nailed it and how consistent he was.

For a long time, I was conflicted about the recording process. It was as if there were too many options. You could spend weeks and weeks perfecting one tune, or even one part of one tune, or you could throw caution to the wind, record tunes in two or three takes, and just accept what you played. That's jazz, that's what we played, and over time you learn to live with the things that made you cringe during the initial playbacks.

It was as if all the advances in technology were getting in the way of your original intent—which was, basically, to learn how to play, get good enough to be a recording artist, and then make some records. Period. The hidden drawback of the technology, for me, was this: having the luxury of editing and having the opportunity to make every solo technically "perfect," you can overlook the organic nature of playing. Better to be a little loose and keep the good feeling of the improvisation than to clean up everything to a point where it's cold and mechanical.

To be sure, a little editing is acceptable even within these parameters, but it is best to keep it to a minimum. For example, to get all the ensemble sections of a newly composed piece to an acceptable level, you can copy a correctly played version of a passage that's repeated in the arrangement and drop it into the appropriate spots. That way you don't have to re-record the ensemble parts. You keep the integrity of the "heads"—the written parts—but other than that, baby, just live with what you blew. You'll get over it—that's jazz.

I see now that this is a matter of allowing yourself to be subjected to some necessary ego-reduction. In other words, "Yeah, I'm the expert on my playing. Wait a minute, maybe I'm not—maybe I just have to do my best to improvise, but after that, as the Beatles tune says, 'Let It Be.' "

Do your best, then go on to something else—seriously. One problem I seem to have is playing the same tunes over and over again due to gig requirements—the public expects to hear certain things—but then the music starts to get stale, or, more correctly, it may get stale if you don't pay attention. As musicians, we always have to strike a balance in the endeavors we undertake while performing live. We can't be too concerned about the public's perception. It's up to us to set the trend. We can't get too comfortable.

Sometimes it's better to throw caution to the wind and play some stuff that's not so well prepared, to challenge yourself. Often, when you're trying to work through a new set of changes, you play your most honest and spontaneous stuff—it just requires courage. I used to supply the courage with chemicals—now I just do it on my own. I roll the dice and see what the Muse comes up with. It can't be that bad, especially if you get out of your own way.

Here's what I mean by that: sometimes I would be recording a blowing date at Rudy's, and I would let somebody else's opinion take precedence over mine when there was a passage in doubt. It could have been the producer, the engineer's assistant, or just about anybody in the studio who was passionate about the music but—this is key—objective. We'd hear a take, it would be acceptable to the majority of listeners in the studio, and we would move on. Left to my own devices, I would try to get it "just so," and we might be in there for two weeks just trying to get one tune—or even just one eight-bar phrase—"right."

The record with Kenny Barron was one good example of this, and we followed that with a date where we played some Monk and some Miles, and we also did "Naima" by John Coltrane. Pianist John Hicks played so great on "Naima"—it was a special moment in my music life. "Naima" is such a delicate, passionate ballad, and we played it rather simply, almost minimally. When the final notes of the piano settled after the last chord, it was so quiet—so intensely silent—in Rudy's studio that I actually broke down and cried. The emotion was that strong. Initially I felt a little embarrassed, but what the hell, I couldn't help it—and I have concluded that crying is a good thing. We called that CD *Monk, 'Trane, Miles and Me.*

One night I was hanging out in Brooklyn with my friend Nobu and we called WBGO—it was really late—and asked them to play a tune from *Monk, 'Trane, Miles and Me:* our version of Miles's "All Blues." That tune has been recorded many times, of course, but our version had its own thing. I played fewer of my usual stylistic phrases and instead tried to get more into the pure elements of the composition. I enjoyed hearing that on the radio. Sometimes it's fun to hear yourself—just don't let it go to your head. I've discovered that usually after I hear one of my things on the air, the next thing they play knocks me out and I say, "Wow, who's that?" There are lots of good players out there, and when you're in New York you are quite aware of that. That has always helped to keep me right-sized, I hope.

# *Chapter 39*

## *Orchestral works*

IN THE EARLY 1990s, I was commissioned to write a piece that eventually became known as "Concerto pour Cote d'Opal," named for the area in northwestern France near the English Channel. The promoter who asked me to do it, Patrick Drehan, was a guy I really liked, and he felt I could do something with guitar and orchestra that would be a bit different. The bread was pretty good, too, so I set out to compose my first extended orchestral piece.

I knew that projects like this had been done quite a few times before in jazz, and I was a bit afraid that it would sound pretentious or stiff or—hey, just "wrong." But in the end I put in so much work that I was able to avoid those feared qualities. The piece wasn't great, but I think it was good. What it made me do was work. It was a lot of effort to compose the main themes, and then to orchestrate them, and then to fine-tune the solo guitar part.

The first performance—the world premiere, as it were—took place near Boulogne, France, with a youth orchestra. They gave it their best shot, and I gave it mine, and, well—we got through it. I was grateful just for the opportunity to have done such a large-scale project, even though it was not great. It was just too long, too involved, and little bit too far-reaching to be successful.

A few weeks later, I did a radio show on the *New York Times*'s FM classical station and played the whole thing—or, rather, approximated the whole thing—on guitar. It was recorded, and I got a DAT, but something happened to it, and there are huge glitches that make the recording useless. But it sounded like the concerto—at least the parts that I could hear. It was as if I needed to fall short with the initial presentation with the orchestra in order to go back to New York and play it in reduced form to make it work better. All in all, with regard to the "Concerto pour Cote d'Opal"—no regrets.

My second concerto for guitar and orchestra was commissioned by a group of Italians in 1999. It was to commemorate "Due Agosto"—August 2, 1981—when there was a terrible terrorist bombing in a train station in Bologna. The guy in charge was an excellent musician named Fabrizio Festa. As good as he was at music, he was just as good at administration, so everything was well organized. Part of the deal was that my composition was to be included in a program of winners of a composition contest—and the winners, from all parts of Europe, were excellent. There were varied compositions, all involving guitar and orchestra, with styles ranging from the Romantic to the avant-garde. I was also commissioned to play the guitar part for a contemporary composition written by an Italian musician—this was also quite good.

My concerto was to be a double concerto with Al DiMeola; he would play an Ovation nylon-string guitar, and I would use my Cort signature archtop jazz model. In writing the piece, I fashioned a large part of the long ending movement in a style that I thought would be right up Al's alley. It was a tango in A minor intended to showcase Al's proclivity for excelling in the Mediterranean style of improvisation. When we played it, he kicked butt. I didn't do so badly either, and one of the unexpected benefits of this gig was that after we played the concerto with the orchestra Al and I went out and just jammed for the capacity crowd. They went nuts—to be spontaneous after all that planned music was a great and uplifting release.

During the months-long process of composing the second concerto, which was eventually titled "Sentenza del Cuore (Sentence of the Heart)," I used my Buddhist practice to get me through the rough spots. For example, since this concerto was to be a positive response to a negative situation, the Bologna bombing, I chanted about the emotional content of the event. I chanted to really feel the tragedy, to feel the outrage, and also, after that, to try to arrive at some higher level of consciousness to deal with the aftermath: the loss of life, the destruction, the trauma—in short, the horror of the terror.

I read articles and stories about the tragedy (in Italian) and was able to obtain photographs of almost every victim. I took each photo, placed it on my altar, and chanted for the repose of the person killed. I then chanted for the consolation of their loved ones left behind. Later, when we went to Bologna to prepare for the concert, I was able to meet with the organization of the families who had lost loved ones in the disaster. This was an especially uplifting and lesson-teaching experience; in other words, yes, the music is important, it's why I'm here, but in this case the music became a means to see another, truly more serious, side of life. The reality of killing and hatred was juxtaposed with the love and caring that go into a large musical event designed to ward off the evil that created the event. And it was a great privilege for me to witness all this taking place within the framework of the beautiful, rich, utterly humanistic Italian culture.

During one of my visits to Bologna to prepare for this event, I heard a solo concert by expatriate American guitarist Elliot Fisk. It was incredible, especially when he played a transcription of music by the great Paganini. Bireli LaGrene had been carrying around a CD of Elliot playing Paganini during our 1996 tour, and I remember being blown away by it then. But to hear it live, as Elliot's encore, was a treat beyond description. Elliot also spoke perfect Italian while announcing his program to the audience. It made me proud to know him.

"Sentenza del Cuore" went well enough in that first performance to warrant another performance about two years later, in Athens, as part of a special concert organized by the great Greek guitarist Costas Cotsiolis. For that, Al and I played with the Volos (Greece) Symphony.

A third performance took place in Cordoba in 2003 with the Cuban composer and conductor Leo Breower, who is an incredible person and, in my opinion, the best conductor there is for guitar music. I teamed up with Randy Brecker on trumpet rather than another guitarist, and the way he interpreted it gave the piece more of a Spanish flavor. It was reminiscent of Miles's work on *Sketches of Spain,* but Randy played with a lot of originality, too—so even though you could hear the Miles influence, it was all him. It worked like a charm. Leo, genius that he is, rearranged the instrumentation (reduced it, actually) and reinterpreted the attack on the notes in the tutti sections, thereby enhancing the rhythmic forward motion of my composition. By doing so, he improved "Sentenza" a heck of a lot.

In my experience with guitar and orchestra events, one conclusion has clearly emerged: this is a good path for the future of our music. By "our music," I mean more or less those who improvise based on the foundation of jazz. I believe that each succeeding generation of listeners needs to hear not only the "Three B's," as well as Mozart and the French school that includes Ravel and Debussy, but also the logical "next thing" that comes from those great required-listening composers of the past. One of the most heartwarming compliments I got when we were rehearsing "Sentenza" in Parma came from Fabrizio Festa. He had been making suggestions to me over the summer of 1999 about reorchestrating parts of "Sentenza," and I had made revisions to the bridge of the "Tango" movement. Fabrizio said he liked it and that it reminded him of Ravel. Well! That just about made my day—an artist can progress in spite of himself, after all.

In 2000, when I was asked by Chesky Records to record a CD with my sons, we played scaled-down versions of excerpts from "Sentenza." We reduced the prelude to three guitars plus the excellent bass of Brian Torff and the dominating presence of Alphonse Mouzon on drums, this time in a more subtle, supporting role. My younger son, Julian, played Al DiMeola's part on the "Adagio" movement and acquitted himself beautifully. That record was called *The Coryells.*

As I write this, my sons are doing well. Murali lives in upstate New York, Julian is in L.A., and they both have successful careers in this crazy business we call music. Murali has given me two grandsons. I'm waiting for Julian to follow suit, but there's no hurry.

# *Chapter 40*

*Do the better players really get overlooked? Does it matter?*

As I near the end of this tale, I'd like to address a topic that may be meaningful to any of my fellow players who are reading this and perhaps struggling with their life in music. How many times have you been sitting around, discussing the things you like about music and musicians, and the conversation goes to how unfair it is that John Tesh or Kenny G (or whoever!) is successful while so many others are struggling. The response is usually, "Well, their music is commercial, it's easy to digest," or some such explanation, and from that point some serious dissing can take place: "They can't play nearly as well as Coltrane" or some such remark. Of course, nobody can play as well as Coltrane, but we shouldn't begrudge anyone's success. This stuff happens because we're all artists, but at the same time we're all human, and we can get morose about the unfairness of the business.

I was once in New York watching a concert with my son, Julian, and there was a guitarist who shall remain nameless up there who, according to Julian, shouldn't even have gotten the gig. I knew what Julian meant, but I told him that he shouldn't be affected by something like that. Over time, everything evens out.

That instance made me think of some experiences I've had in my life. I'd be in a jam session or at some kind of loosely organized gig, and somebody I had never heard of—usually a guitarist—would come out of the woodwork and blow everybody away. Bill Conners comes to mind, when he emerged to play with Return To Forever in 1973. Another time—I think it was in the early 1990s—the saxophonist Vincent Herring invited me play with his group, which included my old friend, the late Beaver Harris, on drums. Well, Vincent had this guitar player whose name I can't even remember. He was a white guy, diminutive stature, maybe wearing glasses, and we were playing "Caravan." The tempo was up there. It came time for this guy to play a solo, and he tore it up! Great ideas—bebop, for sure, but some good contemporary phrasing with excellent, subtle string bending on a Fender Telecaster. This guy was flyin'! I was so impressed that I invited him down to my gig at the Village Vanguard the following week, and he sat in and played his tail off. I never heard from him again, and I wish to heck I could remember his name.

A few years later, I was at the NAMM show, the big music industry trade show in Anaheim, California. On the last hour of the last day, this guitarist I knew, an Israeli named Mordy Ferber, struck up a jam session at the Cort Guitar booth with bassist Jeff Berlin and drummer Danny Gottlieb. All Danny had to play was a ride cymbal, I think. They played "Solar," a composition attributed to Miles, and Mordy said to hell with the melody—he played what I would call his reaction to the melody. Jeff and Danny were so tight with the time it was scary, and Mordy was just burning. There were no clichés in what he was playing. I like players who either use clichés tastefully or go the other way and become "anti-cliché" players. Mordy did the latter—it swung, it was fresh, it was art, baby. Fortunately, somebody videotaped that impromptu performance and gave the tape to Mordy. On the strength of that, he got a gig with Danny and Jeff in New York—but he later told me that the gig in the City wasn't quite as good as that magic moment at the NAMM show.

Sometimes the Muse of creativity only gives you one good shot every once in a while. Good music is elusive! To us players, that is—who knows if the general listenership can tell the difference—but that's a subject for a different discussion. I mean, you have somebody like Carlos Santana, who is a legendary melodist, coming out of a rock-blues technique with a Latin foundation, and you compare him to somebody like Mordy. Well, Mordy plays more abstractly, and his music is more complex. At the same time, Carlos's music is totally sincere and definitely of sufficient depth to attract the attention of greats like Wayne Shorter and Alice Coltrane. There's room for both types of players on the scene. A player like Mordy always has the satisfaction of knowing what he knows—and, in the end, is it really about how many gigs you got and how much bread you made, or is it about how deep into the music you penetrated? To me, it's about the depth—and different players have different standards of what is important to them musically.

The ideal would be—and I'm just thinking out loud here—to lead, or just be in, the world's best jazz band, play all your own tunes and maybe some choice standards, get paid what we call "stupid money" (lots and lots of bread) for huge crowds—every time—every gig—sold out, standing room only, and on top of that get rave reviews in the jazz press, and, along with the positive press, really flattering photos of yourself on the gig, preferably in color. Does this happen every time? Yeah, right!

Having said that, there is a corollary to this discussion. There are two states of mind that we as artists can adopt when operating on a conscious level. One is what I call the "Salieri consciousness," and the other is the "Mozart consciousness." If you recall the play *Amadeus* (later made into a movie), there was this composer, a contemporary of Mozart's, named Salieri. Salieri was a pretty successful musician in his time, got some good gigs, and had his music played extensively. Because of all this, he had a good reputation. But Mozart was always getting better gigs, was more successful, and when the man on the street would hum the beginning of one of Mozart's melodies, the second man on the street would finish the phrase! Mozart was, in short, a better musician—a genius. Salieri found this hard to take and was always comparing himself to Mozart. He fretted about whether or not he measured up to Mozart, not only in creativity, but in all aspects of the music game. Well, we can be like Salieri: full of ego and constantly worrying about how we're doing. Or we can be like Mozart and live in the moment—what am I composing now, what will I compose next? What was done last week or last year is of no immediate consequence; let's go straight ahead and dive headlong into the music-making process.

I've learned that I always have to be on guard to avoid lapsing into the "Salieri consciousness" when I hit rough waters. I have to remember the lesson of this story—stay in the moment, do the creating, and let other people be the judge. Judge yourself only when you are within the parameters of your personal music standards; in other words, don't be afraid to be self-critical, but make sure it leads to improving your music. Music, ultimately, will stand on its own. The same principle applies to improvising and the degree of quality thereof. I am my own harshest critic, and I assume my colleagues feel the same way. But we should use our self-criticism only in a non-egoistical way—there's a point where you have to say, "That's the best I can do" and move on—enjoy someone else's music instead, for example. You can't hit a home run every time, but you can keep stepping up to the plate. Do your best. Be like Mozart. Create. Be in the moment.

The music comes first.

Peace.

# *Epilogue*

**M**Y STORY HAS TO STOP SOMEWHERE, so I now prepare to put down my pen. I'm 63 years old as I write this, and I think I'm in pretty good shape. I've had a rather checkered personal life, but even that aspect of my "insanity" is starting to stabilize. My second divorce became final mid-2005. After two divorces, I have finally found the right person for me. Her name is Tracey. She's a gorgeous knock-out of a woman, a beautiful singer, and a fantastic, original songwriter. When I met her, I fell in love immediately. I couldn't stay away—she was mysterious, she was quiet, she was gentle and intelligent. I could somehow hear a voice telling me, "This young lady is going to be my partner." My heart was telling me I had to do this.

We began to do things together, and I found that we got along well. I felt that we could somehow come to a mutual understanding about how to make music together, although she was more pop-oriented, and I was a jazz musician. I even started singing songs to her. I was falling head over heels; I hadn't sung like that to a woman in a long time, probably never. She started writing songs about me—and, well, I was hooked.

Eventually I was able to start a new life with Tracey and include her in my travels, which makes life on the road much easier for me now. We're also recording music together and performing in public on a limited basis. She's a guest vocalist on my latest release from Rhombus Records, called *Laid Back & Blues: Live at the Sky Church in Seattle*. She performs a folk-blues thing written by Tracy Chapman that I like to include in my stage show as well. I'm also helping her to produce her next project, sort of a pop-jazz thing. The first track has Paul Wertico and Danny Gottlieb on drums plus Mark Egan on bass, also to be released on Rhombus.

It's been difficult for Tracey and me to make ends meet because the alimony and child support are pretty hefty. But that was to be expected, and I have learned to get along on less money for a while. I never needed that much anyway—I always just wanted to play the guitar. Modern life's realities require us to be at least a little bit materialistic so we can do the things we need to do as artists—you know, plane tickets, instruments, live under a roof, sleep in a bed, stuff you need.

I've always had a problem with the women in my life—I'm so obsessed with the music that sometimes I forget the little details of decency required in daily life with another person. It takes time to build trust, but I think I can get it together this time because I know I love Tracey. I see tremendous potential in us and in her music. Plus she's already learning more of the subtleties of jazz! With her, I have faith in the relationship. We got engaged on Saint Patrick's Day of '06—now we're just waiting for the right time and place to tie the knot.

I'm still busy playing in a lot of situations. I started 2005 with some trio gigs in Connecticut with Mark and Paul. As I said earlier, we went to Seattle, where we recorded a performance at the Sky Church, which is part of the Experience Music Project complex. In addition to Tracey, I had my old friends from Seattle in the band: Dean Hodges on drums, Chuck Deardorf on bass, and Mark Seales on piano. It was good to come back to Seattle after all those years on the East Coast. I was able to bring together various elements of my approach to jazz—some solid straight-ahead, coupled with copious salutes to the blues.

I also played with the Three Guitars: John Abercrombie, the Brazilian Badi Assad (the younger sister of the great Assad Brothers classical guitar duo), and me. Those gigs were great because it was all acoustic. We had recorded for Chesky in 2003, but it took us a while to find some gigs. The material is mostly compositions written by John and Badi; John leans toward bebop, and Badi (naturally) composes in the Brazilian style. I added a couple of my things, too, so the compositional mix is good. It's pretty much all original material—no standards to speak of—and I think that's been a good selling point for the trio.

We went to Italy in February and then continued to play in Europe, mostly Spain, where I was robbed for one of the few times in my life (it was strange, but I lived to tell about it—that's all that matters). After that, I formed another trio with bassist Victor Bailey and drummer Lenny White. We cut a CD called *Electric* on Chesky Records and followed that with a trip to Japan. I did several mini-tours with the Mark Egan–Paul Wertico tandem as well, between my stints with Victor and Lenny. With Mark and Paul, I have been playing mostly my originals plus some standards, like "Well You Needn't" and "'Round Midnight"—Monk remains a favorite of mine. It seems like every time I do a Monk tune on a record it brings good luck. As a matter of fact, Coryell, Bailey, and White just made a follow-up CD for Chesky that included Monk's "Mysterioso," which found me using a slide, something I rarely do. Called *Traffic*, it was released in September 2006 in tandem with a U.S. tour. This time we did some acoustic stuff, including a guitar solo called "Jake's Lullaby", in addition to the usual high-powered electric approach of the first date.

At this point I am still planning to do another recording with Mark and Paul, but first I have to tend to my latest releases on Rhombus and Chesky. I want to record in an Indian context again, too, but that's on the back burner until I take care of the other projects. I have been playing with practitioners of the Indian wooden flute, the bansuri, in the last few years. Some of those gigs have been with the amazing Hari Prasad Chaurasia, who is considered the dean of that instrument. There is also a younger bansuri player, Ronu Majumdar, who is quite incredible. He and I have hooked up with a tabla player named Vijay Ghate and an American tenor player, George Brooks, whom I met when playing with Hari Prasad; we've done concerts both here and abroad. Playing Indian music is a real challenge. Even the way they play 4/4 is tricky—the Indian artists can create various groups of uneven beats inside the main 4/4 beat. It's a wonder to behold.

In October 2005 I participated in a retrospective of my original jazz-rock material (which included singing) from the late '60s and early '70s. We tried to create the old scenario as faithfully as possible by using—or trying to use—the original players from that earlier era. We *did* get Bernard Purdy to play drums, but we had to use other players to fill in the other roles, and it worked fine. We did it at the Avalon Theater in Hollywood. As guest guitarists I had James Valentine from Maroon 5 (who was taking guitar lessons from my son Julian) and David Hidalgo from Los Lobos. I had wanted Santana; he couldn't make it, but he did send a very gentlemanly message—that was nice. Special thanks to Julian for his superb guitar and keyboard work and participation; without him things would not have gone so smoothly. He pulled most of the musicians together, found the recording engineer, supplied essential equipment including some killin' guitars, *and* got me his guitar tech from Aimee Mann's band. This concert was originally supposed to be a part of a film documentary on my life. At this point however, it is slated to become a concert DVD. At least there will be a high-quality document of those early years—albeit as a retrospective—before the Eleventh House.

There's much more to be written about the music, and I will write again when the occasion calls for it. For now, it's important for me to look at some events that occurred during the writing of this autobiography, to share them with you, and to draw some meaning from these events. My Buddhist practice of more than 21 years has helped me as I try to understand what happened.

In 2005 I lost two people with whom I was close: Steve Marcus and Eric Fuchsman. You may remember reading, early in my story, about Steve and me playing with Gary Burton during the creation of jazz-rock fusion in the late 1960s. Steve was a great jazz saxophone player, and when we first met on the Lower East Side in 1966 I found that he had a similar concept to mine—that is, he was trying to blend Coltrane with the Beatles. He came into Mike Nock's apartment on the ground floor of 198 Eldridge Street on a hot day in the summer of 1966, bringing an arrangement of "Eight Miles High" by the Byrds. We later recorded it on his album *Tomorrow Never Knows* on Atlantic Records. Steve did some great Coltrane-inspired modal soloing in the section where Jim McGuinn had played his electric 12-string guitar solo. Steve—"The Count"—brought another jazz-meets-rock arrangement with him that day: "Paperback Writer" by the Beatles. It never was recorded, but I remember that it was killin'. By working off George Harrison's guitar motif, the Count created a compelling and original improvisatory framework (and we always liked new things to play on). Steve Swallow played the bass part that day—I think it was his arrangement—and I think the Count had someone record it, but I've no idea whom or where the tape might be.

I remember that Jim Pepper, who lived in the building, came down and jammed on that Beatles arrangement. I marveled at the opportunity to hear the Count and Pepper together—two great tenor players from my generation. The contrast was amazing: the Count being more straight-ahead but still adventuresome and Pepper coming from a core of pure freedom, blending ingeniously into the straight-ahead genre. Each had a sound that matched his personality: Pepper's was big and raw while Steve's was sophisticated yet still powerful.

I was close to Jim but even closer to the Count—we were friends longer, and we connected off the bandstand as well as on. He was really funny, and we'd have a ball just shootin' the breeze. Steve was like jazz's version of Woody Allen—he used a lot of good-natured sarcasm punctuated by Yiddish humor. Sometimes he'd make me laugh so hard the tears would come. Toward the end of his life, I got him to chant with me at some gigs, right before we went onstage—and he said he liked chanting. For this I am grateful: that Steve chanted Nam-Myoho-Renge-Kyo together with me. It was a way of invoking the Law of the Universe; a way to connect with that which is the Essence of Life. What we did as players was not unlike that—a cosmic hookup that transcended time and space and at the same time established a relationship of the spirit: an environment of mutual respect for our own (and others') deepest humanity.

Steve passed away in his sleep at his home in Pennsylvania in September 2005. I got the call on a Sunday afternoon from his daughter, Holly, and I knew I had to go to the funeral. It was held a couple days later in Westchester County, and it was a wonderful celebration of Steve's life and music—there was a great photo on the casket of Steve playing with his mentor, Buddy Rich. My heart went out to Holly and to Steve's wife, Eleanor, another close friend for years. The Jewish service was beautiful—stories were told by Steve's brother and his bandmate, Andy Fusco, and I added a message from Mike Mandel, our keyboardist in the Foreplay band. Mike couldn't make it, so I carried his message. Afterwards, as I drove away from the cemetery, I realized how grateful I was that Steve and I had chanted together.

We had a memorial service for the Count at the "Jazz Church" at 54th and Lexington on May 28, 2006, with the Buddy Rich Alumni Band in attendance, which also included drummer Steve Smith and the "Buddy's Buddies" small group. Steve is the driving force behind keeping this configuration going in order to help the public remember how great Buddy Rich was. Originally, I had had a gig booked in Russia for the day of the service, but the Universe knew I had to be in New York to bid farewell to the Count so that gig got cancelled—funny how stuff works out that way.

At the service, Mike Mandel and Harry Wilkinson from the Fourplay band showed up, Harry all the way from Nashville. Eleanor and Holly asked me to say a few words, which I did—then I played Gershwin's "Our Love Is Here to Stay" on acoustic guitar as a tribute to the Count. At the end they ran a video of the Count soloing with the Buddy Rich Band—it was a fitting coda to the event, since it displayed Steve's prowess on tenor to the max. There was a series of held chords at the end of the piece, and the Count soared over the top with his cadenzas, and these cadenzas were so characteristic of the Count's unique voice—he was coming out of Coltrane, for sure, but the originality was there. It was exciting and sublime at the same time. It's good to have video documents like that so succeeding generations can get an idea of how deep the music is, and has been, and will be.

I mentioned Eric Fuchsman, too. Eric's name hadn't come up before, so let me tell you about him. Eric worked for the Cort guitar company, and he had gotten me an endorsement for a Larry Coryell signature model. We had a pretty good run with that guitar, and Eric and I became friends. Before he went to work for Cort, Eric ran a club in New York called Zanzibar—not for profit but because he loved the music and the musicians. It was hilarious to call him at the club; the place was always packed and the band would be blasting away, so much so we'd barely be able to understand each other. Eric liked electric fusion and hired great groups who played that style, but sometimes their sound was a little too big for the room. All the musicians dug him because he always put their needs before his own. Eric really cared about other people. He wasn't pretending to care—he was truly interested, which is a rare quality in today's atmosphere of superficiality and consumerism.

Unfortunately, in 2003 Eric began to have seizures that betrayed the presence of brain tumors. He went to see specialists and had operations on his brain—and all the while he tried to keep working as director of sales at Cort. He was in the fight of his life, and I started chanting for him. I would send him daimoku (the repeating of Nam-Myoho-Renge-Kyo) for hours on end, then call and ask him if he felt anything. He said he felt better—my chanting was reaching him, helping him, at least on an emotional level. This went on for months. I kept chanting for Eric and he'd say it was helping him, and then he converted to Buddhism and joined the organization (SGI-USA) of which I'm a member. He received his own Gohonzon, the scroll that is the object of devotion in the practice of chanting. All of sudden there were SGI members in Chicago, where he lived, who were chanting with him and supporting him. They were there with him until the end, which came in November 2005.

I was glad that I had been able to chant with Eric—we made a mystical, eternal connection that complemented our devotion to music. With Eric gone from Cort (a very good company), the atmosphere for me changed and I decided to make a move to another company. I thought long and hard about what I wanted to do concerning designing and developing signature guitars and made a decision to sign on with Parker Guitars in July 2006; I felt I could do my best work in their environment. But my friendship with Eric was a "treasure of the heart" for me. It's so important to appreciate our friendships. I've lost a great many friends during my career, especially in the last year or two—among them: Billy Higgins, Joe Henderson, Kenny Kirkland, Tal Farlow, Grover Washington Jr., and Niels-Henning Ørsted Pedersen. I have chanted for all of them, not just for their lives but also for the music they gave to our generation. I continue to chant for their return to this earthly realm in order to work more on their music and their lives. The road to music is endless—my classical guitar teacher Leonid Bolotine told me that in 1966, and I hope I never forget it.

Musicians are special people. The really good ones are always working on the next thing. The special players I've encountered while being on the scene for more than 40 years all have one thing in common: when they walk into the room, you know there are some unique vibrations—positive and strong—about to emanate. You can call it charisma—I'm told Bird had it; Miles definitely had it. Wayne

Shorter and Herbie Hancock have it. I've seen them in special duo performances after we have all chanted in a large group at Buddhist meetings, and their music took on extra-dimensional characteristics. I hope that can happen to me, especially when my life condition is strengthened through my practice.

It's a lifetime practice, and I will never graduate. I will never really "be there" or be mistake-free or be immune to character defects or shortcomings. And, of course, life is always a little bit insane no matter how hard we try. The important thing is to have the determined faith to live a life that ultimately will be free of regret. I want to have that kind of life. My life has been intertwined with creativity—the arts, especially music—and I will never be able to fully repay the Universe for this gift. What I can do, and what I will do, is give every ounce of my strength, and make every effort, so that when I get to the end I can look back and say I understood the blues, that I understood what jazz is, that I understood what great classical music is, and that I played some of those things in this existence that couldn't have been played by anyone else.

I no longer live in New York City but in Orlando, Florida. I've taken what I learned about musical self-discipline and the rules of pursuing a career as a serious musician in New York and have discovered that with the right attitude I can continue to grow and evolve as an artist anywhere. But New York remains the epicenter of the energy and creativity, and I will always go back. I love it there, but at my age it's nice to live where there's better weather and a less stressful urban environment.

My quest goes on. I have so many projects—I'm just now rediscovering the genius of the great Brazilian guitarist Hector Villa-Lobos; after I heard Elliot Fisk play Villa-Lobos's "Twelve Etudes," I went out and got them and they're kickin' my butt. I need that. The other thing I want to share with my fellow musicians is something that Billy Taylor once told an interviewer. He said, "If you're too busy to practice, then you should get out of the business." Right on, Doctor Taylor! I mention the "Taylor axiom" only in reference to myself—I know lots of cats who simply don't need to practice: they get to the gig, and they hit on all cylinders without ever having touched their instrument. But I'm not one of those people—I got to keep the fingers wrapped around the guitar at least an hour a day between gigs.

In 1966, Jimmy Garrison told me that "the white boy never steps in a hole." Well, this is one white boy who tried like hell to step into that hole and almost didn't make it out. I had skewed values for a long time, and I am lucky that I'm slowly coming around to being able to distinguish the real thing from all the b.s. that permeates everyday life. It just takes practicing life's basic rules and the willingness to learn from mistakes—and then it takes the strength to change and to propel oneself forward as an artist. I love music that makes me laugh, but I revere, I bow down to, music that makes me cry—the string quartets that Beethoven wrote near the end of his life come to mind. And, of course, anything by Miles and 'Trane, Monk, Stan Getz, Lester, Mingus, Jimi, Stevie Ray—my teachers, my inspiration. I must continue to practice my instrument. I love the blues—I will understand the blues completely one day. Life is the blues. The blues is life.

Thank you from the depths of my life, O great gods and goddesses of music. May I continue to serve you upon my return, whenever the Universe wills it.

Orlando, Florida
September 18, 2006

# *Appendix*

*Selected* Guitar Player *columns, 1977–1989*

# Larry Coryell's
# CONTEMPORARY GUITAR

## The Lydian Mode

Last month, in our discussion of repositioning, we introduced the lydian mode which differs from a regular diatonic scale in that the perfect 4th is replaced by an augmented 4th (flat 5):

This particular mode is interesting in that it works well to cover the dominant 7th vamp so often found in contemporary music. If we were vamping on G to F, for example, the F lydian scale would cover the entire "modal shift," since the tones are the same as are found in the two chords (F, A, C for the F chord and G, B, D for the G chord):

Here's a useful rule: 9th chords and half-diminished chords a major third up can also be single-noted by the same lydian mode. For example, to play either G9 or Bm7b5, you play the lydian mode beginning on F.

Another way to remember this is to use the following formula: for a 9th chord select the lydian mode one step down from the chord's tonic or root; for a half-diminished chord select the lydian mode found an augmented 4th (or flat 5) up from the chord's tonic or root. For example, as shown above, for a G9 and a Bm7b5 you would use a lydian scale beginning on F; for a G#9 and a Cm7b5 you would use a lydian scale beginning on F#; for an A9 and a C#m7b5 you would use a lydian scale beginning on G; and so forth.

In Example 1, we see how to apply the lydian half-diminished formula in a song context. In order to navigate the F# half-diminished (F#m7b5), we play off a B# (or C) lydian scale. To continue on to the E half-diminished (Em7b5), we play off an A# (or Bb) lydian. Note the relationship between the half-diminished root and the lydian converted root stays the same—a diminished fifth (or augmented fourth) away.

Example 1 involves a more or less "standard" application of the lydian principle. A less common usage is described by Example 2. In the key signature of E major, we are using an A lydian to traverse the ubiquitious presence of the II minor 7th chord. This lydian conversion can be useful for those of you who are tired of being starved inspirationally by thinking you have to develop each chord scale from the root! In this case, we start on the minor 3rd (G) above the root (E) and play off F# minor's relative major, A, which we also "lydianize" (using D# instead of D-natural).

Example 3 shows two things: 1) the lydian scale is a beautiful melody in and of itself, and 2) it is the modal glue that brings together such foreign sounding changes as Gbmaj7b5 over F natural. As illustration we use part of "Adam Smasher," a song written by pianist Mike Mandel, from The Eleventh House [Vanguard, VSD 79342]. This section also employs alternating bars of six and seven beats to contrast with the uniformity of the Gb lydian scale. Remember, this key signature has two flats in it already, so be sure to include Bb and Eb in your list of accidentals. You might try counting it like this (note the accents): one and two and three and four and FIVE SIX (last two notes are Bb); one and two and three and four and five and six and SEV'N (pronounced as one syllable).

There are many more uses for the lydian mode. Can you think of any? Don't hesitate to apply this knowledge to chords, as well as single notes. Remember, open strings five through two make for a G chord over an A in the bass. Open strings five through one make for an Em7 chord with an A bass. The lydian scale beginning on G works with either (see Example 4). You take it from there, guitar players! Good luck, lydian users!

## June 1977, "The Lydian Mode"

This was one of my first columns, and it dealt with the idea that one scale can cover more than one chord. Many players, at least in their early development, think that there must be a separate scale for each chord; then, as their harmonic wisdom evolves, they start to see that with, say, *C* and *Am*, both chords can be covered with the *C* major scale.

With that concept in mind, I wrote this column to share my thinking on how well the Lydian mode fits with certain chords—in this case some dominant 7th and half-diminished chords, as well as a straight-ahead maj7♭5 (see Ex. 3, with a *G♭maj7♭5* over an *F* bass). If I were to teach the same lesson today, I wouldn't put quite so much emphasis on the Lydian mode.

After this column came out, there was a rather derisive letter to the editor from some guy making fun of "Lydian Larry" Coryell and "Aeolian Al" DiMeola, one of my partners in crime in the fusion movement of that era. The letter writer made a good point—and now, when I look at the *F♯m7♭5* in Ex. 2 of this column, it strikes me that I would simply tell a student to play the Locrian mode from *F♯* with that chord, to get a better idea of that particular chord-scale relationship.

# Larry Coryell's
# CONTEMPORARY GUITAR

## Lenny's Lesson

For several years, I have wanted to learn how Lenny Breau played something called "Tuning Time," from *The Velvet Touch Of Lenny Breau—Live* [RCA, LSP-4199]. In April 1977, I had the privilege of performing with Lenny at Nashville's Exit Inn. We went to my hotel afterwards, and he showed me the amazing technique that created those heavenly sounds which had haunted me for so long. It involves alternating back and forth between fretted notes and harmonics. As an example, choose a chord (preferably one that employs all six strings), and pick the fourth string with the little finger of your right hand; then play a harmonic on the sixth string (12 frets above the fretted note), lightly touching the string with your right index finger while simultaneously picking. (You'll have to hold the pick with your thumb and middle finger.) In a similar fashion, alternate between other fretted notes and harmonics (third and fifth strings, second and fourth strings, and first and third strings), playing through the whole chord in an arpeggiated fashion. When these series of notes start to sound like you're playing a harp, then you've got it. I haven't recorded this technique yet, but if you listen to Lenny or Chet Atkins, you'll have some recorded samples of this beautiful phenomenon.

In the illustration below, notice the positions of the fingers: the index finger is pointed forward, ready to touch the string lightly as the pick sounds the harmonic, the 4th finger is ready to play the alternating fretted note.

When attempting these artificial (closed) harmonics, the index finger of the right hand should only touch the string at the instant you pick. As soon as the pick leaves the string, remove the 1st finger. Also, a light touch is necessary to make this technique work most effectively, since it allows the harmonics to be heard at about the same volume level as the notes plucked with the little finger.

What I have described is the *simplest* form of this technique. People like Lenny and Chet do all sorts of wonderful things with it. Chet told me that he sent a summary of the technique to Johnny Smith, who probably has developed some new extensions. You'll likely find plenty of variations on the basic idea, once you've done some experimentation. It's not really hard—it just takes practice and patience. Once you get the mechanics of it, try beginning the alternation with a harmonic. Certain chords provide added possibilities for open-string harmonics (see *Em9sus4* below).

The following nine chords are good to start with, and by working with them you'll find that there are endless possibilities that can be realized using this technique. It is truly a different way (at least, it is to *me*) to extend the range of the instrument and add to the variety of textures that guitarists can produce. It works great on acoustic guitar, but I think it's even better when applied to the electric. One warning, though: on the electric guitar, make sure that your volume is lower than normal; otherwise, the overtones may distort, destroying the purity of the effect.

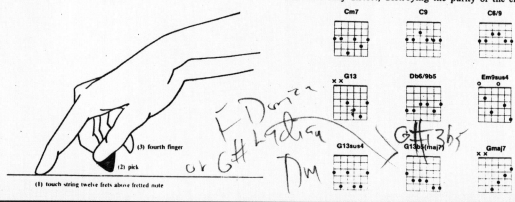

(3) fourth finger

(2) pick

(1) touch string twelve frets above fretted note

## January 1978, "Lenny's Lesson"

Wow, how time alters our perception! In the last sentence of this column I wrote: "make sure your volume is lower than normal; otherwise the overtones may distort, destroying the purity of the effect." This has *not* proven to be true for me in the years since, when I've used this technique. When I wrote this, I was still green as a columnist—although that's the only thing I'd change in this lesson.

As the column explains, Lenny Breau and I hung out after a gig one night, and he laid a lot of stuff on me (including how to navigate some of the "Giant Steps" changes) in an hour or so. What a generous soul Lenny was. He continued to do innovative stuff with the instrument right to the end of his life. Around 1986, I saw a video of him in a solo concert, and he was playing a 7-string guitar, only the seventh string was an *A*, up a 4th from the first string. That set was the deepest solo guitar playing I've ever heard in my life in terms of emotion and artistry—it's as if he may have known, somehow, that his days were numbered. The music was sad, but in a profound way, not wishy washy—and not a cliché was played.

I was not in such good shape on the night we got together in Nashville, but at least I had enough capacity to pick up this "trick" of alternating a normal note with an artificial harmonic. I have shown it to many other players, and many of them do the right-hand thing without the pick, more in the classical guitar style—and that's just fine. Russell Malone got this down well, and he uses it with more alacrity than I do, I think. Bireli LaGrene also does wonders with this technique—of course, he does wonders with everything.

I've composed entire pieces using this artificial harmonic technique; examples include "Opus One," from *Visions in Blue*, and "Transparence," which I have recorded several times and is covered in the last chapter of my instruction book *Power Jazz Guitar*. As I've told guitarists who are learning this technique, once you get the hang of it and start producing what Stefan Grossman calls the "ripple effect" (kind of like a harp), the sky's the limit—and it works absolutely great on an electric guitar all cranked up!

# LARRY CORYELL
# CONTEMPORARY GUITAR
## "Lines," Part I

**T**HIS IS THE FIRST INSTALLMENT of a two-part lesson devoted to a composition of mine called "Lines," which was written in 1967 and recorded by the Gary Burton Quartet on *Lofty Fake Anagram* [RCA Dynagroove, 3901]. This month I'll analyze the melody and save the improvised section for our next column. [*Ed. Note: In the following tablature, the horizontal lines represent the strings (the top line is the high E), while the numbers indicate the fret to be played.*]

The intro starts with free rubato (out of tempo) in a pseudo-classical mood and makes use of the open third string. The *A(add 9)* chord just before the 12/8 time signature utilizes the open first, second, and fifth strings. Be sure not to rush the rhythm; it's very light-feeling and employs hammer-ons, pull-offs, and slides. Note the slide from beat nine to beat ten in the third measure.

Section A assumes a fast 4/4 tempo and is a big change in mood from the intro. It has the feel of a country hoedown and uses a 15-bar structure: twelve in 4/4 and three in 2/4. You may accent the points where there are hammers and pulls by hitting the strings with extra force.

The first three measures of Section A can be looked at as one long

line, and the following measure as another phrase. Both lead into the 2/4 part (measure 5), which connects to the four-bar bridge. Before you examine the bridge, practice the opening phrases until they're smooth. Don't let the 2/4 bars throw you; be careful to count them accurately, especially the first 2/4 measure and the eighth-rest that precedes the *G* chord. And feel free to add a few bass notes with your thumb (such as the *E* on the 1st fret of the sixth string in the second bar of Section A, and the *G* in the 2/4 bar that follows).

In bar 7 I suggest you get the *C#* and the *A* fingerstyle by holding the pick normally but extending the 3rd finger of the right. The intro can also be played this way.

Notice the ritard (*ritardando*, slow down), and the subsequent *a tempo* (return to the original tempo) indications in measures 8 and 9. With bar 10 we recapitulate the theme with two country and western-tinged phrases comprising two bars of 4/4, one of 2/4, and another of 4/4. The final two measures change mood slightly into a gentle easing off. (The *coda* sign in parentheses pertains to the end tag, which will be included with the improvised section in next month's column.)

**Next month:** The improvised solo to "Lines."

## "Lines"

By Larry Coryell

## September 1983, "Lines, Part I"

This was done in two parts, but I will treat it as one lesson, appearing here and on the following two pages. "Lines" comes from a period in my creative evolution where I was greatly influenced by country music and thinking about how to relate it to jazz. I was with the Gary Burton Quartet, and we were listening to the radio as we traveled around the country in a Volkswagen bus—and we drove through many rural areas. We were attracted to the sound of groups like the Beatles and the Stones, and especially to Bob Dylan's backup group, The Band, which had a lot of country influences. And Gary had done the *Tennessee Firebird* project with Chet Atkins about a year before.

We recorded "Lines" on the Quartet's *Live at Carnegie Hall* album on RCA, and I recall that Steve Marcus was disappointed that I had so much low end on my guitar on the recording. I haven't heard the live version since we did it back in the late '60s, but I do recall the original version on *Lofty Fake Anagram*. I really struggled on my solo—meanwhile, Burton was throwin' it down like he was pitching hay. I guess his country roots were deeper than mine. Today, I have to laugh at my comments on my solo in the text: "bars 10–15 are a bit unorthodox theoretically; such is the nature of swift-footed improvisation." Yeah, right—what that means is that I was just going for it.

# LARRY CORYELL
# CONTEMPORARY GUITAR
## Lines, Part II

LAST MONTH I PRESENTED the head to my tune "Lines," which was recorded by vibraphonist Gary Burton on his LP *Lofty Fake Anagram* [RCA Dynagroove, 3901]. This lesson features an analysis of the song's solo section. [*Ed. Note: In the tablature, the horizontal lines represent the guitar's strings (the uppermost line is the first string), while the numbers denote the frets.*]

For the most part, the solo sticks faithfully to the changes, except towards the end where it begins to expand on the tune's harmonic limits. Keep in mind that it's especially important to observe the various time changes that occur.

Bars 6 and 8 of the solo are an interesting study in repetition; bar 8 copies the *D B D B* pattern of bar 6, but later changes to a *D B A G* sequence. Notice the use of space—rests—in bars 7 and 9. These pauses are important and give balance to the solo.

Starting at measure 10, the line strictly follows the changes, but by

the beginning of bar 11 develops a life of its own: It's not clashing with the *E7*, but plowing through it to reach the subsequent *Am*, *F*, and *G*. At this point (into bar 13), the last four eighth-notes outline more of a *Cm* rather than the *C* that's called for.

The solo continues to break the conventional harmonic limits into bar 14 by anticipating by two beats the *Bb6/9* appearing in the second half of the measure. What's interesting in measure 15 is how the little phrase with grace notes sets up a pattern that continues on into the next chorus (not shown here), which demonstrates that you don't have to stop once you get to the end of a chorus. (Don't forget that you need last month's column in order to play the *coda*.)

While bars 10-15 are a bit unorthodox theoretically, such is the nature of swift-footed improvisation, especially as done in the harmonically iconoclastic '60s. See you next month.

## "Lines," Part II

By Larry Coryell

## October 1983, "Lines, Part II"

In 2001, when I was artist-in-residence at the University of Washington, I played this with the mallet professor there, Tom Collier, and it kicked butt. When "Lines" is played right, it's what is known in the business as a flag-waver. People love it.

One of the most interesting characteristics of this piece is the involved way that "simple" (straight major and minor) chords are used. Plus, there are many arpeggios. The message here is that if you don't know your arpeggios backwards and forwards, you run the risk of being stumped.

# LARRY CORYELL
# CONTEMPORARY GUITAR
## Melodic Minor Modes

HEARING FLAMENCO MASTER Paco de Lucia play the phrase in Ex. 1 impressed upon me the importance of the ascending melodic minor scale (also known as the jazz minor scale) shown in Ex. 2. When broken down into modes, this indispensable tonal sequence can be used to improvise over many advanced altered and extended harmonies. [*Ed. Note: For a look at scale construction and fingerings, see Scale Systems in the July '84 issue of* Guitar Player. *For more on the jazz minor scale, see Arnie Berle's column on page 136.*] Now let's turn our attention to Ex. 3, which illustrates the melodic minor's modes and shows a few of the chords they fit.

The ionian melodic minor mode in Ex. 3 works well with minor/ major 7th-type chords; that is, chords having a lowered 3rd and a major 7th. (Notice that the only difference between *F* melodic minor and *F* major is the lowered 3rd.) In contemporary improvisation, the dorian version of the melodic minor scale can be used to produce a *G6sus4b9* sound. I like to mainly use the phrygian melodic minor for maj7b5-type chords; however, it has other uses as well.

Next, we have the lydian-mixolydian scale (also known by the names dominant lydian and altered lydian). Notice that it's a combination of the lydian mode, which has a raised 4th, and the mixolydian mode, which has a lowered 7th. This scale fits several types of dominant harmonies employing a lowered 5th (same as the raised 11th).

While the voicings I've shown for the supermixolydian mode omit the lowered 7th, the scale is dominant in nature. The aeolian melodic minor can be used as an alternate for the conventional locrian mode, which fits m7b5 chords. Whereas the usual locrian mode begins with a half-step, the aeolian melodic minor begins with a whole-step. The final mode in Ex. 3 is the superlocrian, which works well for dominant 7th chords with a raised 9th and a raised 5th.

Of course, if you don't have a basic understanding of the major scale and its modes, you won't have an easy time grasping what this lesson is all about. If you aren't acquainted with modes, many books about them are available (consult your local music store or library). Next month will be devoted to the melodic minor's fingerings and some examples of how they're used. See you then.

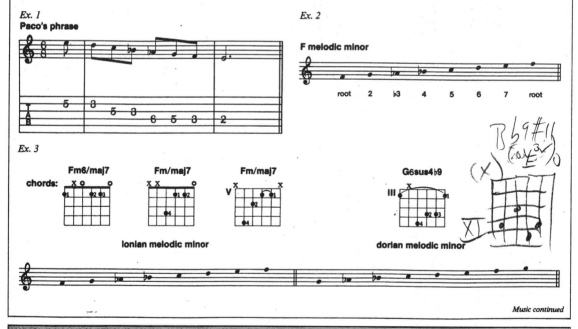

*Ex. 1*
**Paco's phrase**

*Ex. 2*
**F melodic minor**

root    2    b3    4    5    6    7    root

*Ex. 3*

chords:    Fm6/maj7    Fm/maj7    Fm/maj7    G6sus4b9

Ionian melodic minor    dorian melodic minor

*Music continued*

## November 1984, "Melodic Minor Modes"

I may have tried to be a bit too erudite in this column, but I think it was important that I got this information out there for young guitarists in the mid-1980s, when there was a groundswell growing to get more harmonically sophisticated. At that time, I was in the habit of naming every chord based on its root, hence the "*G6sus4♭9.*" I could have easily spelled that chord "*A♭maj7♭5/G*"—just as complicated but more descriptive, I think, due to the cozy connection between *A♭* major and *F* minor (after all, this was a Dorian declination of an *F* melodic minor).

I still think you need to use the names of the modes for quick communication with other players, but—as we will see as the columns progress—I ended up following the wisdom of my mentor Jerome Gray in Seattle and started to view all improvisatory phrasing as "interval shapes" rather than always talking about this mode or that scale.

I didn't recognize that there were alternate approaches to using this scale until I heard Paco de Lucia use it in one of his tunes. He used it as a melody—flamenco-sounding, of course. We jazzers use it to enhance the chords that support the melody, so everybody wins with this scale.

# LARRY CORYELL
# CONTEMPORARY GUITAR
## Melodic Minor Applications

THE FOLLOWING FLAMENCO PHRASE by Paco de Lucia led me to explore the modal system of the melodic minor scale:

In addition to flamenco lines, this indispensible scale can be used to generate many of the sounds common to contemporary improvisation. If you're still a little unsure of the melodic minor scale, remember that it's constructed like a major scale, except with a lowered 3rd:

Last month, I discussed the melodic minor modes and the harmonies they can be superimposed over. Now let's turn our attention to analyzing some of their uses, and learn some common fingerings.

Like the conventional locrian mode (generated from the major scale), the aeolian melodic minor also can be used for half-diminished chords (m7b5). Whereas the locrian begins with a half-step, the aeolian melodic minor begins with a whole-step (from there, the scales are the same). You can determine where to use the melodic minor modes by analyzing tunes and their progressions. For instance, the G aeolian melodic minor is suggested in bar 9 of Chick Corea's "Captain Marvel," and works well over the changes since they resolve to F:

© 1979 Thailan Music.

Fm/maj7-type chords (built from the F melodic minor scale; see last month's column) have a very intriguing sound and are highly useful. This example is a sample solo to bars 21 and 22 of the old standard "Stella By Starlight." Thoroughly analyze the Ebm/maj9 and my triplet phrase (not all of the notes of the Eb melodic minor scale were used):

bars 21 and 22:

Next, I have included some ways to play the superlocrian mode. Since this scale is characterized by a half-step/whole-step section (and a whole-tone section), it's tricky to finger. Ex. 1 covers one octave, and begins on the fifth string, 7th fret. Ex. 2 is played in a higher register. Watch out for the C at the 13th fret, second string—it's played with the 2nd finger. Ex. 3 begins on the sixth string. Notice the six-fret stretch with the three notes before the octave. [Ed. Note: For more on scale construction, see Scale Systems in the July 1984 issue of Guitar Player.]

Due to their complexity, melodic minor modes are difficult to assimilate, so remember that they're not much different from the major modes. As a final tip, when you practice scales or modes, always keep the sounds of their corresponding chords in you head. That way, you train your ear as well as your fingers. ∎

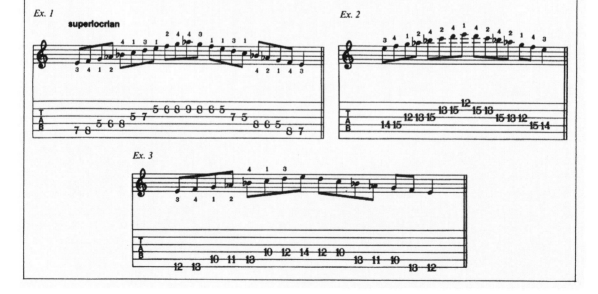

## December 1984, "Melodic Minor Applications"

The logical column to follow "Melodic Minor Modes" was one on applications of that mode. I have to credit my bass-playing friend, Bunny Brunel, for hipping me to the details of fingering the Superlocrian declination—this is what happens when you travel around Europe on trains and sit in the compartment with your axes, trading ideas. Bunny and I were on tour, with Alphonse Mouzon on drums, and we made the most of our travel time by practicing and workshopping.

This column holds up well for me because a couple of the examples show the versatility of the melodic minor. For instance, the "Captain Marvel" excerpt is scale-like, while the "Stella" example is more arpeggio-like. Both ideas sound beautiful to my ear. This column also expressed a useful idea in the last paragraph: "When you practice [this] always keep the sounds of [the] corresponding chords in your head. This way, you train your ear." Several years later, I expanded on this idea in my book *Jazz Guitar Creative Comping, Soloing, and Improv*, on pages 72–73. I tell my students that if they can play those two pages—maybe not perfectly, but with comprehension—then they will "get" the chord-scale relationship vis-à-vis the melodic minor (also known as the "jazz minor").

# Larry Coryell
## Harmonizing The Phrygian Mode

CHORD SCALES IN MORE COMMON modes such as the Ionian or the Dorian usually produce straightforward results, as long as you remain faithful to the relevant notes. [*Ed. Note: For more on chord scales or harmonized scales, see Music Theory Seminar in the Jan. and Feb. '83 issues of* Guitar Player.] However, you can explore some pretty interesting territory once you begin to superimpose chords and use unorthodox voicings. The Phrygian mode especially can produce some intriguing harmonies because of the half-step between its first and second degrees, its minor intervals, and its Spanish flavor (the familiar flamenco-style progression *Am, G, F, E* is most often associated with the Phrygian mode).

This month, I have included two examples of Phrygian chord scales based on the *E* Phrygian mode (*E, F, G, A, B, C, D*), which can be derived by starting on the third note of the *C* major scale and playing to *E* an octave higher. [*Ed. Note: For more on modes, see Scale Systems in July '84, and Questions in July '85.*] Ex. 1 employs the *F* major and *G* major triads. Ex. 2 starts with a *Bm11b5* superimposed over the tonic (*E*). To produce subsequent chords when harmonizing a scale, once your first chord is established, it's common to move each note up to its next scale tone. However, in Ex. 1 and Ex. 2, I've made a few alterations to keep things within the Phrygian character. There are many possibilities, so feel free to experiment on your own.

Ex. 1 starts with an *F* major triad over an *E* root. The next chord features an *F* root with a *G* major triad on top. Then you have what I call a *G11*, which is an *F* major triad over a *G* bass. The *A9#5sus* is like a *Ddim* or a *G7* suspended over *A*. Next, you have an *F* major triad over a *B* tonic, resulting in a *B7b5b9* (the *F* is the lowered 5th of *B*, and the *C* is the lowered 9th). The *Cmaj9* features a *G* major triad over *C*. At this point, I kept the *G* triad, but changed the order of the notes from *G B D* to *B D G*, low to high. This sets up the *Fmaj7/E* that completes the scale. I have included an optional last chord that also sounds unmistakably Phrygian.

In Ex. 2, the bass ascends exactly as in Ex. 1, but the starting chord is *Bm11b5* instead of an *F* major triad. The second chord is a *Cmaj7* over *F* (or *F9b5*). Next, you have a *G11* minus its lowered 7th. Observe that the *A7#5sus* lacks a 3rd. Next, *Bm11b5* reappears. Then, you have a *G7* over *C*, producing a *Cmaj7sus* (no 3rd). For the *D* bass note, I've included a *Dm11* and an alternate (*D9sus*), which is easier to finger. Finally, you return to the first chord (*Bm11b5*), but with its root an octave higher on the fourth string.

Remember that all of the preceding chords employ notes from the Phrygian mode. If you want to continue on your own, take things out of the "white keys syndrome" and work in a variety of keys. Have fun!

*Ex. 1*

| F/E | G/F | G11 | A9#5sus | B7b5b9 |
|-----|-----|-----|---------|--------|

| Cmaj9 | G/D | F/E | or |
|-------|-----|-----|-----|

*Ex. 2*

| Bm11b5 | F9b5 | G11 | A7#5sus (no 3rd) | Bm11b5 |
|--------|------|-----|------------------|--------|

| Cmaj7sus (no 3rd) | Dm11 | D9sus | Bm11b5 |
|-------------------|------|-------|--------|

## September 1985, "Harmonizing the Phrygian Mode"

I recall watching Steve Kahn working with a student back in the 1970s. He told the young man, "You have to be able to play chord scales." I thought that was a good idea, because it forces you to learn different voicings, plus you must be consistent with the scale-color, or mode, with which you are working. Hence, we have this exercise in the Spanish-influenced Phrygian mode. This one was really good for me when I went back and played it.

One extra benefit in devising this column was that it made me find some chords that I didn't usually play or hadn't even known before, such as the fifth chord in Ex. 1 (*B7♭5♭9*) and two of the chords in Ex. 2, *A7♯5sus/no 3rd* and *Cmaj7sus/no 3rd*. Then there was the first choice of the top of the scale (the eighth chord in the example), the *D9sus* with the big stretch of the 1st, 3rd, and 4th fingers—that's going to prepare you to play with Alan Holdsworth, if you play your chords right.

# Larry Coryell
## Right-Hand Independence

**M**UCH HAS BEEN MADE OF THE left hand's importance—and for good reason. But to achieve smoothness of time and feel in jazz-oriented passages, the right hand, which holds the pick, has to do some

*Larry Coryell helped pioneer fusion in the late '60s and has recorded with numerous legendary musicians, including John Mc-Laughlin, Sonny Rollins, and Stephane Grappelli.*

difficult things. This installment covers alternate picking and how it applies to musical situations where successive up- and downstrokes are employed.

Ex. 1 is a warm-up exercise to get you into the feel of up- and downstrokes without any break in the picking pattern; it's in the key of B minor (which is related to D major) and uses a B minor pentatonic scale. To help you develop control, the pattern shifts up a half-step and then back down.

Once you get Ex. 1 under your belt, go to Ex. 2, which begins as an ascending B minor scale (it's the B Dorian mode), with successive downstrokes occurring on the third and fourth notes of measure 1, and the last note of bar 1 continuing into the first note of bar 2. Observe that you use strict alternate picking in bars 2 and 4.

## April 1987, "Right-Hand Independence"

The idea here was to get an advancing player to go back to the basics of being rhythmic with picking and to try as much as possible to use alternate-stroke picking. There are exceptions to every rule, however, and this exercise was also meant to show that the exceptions are important—especially, when going from higher strings to lower strings, to use two successive upstrokes (followed by a downstroke if it's a three-note phrase). The $C\sharp$ on the first half of the third beat in bar six of Ex. 2 should be an $A\sharp$—I didn't catch that back in 1987. Sorry!

What's interesting to me now, almost 20 years later, is the incursion of the use of the plectrum-less right hand—that is, just using the right-hand fingers and/or the thumb. My esteemed colleague John Abercombie stopped using the pick a few years back, and he's doing just fine, especially on electric. When doing an acoustic gig he has to be careful not to ruin his thumb, but I've done some tours with him, and it's been a real joy to work together in this manner—sometimes I'll join him in the "pick-less" department for a few choruses, but I reserve the right for the "return of the plectrum," as it were, when the going gets tough. The whole point of playing, whether you're working on the examples in this column or on the bandstand, is to achieve a solid time-feeling, swing, and play some music—pick or no pick.

# Larry Coryell
## Left- And Right-Hand Coordination

THE IDEA THAT PLECTRISTS (PICK-wielding musicians) should play all down-strokes, upstrokes, or alternate strokes isn't always true (see last month's column). This month let's look at an example that uses certain fingering and picking concepts to bring out specific lines and their internal dynamics.

This exercise works through 11 bars of *Em7* before shifting ever so slightly to *Em7b5* and *A7* (provide your own resolution to *D* or *Dm*). The initial ascending run is a little surprising; the pick-up begins with a downstroke, while the following downbeat begins with an upstroke. Work on starting phrases with either stroke to

*Larry Coryell helped pioneer fusion in the late '60s and has recorded with numerous legendary musicians, including John McLaughlin, Sonny Rollins, and Stephane Grappelli.*

make your playing more varied (you'll also get more control). Also observe the small barres used in measures 1 and 2 (these involve either the 1st or 2nd finger).

In bar 2, the pull-off that begins on an upstroke is very important; equally important is the upstroke on the *B* note, which enables you to start the next downbeat with a downstroke—notice how you can use successive downstrokes when going to a higher string (the third to the second, for example). Now look at the upstroke used for the last note in measure 4; play it strongly so you can hear the *C#* that follows (this is a good example of a downbeat that isn't picked).

Measures 5 through 7 feature a straight *D* major scale. Bars 8 and 9 get into some chromatic passing tones; the last note of measure 8 is like the last note of bar 4, only this time it's a

downstroke leading to a strokeless downbeat. The pull-off and hammer-on in bar 9 are done with an upstroke and a downstroke, respectively; this is a little tricky, but you can get it (don't forget the accents).

The rhythm breaks up a bit in the remainder of the exercise, with an eighth-note triplet on the fourth beat of bar 10 and a nice grace-note slide on the third beat of 11. The last note of measure 11 (*A#* on the fourth string, 8th fret) anticipates the *Em7b5* to *A7* in bar 12.

If you have trouble coordinating the picking with the slides, hammer-ons, and pull-offs, just play slower, using all downstrokes until you can tackle my suggestions (different strokes for different folks); but if you want to bring dynamic interest to your improvisations, learn how to coordinate these important variables.

## "Picking Exercise"

By Larry Coryell

## May 1987, "Left- and Right-Hand Coordination"

This column provides more information about situations where strict downstroke/ upstroke picking doesn't apply and also covers things like the slide into the downbeat in measure 5. Ignoring for a moment the possibility that these ideas can be played fingerstyle, this exercise is quite straight-ahead in terms of the traditional approach to jazz guitar that existed when I was a teenager. As a matter of fact, the opening *Em* idea is something I learned from John LaChappelle, my first jazz guitar teacher, in my second or third lesson from him. At that time, as a youngster, I waxed ecstatic about playing a long minor-chord idea like that—I didn't know that kind of stuff was possible.

This column was written around the time when I was working with the late (and great) Emily Remler, and I used a bebop phrase I had heard her play—the aforementioned idea, which starts in measure 4 and slides into the downbeat in measure 5. I refer to that idea again in measure 11. Emily was the ultimate natural player. In my musical life—almost 50 years now as a professional—I have encountered only a couple of players who had that special "thing" about how to play and how to swing, and how to use chords in a unique way, that cannot be taught.

I always tell developing players to be as comprehensive as possible vis-à-vis scales, chords, arpeggios, and the study of solo transcriptions of great players, but also to know that if you can turn your mind off (or at least way down) and get into a zone where you just *play* and you're not really conscious of what you're doing—oh, it comes out great!

# Larry Coryell
## Left-Hand Prowess

TO HELP YOU GET YOUR LEFT-hand chops together, let's work with a variety of scale fragments. First we'll start with a relatively simple pattern, and then we'll expand it and move it up and down the fingerboard.

Ex. 1 is a repeating lick in *D* minor that uses a basic pull-off; practice it until it's

*Larry Coryell helped pioneer fusion in the late '60s and has recorded with numerous legendary musicians, including John Mc-Laughlin, Sonny Rollins, and Stephane Grappelli.*

even-sounding. Ex. 2 is four bars long and introduces a two-note hammer-on—nothing fancy, but it's very effective for adding smoothness to a phrase. Don't pick the first note in bars 2 through 4 of Ex. 2; let the momentum of the slides do all the work.

To spice things up a bit, a few combinations are featured in Ex. 3. The important thing to remember here is to negotiate the position shifts with fluidity so that you can keep the smoothness happening. Also observe that some of the pull-offs are whole-steps instead of half-steps (this takes place in the second and third measures).

Now experiment with your own combinations of scale fragments, and build some lines that are longer than Ex. 3. Remember that you are not only exercising your fingers, but also creating phrases that can be used in many playing situations. For instance, Ex. 3 can work well in certain modal-based fusion contexts because it implies tonalities a half-step away from what's already there (when you play this quickly, it gives the impression of soaring and diving). Good luck, and see you next month. ◗

Ex. 1

Ex. 2

Ex. 3

## June 1987, "Left-Hand Prowess"

Okay—because this was written nearly 20 years ago, I'm not going to attack myself for being a bit too obvious in my choice of phrases in this column. When I wrote these lessons, I wanted stuff that was simple enough for aspiring players to grasp. Having said that, if I were rewriting this lesson today, I would change these simple phrases (which involve a lot of pull-offs) into ideas that would challenge the student more with the content of the phrases themselves, as well as the technique. In Ex. 1, for instance, I would move the idea up the neck and do the pull-offs on the third string.

What I used here were some major and minor clichés, and I think the true idea of prowess in the left hand would have been better served if I had had tougher content. But that's just how I see it all these years later. Maybe some young player starting out got something out of this column—I hope so.

# Larry Coryell
## Using The Jazz Minor Scale

**R**ECENTLY I DISCOVERED *Jazz Improvisation* [1984, A. Garrison Fewell] by Garrison Fewell, who has taught at Boston's Berklee College of Music since 1977. The book has some excellent examples of how to use the jazz minor (which is the same as the ascending melodic minor scale) with a basic II, V, I progression. The material that caught my eye was on pages 38 and 39, where he took a II, V, I in the key of *C* and changed it to II, bII7, I—in other words, *Dm7, G7, Cmaj7* becomes *Dm7, Db7, Cmaj7*.

Instead of reprinting examples from the book, I've written some of my own, which utilize the *D* Dorian mode [*D, E, F, G, A, B, C*] going to the *Ab* jazz minor scale [*Ab, Bb, B, Db, Eb, F, G*] going to the *Cmaj7* chord. Why should you know how to play this progression? Because it occurs often, and the more work you do on this relatively easy exercise, the more proficient you'll become.

All of this month's examples are in the key of *C*; I've kept things simple by using all eighth-notes (with the exception of the sixteenth-note pull-off in Ex. 1). Ex. 1 doesn't require that your left hand move around much; there's just a little shift up a fret at the juncture of bars 1 and 2 with the 1st finger. Next comes another shift (down a fret) at the juncture of measures 2 and 3.

In Ex. 2, your 3rd finger is used for a shift, and then it's flattened to go from the third string to the second. When you get to the 12th-fret *E* on the first string, shift up with the 4th finger. Ex. 3 has the 2nd finger playing four notes in a row (for the *Db7*)—you might need to work on this a bit to get it together.

Ex. 4 gives you a choice of fingerings; observe that the first note of bar 1 (an *A*) should be accented, otherwise it will feel like a pick-up and throw you off. This example is more arpeggio-like than the others, but it's still very playable (notice how it ends on *D*, the 9th of *Cmaj7*).

Look back at the last note of every example, and you'll see a variety of resolutions. If you end every phrase the same, your improvisations will sound static. Strive for variety! Have fun!

*Larry Coryell helped pioneer fusion in the late '60s and has recorded with numerous legendary musicians, including John McLaughlin, Sonny Rollins, and Stephane Grappelli.*

**PAGE 32**
# Control Your Technique

## August 1987, "Using the Jazz Minor Scale"

Jazz harmony is rife with II-V-I progressions, so this column opens up new ideas for players who are serious about developing their skills at improv on this most common of chord resolutions. The jazz minor (I had called it the melodic minor before but changed the name for simplicity's sake) was a good scale to cover the altered chords in the progression. Another way to explain the II-V-I in *C* using the ♭II7 as a substitute is to tell the student: play *D* Dorian for the II, then the Lydian declination of the *A*♭ jazz minor for the *D*♭7 (♭II7), followed by the resolution to *C* major. Then I would add: think of a simple interval shape—for example, start from the *G* on the 5th fret of the fourth string, then up a half-step to *A*♭, then up a major 7th to the *G* on the 8th fret of the second string for the first two chords, and then resolve it to the notes (no more than two or three) of your choice for the tonic (*C* major). This is more horn-like, which is never a bad thing when working out single-string ideas on the guitar. These four examples were a bit academic—they were all eighth-note ideas with no rests or syncopation. The point was to focus on the correct scales that go with the chords. Once you get that down, you can get more organic with your II-V-I ideas, using more space in putting the phrases together.

# Larry Coryell
## Scale Routes

INCORPORATING OPEN STRINGS IN your scale fingerings can add a vibrant, ringing touch to your improvisations. In addition, when you work in the higher positions on the fingerboard, thinking in terms of both open and fretted notes can also help you to get a better mental picture of where things are located.

This month let's discuss a new way of playing two modes: *E* Dorian and *C* Ionian, which is the same as the *C* major scale. If your immediate reaction is, "I already know those scales, so I think I'll skip Coryell this month," remember that this approach is different than playing straight fingerings. Here the goal is to intersperse open strings and natural harmonics along with the fretted notes, which can make for some great effects.

Do I have your attention? Look at Ex. 1. The first bar is in 7/4, and the notes are located in the first position (1st-fret area) with open strings. (On guitar, a "position" is defined by the relationship of your left-hand 1st finger to a given fret, with your remaining fingers falling into a finger-per-fret alignment.) On the third beat you shift to the fourth position, while you move down one fret on the seventh beat.

Measure 2 of Ex. 1 is in 4/4, and it features a combination of fretted notes and natural harmonics played by lightly touching the string with the appropriate left-hand finger directly over the indicated fret, and then sounding the harmonic with your right hand. The most difficult note to play in Ex. 1 is the *C#* harmonic located on the fifth string at the 9th fret, which usually has to be plucked a little harder than usual. Strive to let every open string and harmonic ring for as long as possible, and observe that some notes can be played more than one way.

Ex. 2 is more straightforward, because it doesn't jump around so much. Again, I indicated where there are two ways of playing the same note. For example, in bar 2, you can play the *E* open or as a harmonic located on the fifth string, 7th fret. The last note of bar 4 can be played on either the third string or the fourth. The placement of the last note is also optional, but it will ring longer if you play it on the fifth.

By now I hope that you're getting an idea of how versatile the guitar is. If you feel as if your playing is in a rut, look for new ways to do things—they're there just waiting to be found. ∎

---

*Larry Coryell helped pioneer fusion in the late '60s and has recorded with numerous legendary musicians, including John Mc-Laughlin, Sonny Rollins, and Stephane Grappelli.*

Ex. 1

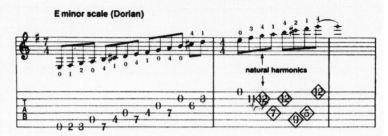

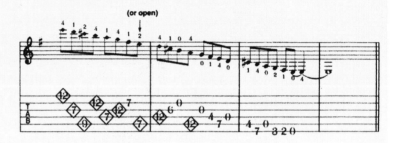

Ex. 2

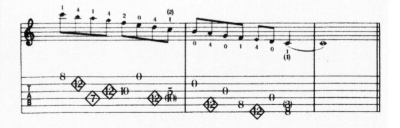

## December 1987, "Scale Routes"

This lesson is about natural harmonics, the ones that occur at various places on open strings, most notably the 5th, 7th, and 12th frets. Early on, I was attracted to the sound of harmonics, first from my teacher John LaChappelle and then from hearing Tal Farlow on record. Later, when I was in New York studying with Leonid Bolotine in 1965–66, I was introduced to the world of Villa-Lobos and subsequently the beautiful way he used harmonics. And then Jaco Pastorius started playing natural harmonics in unexpected places on the electric bass. Bireli LaGrene was a disciple of Jaco and practiced electric bass, playing along with Jaco's records. Then Bireli would switch what he had learned on the bass to the guitar and—*voilà*—he extended and expanded the use of natural harmonics on the guitar.

After Bireli, along came a generation of (mostly) acoustic guitarists—Badi Assad comes to mind—who have become fluent in the language of using natural harmonics in a musical way. I've been playing alongside Badi onstage in situations where we were both interspersing harmonics in our playing, and you couldn't tell from which guitar the "bells" were coming—a beautiful chaos of chimes.

"Scale Routes" was also designed to get guitarists more familiar with how the same note can be played in more than one place. The other plus with this exercise is the nice effect achieved when you use open strings to execute otherwise ordinary scale fragments—the ringing of the open string while the next note is being played often sounds nice.

# Larry Coryell
## Mixing Natural Notes And Harmonics

THOSE OF YOU WHO HAVE NEVER played scales with a mix of natural notes and harmonics should refer to last month's column, which dealt with *natural harmonics* played on the open strings mixed with normal notes. Now let's turn our attention to mixing natural notes with *artificial harmonics*, where the left hand frets a note and the right hand not only stops the string a given number of frets above the right's position, but it also does the plucking. If you're unfamiliar with this technique, check out my column Lenny's Lesson, which was reprinted in the Jan. '87 issue (the original appeared in Jan. '78).

Before we get under way, here are two important things to keep in mind. First, all of the music's right-hand touch points (normally executed with the index finger) are 12 frets above the right-hand's position. Second, if you use a pick, hold it between your right-hand thumb and middle finger, using your pinky to pluck the string with an upstroke motion (it helps to have a long nail on your little finger). Fingerstyle players can pluck the string in classical style with the ring finger, or with the thumb, a la the late Lenny Breau.

Ex. 1 shows a G major scale starting with a harmonic. Right away you should see that you need to divide your field of vision between the left hand doing the position shifts and the right hand pinpointing the artificial harmonics. The best way to deal with this is to try doing the left-hand shifts without looking—you might flub things for a while, but stick with it so you can watch for the harmonic points, which *must* be accurate.

The same scale is featured in Ex. 2, only you start off with a normal note—the reverse of Ex. 1. At the top on the scale, you have to make an extra stretch from the 11th fret to the 15th (on the third and first strings, respectively). Observe that barre positions can be employed at various points in each example. You can make the scales sound either legato, where the notes over-ring, or staccato, with each note played short and separate. I like both approaches, but I lean toward the staccato.

Ex. 3 takes you up and down a little bit, so you can see the melodic possibilities of the technique. It takes getting used to, but once you get the hang of it, the opportunities are numerous. One thing you may want to do concerning Ex. 3 is to play the first four notes over and over, so you can really get a feel for the groove. Stationary use of the technique is shown in Ex. 4, played in open position. Notice the interesting melodic effects that can be produced by skipping various strings, which is demonstrated by the last six notes of Ex. 4: an open second string to the C harmonic on the

---

*Larry Coryell helped pioneer fusion in the late '60s and has recorded with numerous legendary musicians, including John McLaughlin, Sonny Rollins, and Stephane Grappelli.*

fifth string, an open G string to the open sixth harmonic, and the open D to the open sixth.

There are a lot of possibilities here, especially if you play a solidbody guitar. With a few effects, such as chorus and reverb, you can really go into the stratosphere with this thing.

Before we part, Ex. 5 in my Oct. '87 column was mislabeled. It should read: G Super Locrian, which is the seventh mode of the A♭ melodic minor scale. Sorry for the confusion.

Ex. 1

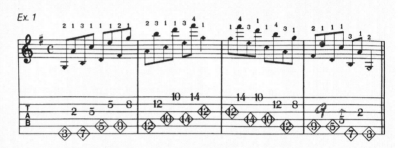

Ex. 2

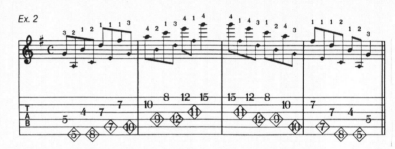

Ex. 3

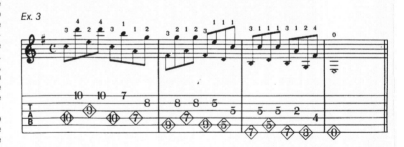

Ex. 4

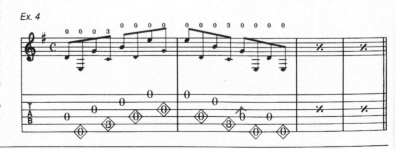

## January 1988, "Mixing Natural Notes and Harmonics"

What was I thinking when I wrote this one? Holy cow! I know I wasn't smoking any-thing—*that* lifestyle was behind me. First, let's clear up the errors in measure 4 of Ex. 1: the second eighth-note of the first beat should be *E*, 9th fret, third string; then the second note of the second beat, a *C*, should be played on the 5th fret of the *third* string, not the fourth. Also, there is an alternative to going 12 frets above every note; if you wish, you can play the natural harmonic *A* on the 5th fret of the fifth string rather than going up the string and searching for the imaginary 24th fret. Searching for those imaginary fret points for both natural and artificial harmonics is still a good thing to learn, however—it has helped me in many performing situations. It's just that it never hurts to know it both ways.

I think my motive in writing this column was to help extend the possibilities that were first expounded in "Scale Routes"—i.e., to really explore harmonics, both natural and artificial, and how they can be used musically. There's one more correc-tion to note: in Ex. 4, measure 2, first note of the third beat, the staff is correct but the tab is wrong—it should be open third string, not open fourth; the open fourth is used two notes later.

# Larry Coryell
## Walking Bass Lines

**W**HETHER YOU PERFORM SOLO OR with other musicians, being able to comp and play bass lines at the same time is a very handy skill to have, especially when a bassist isn't around. Last month I laid out a simple progression with bass lines and chords—an ideal accompaniment for the second guitar in, say, a duo. This month let's work with some "rhythm changes," which center around the patterns I-VI-II-V or III-VI-II-V. The focus of this column is not so much on music theory as it is on the "how-to" aspect of this approach.

Keep in mind that the fingerings in my columns work for me, but they're not carved in stone, so feel free to change them. Over the

*Larry Coryell helped pioneer fusion in the late '60s and has recorded with numerous legendary musicians, including John McLaughlin, Sonny Rollins, and Stephane Grappelli.*

years I've discovered that using successive fingers is useful (scan this month's music, and you'll see that I mean). When I'm in the "bass line comp mode," I put down the pick and use just my fingers. Now let's look at the music.

Another way to play the opening chord (Bb7) is to barre the 6th fret with the 1st finger, getting the D note with your 2nd finger. The way I've marked this part makes you hop from position to position, but it works for me because you're not staying in one place for very long.

In measure 4 a two-note chord is held for two beats, while the bass keeps moving; check out the open fifth string (the last note of the bar). It's the only open string in this exercise. Measure 5 features a barre at the 1st fret; you shift from the 1st fret, fifth string, to the 5th fret, fifth string, as you move from Bb/D to Eb7 and Edim7 in measure 6. Notice that the Bb chord in bar 7 does not have a root; this is

because the line is moving upward chromatically, and the chord acts as a passing harmony.

Measure 10 has another shift. Here you go from the first position (at the 1st fret) up to the Eb bass note at the 6th fret, fifth string. This puts you in position for the subsequent Dm7 chord. Measure 11 features some chord substitutions to end the exercise; Db7 is a substitute for G7, Gb7 is a sub for Cm7, and B7 replaces F7.

"Rhythm changes" usually include a standard bridge, which, in the key of Bb, consists of two bars each of D7, G7, C7, and F7. If you want to complete the progression as it's normally played, repeat what's written here, go to the bridge I just described, and then do the first part one more time. This is referred to as an AABA form.

©1988 Coryell Music (BMI).

## August 1988, "Walking Bass Lines"

I recall being on a bill in Toronto with the great jazz violinist Stephane Grappelli where I wasn't the only guitarist. This Scottish guy named Martin Taylor was also on the gig. He played a lot of fingerstyle—and, boy, when they gave him an unaccompanied solo he tore the place up, playing all the parts of a jazz performance: the chords, the bass lines, and the solo line, all at the same time. I found out later that he had been a child prodigy, and we became fast friends. The rest is history—the guitar world knows Martin very well now and is better off for it.

That was the first time I recall hearing walking bass lines played like that. Shortly after that, I noticed Joe Pass was doing it. (He had probably been doing it for quite a while—I just hadn't noticed.) Now the walking bass line technique has been on the scene for about 30 years, and it works well not only in solo situations but in duos—either two-guitar duos or twosomes where it's guitar and, say, trumpet.

This technique gave me a choice in accompaniment styles. I could use the four-chords-to-the-bar Freddy Green approach, or I could use this fingerstyle device that approximates two-thirds of a rhythm section. You don't want it to sound like a good guitar player and a mediocre bassist, though, so put a little extra effort into making the bass lines interesting—and you're sure to get a gig. Ha!

# Contemporary Guitar

## Chord Substitution

**LARRY CORYELL**

**H**OW DID YOU DO WITH LAST month's Ex. 5? As you'll recall, I challenged you to use new chords to harmonize a melody. This month, let's do a quick review and take a look at the solution I came up with.

Barre chords work well for rock, but they aren't used that much in jazz, because (1) you don't need so many notes, and (2) jazz calls for chords that are more colorful-sounding. For instance, the following example pairs common barre chords with hipper, more jazz-like ones:

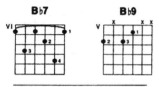

**Bb7**          **Bb9**

*Larry Coryell helped pioneer fusion in the late '60s and has recorded with numerous legendary musicians, including John McLaughlin, Sonny Rollins, and Stephane Grappelli.*

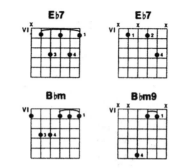

**Eb7**          **Eb7**

**Bbm**          **Bbm9**

Last month's Ex. 5 and this month's Ex. 1 (at the bottom of the page) offer a "before and after" view. Both have the same melodic line, but the treatment from last month includes a lot of rock-like barre chords that can easily be improved upon (there are many possible solutions).

Now take a look at what I came up with in Ex. 1. The *Gm7#5* (it can also be called *Ebadd9*) is a substitute chord for *Eb*, and it's a lot less cumbersome than certain *Eb*

chords. In addition, it's easier to finger than the *Gm#5* I showed you last month. I've also added some subtle passing tones that work nicely. The second chord, *Gbdim7* has a *D* note on the second string, 3rd fret, that resolves to the *C* note a whole-step lower. (As a static form with the *D* permanently in the upper voice, this chord is known as *F13b9* (no root). Passing tones are also a feature of Ex. 1's last two chords: A *G* to an *F* on the fourth string makes the chords *Ab* and *Ab6*, respectively, while *Eb* to *F* makes the coinciding chords *Abm* to *Abm6*, respectively.

By the way, the melody is from my original composition "Tender Tears," which I recorded in 1985 on my album *Equipose* [Muse (160 W. 71st St., New York, NY 10023), WCD-5319]. When you go from rock chords to more sophisticated ones, the contrast is striking. Expanding chordal knowledge is essential for young players who want to go beyond the confines of pop and rock—you may not make as much money, but you'll feel a lot better and probably preserve your hearing for an extra 20 years!

*Ex. 1*

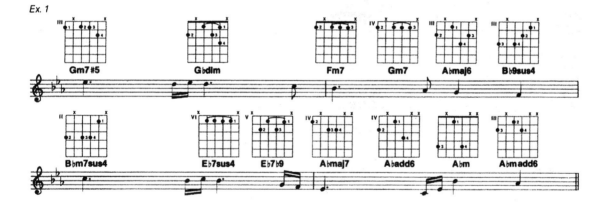

Gm7#5          Gbdim          Fm7          Gm7          Abmaj6          Bb9sus4

Bbm7sus4          Eb7sus4          Eb7b9          Abmaj7          Abadd6          Abm          Abmadd6

## January 1989, "Chord Substitutions"

Hearing chord substitutions in standards such as "Autumn Leaves" and "All the Things You Are" is what initially attracted me to jazz. When I was a teenager, I would go to hear live music and marvel at how a good piano player could play chords that were not the original harmony and make the tune sound better. I still love that. What I did here was take a fragment of a tune that I had composed in the mid-'80s and show how I harmonized it.

The corollary point I tried to make was directed toward newer players, just getting into it, who thought that the more notes in the chord, the better. I wrote out some simple jazz chords that have space in the intervals, to show the difference between the rock approach to harmony and jazz. The actual chords here—there are 13 of them—also have substitutions, more than one in many instances. I wanted to get guitar players to start thinking about and hearing substitutions, so they could make the harmony of whatever tune they were playing become richer.

# Contemporary Guitar

## Preparing for Half-Diminished Improvisation

THIS COLUMN IS DIRECTED AT young players who got into guitar through rock music, but have become interested in improvising with scales other than the minor pentatonic. One such player recently asked me, "What scale does one use for m7b5 chords?"

You can consider the m7b5 a *half-diminished* chord. Take *Em7b5*, for example: You have an *E* (tonic), a *G* (lowered 3rd), a *Bb* (lowered 5th), and a *D* (lowered 7th). If you drop the *D* to a *Db*, you have a

---

*Larry Coryell helped pioneer fusion in the late '60s and has recorded with numerous legendary musicians, including John McLaughlin, Sonny Rollins, and Stephane Grappelli.*

---

diminished 7th chord (*Edim7*). The *Em7b5* is "almost diminished," or "half-diminished."

The Locrian mode best fits the half-diminished harmony because both have the characteristic tritone interval. In the case of *Em7b5*, use the *E* Locrian mode—*E, F, G, A, Bb, C,* and *D*. (Remember, *E* Locrian's "parent mode" is *F* Ionian.)

The examples are designed to help you get into the "color" of the half-diminished. Play Ex. 1 over and over. Notice the designated pick strokes: It's mostly an up-down alternation (with upstroke accents), but there are some successive downstrokes towards the end. Play this until you get it accurately—it's a little tricky. Ex. 2 is the same as Ex. 1, but with a different fingering. This example requires a position shift;

omitting the note in parentheses allows for a smoother transition back to the beginning. Ex. 3 starts lower and goes higher than the first two examples. An alternative fingering is given in parentheses.

Ex. 4 is a sample *Em7b5-A7b9* run. (That's a II-V substitution in *D* minor.) In the first measure, there are two spots where you have to flatten a finger to get notes on the adjacent string, as in Ex. 1. The second measure features a *D* harmonic minor scale over the *A7b9*. We've looked at this usage in the past, but it's not the focus here. Concentrate on hearing the Locrian/half-diminished tonal color. It may take a while, but you'll eventually know what to do when the dreaded m7b5 comes calling. Good luck!

Ex. 1

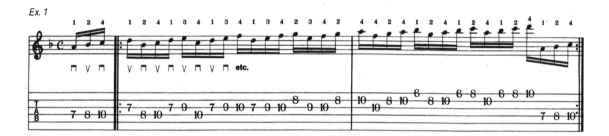

Ex. 2

Ex. 3

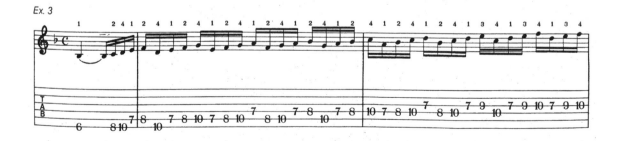

## February 1989, "Preparing for Half-Diminished Improvisation"

Like "Chord Substitutions," this column was intended to help guitar players who had started as rockers to advance into the world of jazz harmony and improvisation. One of the most frequent variations on the II-V-I is the use of the m7♭5 chord as the II, and the scale for this chord coincides with the Locrian mode.

What we have here are variations on the *F* major scale. Because I wanted to put in a little bit of training for playing over the m7♭5 chord, I made the first three examples similar. The aim was to get the student used to playing the *F* scale starting from different notes, like *A* or *B♭* or, as in the sample improv phrase, *C*. What I did when writing this lesson was to play one of the examples and then hit an *Em7♭5* chord and listen to how nicely the single-note lines approximate what I like to call the "color" of the chord. The sample improv phrase, Ex. 4, is for me a clear line that shows the difference between the m7♭5 and the m7 in the II-V-I progression.

I used to marvel at the way Philip Catherine would negotiate the m7♭5 chords—he played beautiful m6 arpeggios. Then a few years ago I heard Mike Brecker in Montreal, on a gig with Herbie Hancock, use Locrian arpeggios plus their extensions in a memorable version of Coltrane's "Naima." The extensions (at least the one I could hear, as Mike was playing rather swiftly) can include playing the 9th degree; with an *Em7♭5*, that transforms the scale from the basic *E* Locrian to *G* jazz minor. I don't think most students would be able to hear that difference unless they became acutely aware of both scales and how to use them—which illustrates why I wrote these *Guitar Player* columns. In all of them, I was trying to share the information that gives a player the building blocks to create good harmony, swingin' rhythm, and burnin' single-note lines. That's a good start to making creative music!

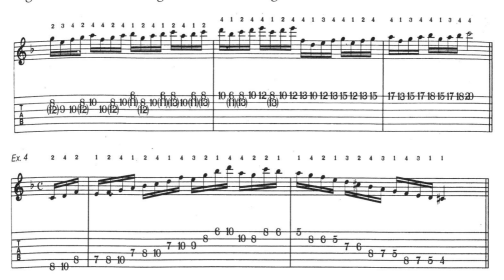

# *Discography*

## 1967

The Free Spirits, *Out of Sight and Sound* ABC

The Gary Burton Quartet, *Duster* RCA

Chico Hamilton, *The Dealer (Introducing Larry Coryell)* ABC

Chico O'Farrill, *Nine Flags* ABC

The Jazz Composers' Orchestra, *Communications* ECM
> This record was a "free" performance, in the spirit of Cecil Taylor, Albert Ayler, and other iconoclastic players who were on the scene in New York. Three things stand out in my memory: (1) The rehearsal was better than the recording (these things happen—nothing you can do). (2) I wore a big felt hat given to me by Hugh Masakela and smashed and rubbed my Gibson Super 400 into the amp to produce screeches, squeals, and other Hendrix-type feedback. (3) In the inside cover, there were some distinctive photos (like the feedback gyrations), including a shot of my first wife-to-be, Julie, sitting on my lap, with me still wearing that blasted hat.

The Gary Burton Quartet, *In Concert* RCA

## 1968

The Gary Burton Quartet, *A Genuine Tong Funeral* RCA

## 1969

Randy Brecker, *Score* Capitol

Herbie Mann, *Memphis Underground* Atlantic
> This was a jazz hit when it came out, and the tune "Memphis Underground" remained a hit for Herbie throughout his career. For me, however, the best track was "Chain of Fools"—I think I was able to express my voice best on that tune, especially because I was able to the get blues phrasing *and* the Indian-type phrasing integrated. Plus, I somehow got a good sound—partially because I tuned my guitar down a major third to *C*.

Larry Coryell, *Lady Coryell* Vanguard Apostolic

Larry Coryell, *Coryell* Vanguard Apostolic

Steve Marcus, *Count's Rock Band* Atlantic

> This was a chance for me to break out of the more disciplined environment of the Gary Burton Quartet and unleash all the blues and rock ideas that I liked to play in jazz-oriented contexts. In other words, we just cut loose and wailed—it was the combined voice of a young generation of jazzers who also loved rock and pop. The version of the Beatles' "Rain" stands out for me on this, plus "Theresa's Blues" by Chris Hills—it was fun-key!

## 1970

Larry Coryell, *Spaces* Vanguard

Herbie Mann, *Memphis Two Step* Atlantic

## 1971

Larry Coryell, *Live at the Village Gate* Vanguard

Larry Coryell, *Fairyland* Flying Dutchman

Eddie "Cleanhead" Vinson, *You Can't Make Love Alone* Flying Dutchman

Jim Webb, *And So On* Reprise

Jim Pepper, *Pepper's Pow Wow* Embryo

## 1972

Larry Coryell, *Barefoot Boy* Flying Dutchman

Leon Thomas, *Blues and the Soulful Truth* Flying Dutchman

Wolfgang Dauner's Et Cetera, *Knirsch* MPS

Larry Coryell, *Offering* Vanguard

## 1973

Larry Coryell, *The Great Escape* Flying Dutchman

## 1974

The Eleventh House, *Introducing The Eleventh House featuring Larry Coryell* Vanguard

The Eleventh House, *Level One* Arista

## 1975

Larry Coryell, *The Restful Mind* Vanguard

With Ralph Towner (guitars), Glen Moore (bass), and Colin Walcott (tabla)—this was three-quarters of the group Oregon; the only guy missing was Paul McCandless (oboe). At the end of this session, Colin Walcott said to me, "Larry, you've joined the acoustic revolution." The idea for this record was germinated in the summer of 1971 when Julie, Murali, and I were living at Garwold House in Scotland. The house belonged to some friends of Julie's who were interested in Tibetan Buddhism, and there was a print hanging on the wall of a Buddhist icon named *Avalalokitesvara*, which means "the restful mind." That was the philosophical basis for the record date. Ralph Towner played a beautiful support role, and Glen and Colin were terrific, plus I did some solo stuff. This was an important record at the time because it was such a quiet contrast to all of the bombastic Eleventh House music.

Michael Urbaniak, *Fusion III* Columbia

Larry Coryell , *Other Side of Larry Coryell* Vanguard

Larry Coryell, *The Essential Larry Coryell* Vanguard

Larry Coryell, *Planet End* Vanguard

Larry Young, *Spaceball* Arista

Lenny White, *Venusian Summer* Emperor

This was the only time Al DiMeola and I played electric guitars together (just one track), and it created quite a stir among hardcore fusion fans, as to who "cut" whom in the frenetic trading between us at the end of the improvisation section. To this day I have not heard it, but I'm sure it was good all the way around. One strong memory of this session (including the rehearsals) was Al's meticulous attention to detail on every aspect of Lenny's compositions.

## 1976

Larry Coryell, *Basics* Vanguard

The Eleventh House, *Aspects* Arista

Larry Coryell, *The Lion and the Ram* Arista

An all-acoustic solo (with overdubs) date, done in a studio way out in the sticks near the Massachusetts/Connecticut border. The record had some singing (which was not appreciated by the critics) and some things that I've never played onstage, including an improvised version of Bach's "Lute Prelude" and an original titled "Stravinsky." I recall being in Jimmy Webb's living room in Los Angeles one afternoon when Jimmy played "Short Time Around" (with me singing) for the late, great Harry Nilsson. He seemed to like it.

## 1977

Larry Coryell & Philip Catherine, *Twin House* Atlantic

Larry Coryell & Steve Khan, *Two For The Road* Arista

Larry Coryell & Alphonse Mouzon, *Back Together Again* Atlantic
Back with Alphonse—this time, he found me a rock guitarist who would lend me his supercharged solid-body guitar (might have been a Les Paul), and I played that for most of the date. Before the record came out, everybody I played it for loved it, but after the record came out, there was a lot of flak—go figure. One Belgian fan didn't like the record because Philip Catherine wasn't featured enough. I could understand that, but I think that Belgian fan missed the point: it was "back together again" for Coryell and Mouzon. There would be more record dates with Philip— like . . .

Larry Coryell & Philip Catherine, *Live in Europe* Atlantic

Charles Mingus, *Three or Four Shades of Blue* Atlantic
Philip was on this record as well. Actually, he got the first call, but when I found out I called Atlantic Records and kind of pushed my way onto this date, because I simply *had* to record with Mingus. He was the man! I remember coming out of the dentist's office in Weston, Connecticut, one afternoon and turning on the jazz station out of New York—they were playing the version of "Better Get Hit in Your Soul" from this record. I was playing a Les Paul Jr. that I later destroyed in a drunken rage—man, that guitar sounded good. Both Philip and I sounded good on this record, I think, and our presence helped to make it a strong seller for Charles Mingus. Yeah!

## 1978

The Eleventh House, *At Montreux* Vanguard

Larry Coryell, *Difference* EGG

Larry Coryell, *Standing Ovation* Mood
This was an offshoot of my friendship with Wolfgang Dauner, with whom I had made the *Knirsch* record in 1972. I found Wolfgang's attitude about music quite

refreshing, and we did a few gigs in Germany over the years. His English was limited (as was my German), but he always communicated what was important: he liked spontaneity and regarded fusion as a tributary of the avant-garde.

Larry Coryell, *European Impressions* Arista

This record was trashed by the jazz police, but my fans dug it. I was using ideas developed from electrified fusion and transferring them to acoustic. I recited an anti-disco poem at the beginning of "Rodrigo Reflections"—fans and friends got a kick out of that.

Larry Coryell with the Brubeck Bros., *Better Than Live* Tomato

Charles Mingus, *Me Myself an Eye* Atlantic

These sessions comprised the who's who in New York at the time—Steve Gadd, Eddie Gomez, Charles McPherson, Michael Brecker, Lee Konitz, Pepper Adams, and more. The list is long and impressive. I was honored to be a part of this, and I thought my solo on "Devil Woman" was pretty good. Mingus was in a wheelchair by then, and the last thing he said to me at the end of the date was, "Larry, I love ya . . . ." I never saw him again. His passing was a truly sad event.

Larry Coryell featuring John Scofield and Joe Beck, *Tributaries* Novus

Larry Coryell & Philip Catherine, *Splendid* Elektra

## 1979

Larry Coryell with the Brubeck Bros., *Return* Vanguard

Sonny Rollins, *Don't Ask* Fantasy

As with my good fortune in working with Mingus, this was in the "I'm honored to do this" category. Sonny was all everyone said he was and more; his sense of what he wanted was impeccable. Plus, just to play with him was to play with arguably the strongest tenor player of all—his strength and confidence, combined with the sheer genius of his concept and execution, put him in the small group of players considered "the most exceptional."

Michael Mantler, *Movies* Watt

Stephane Grappelli, *Young Django* MPS

Philip Catherine got me on this date. In addition to creating a configuration of the Catherine-Coryell duo with the great Grappelli, this was my only recording with Niels-Henning Ørsted Pederson. We had great arrangements and it was a great date—all acoustic, no drums.

## 1981

Larry Coryell, *Bolero*  Evidence

L. Subramaniam, *Blossom*  MCA

Paco de Lucia, *Castro Marin*  Polygram

Kazumi Watanabe, *Dogatana*  Columbia (Japan)

*Fuse One*  CTI

This date united me with Creed Taylor, which would lead to the work we were to do in the 1990s. Put briefly: here was a hands-on producer who was actively involved in the music as well as the recording, and he had both original ideas and the practical know-how to realize them. There was one rehearsal moment at Rudy Van Gelder's studio, where L. Shankar, Stanley Clarke, and I were working on some funky Indian-type idea. Unfortunately, it was not recorded and I don't remember it all these years later—only that it was a great idea.

## 1982

Larry Coryell & Michael Urbaniak, *Duo*  Keynote

Larry Coryell, *Bolero*  Phillips Phonogram (produced by Teo Macero)

Larry Coryell, *Scheherazade*  Phillips Phonogram (produced By Teo Macero)

This music speaks for itself: I came to understand the brilliance of Rimsky-Korsikoff.

## 1983

Teo Macero, *Impressions of Charles Mingus*  Teo Records

Larry Coryell & Michael Urbaniak, *A Quiet Day in Spring*  Steeple Chase

## 1984

Larry Coryell, *L'Oiseau de Feu/Petrouchka*  Phillips Phonogram (produced by Teo Macero)

Larry Coryell, *Comin' Home*  Muse

This was my return to straightahead playing as a leader, and it wasn't sufficiently focused to be as effective as it could have been. But at least it was a start—and each successive straightahead record for Joe Fields got better.

## 1985

Larry Coryell & Emily Remler, *Together*  Concord Jazz

**1986**

Larry Coryell, *Le Sacre du Printemps*  Phillips Phonogram

**1987**

Larry Coryell, *Toku Do*  Muse

Larry Coryell & Miroslav Vitous, *Quartet*  Jazzpoint
I got a terrible review in the French press for this record—the writer said I was a mediocre player, at best. Miroslav and I had been working together a lot at this time, and it was a labor of love. We both played great, and the reviewer simply had his head up his ass. The version of "Nardis" on this date is killin'!

**1988**

Larry Coryell, *Air Dancing*  Jazzpoint

**1989**

Larry Coryell, *American Odyssey*  DRG
This date was intended to follow up on the success of the "Bolero" concept, but it was micro-managed by production and even though I finally got the music together—the Copland was a bitch—it didn't have the spontaneity of *Bolero*. It was great working with Wayne Shorter, though, and our version of "Adagio for Strings" is probably the first instance of jazzers doing this famous Samuel Barber evergreen.

Larry Coryell, *Shining Hour*  Muse

**1990**

Larry Coryell, *Visions in Blue: Coryell Plays Ravel & Gershwin*  Soundscreen
This is the "Bolero" concept revisited, coupled with other Ravel pieces ("Alborada . . ." was really tough) plus some Gershwin, since I was coming off learning the piano solo from "Rhapsody in Blue." It was originally done in Japan for a small boutique label, NEC Avenue. Jimmy Webb heard the Japanese recording, loved it, and made it possible to place this with Soundscreen in the States.

Larry Coryell, *Dragon Gate*  Shanachie

Jack Walrath & The Masters Of Suspense, *Out of the Tradition*  Muse

**1991**

Larry Coryell, *Twelve Frets to One Octave*  Shanachie

## 1992

Larry Coryell, *Live from Bahia* CTI

## 1993

Larry Coryell, *Fallen Angel* CTI

## 1994

Larry Coryell, *I'll Be Over You* CTI

## 1996

Larry Coryell, *Sketches of Coryell* Shanachie

## 1997

Larry Coryell, *Spaces Revisited* with Billy Cobham, Bireli LaGrene, and Richard Bona Shanachie

## 1998

Larry Coryell/Steve Smith/Tom Coster, *Cause and Effect* Tone Center

Larry Coryell, *Private Concert* Acoustic Music (Germany)
This deal was generated by my late publishing administrator, Judith Baldwin, as a follow-up to something Atilla Zoller had done on this German label run by Peter Finger. It's good, because it has the only extant recording I did with Vic Juris, who is a great guitarist out of the New York scene. Vic and I did a lot of duo gigs together in the 1980s.

## 1999

Larry Coryell, *Monk, 'Trane, Miles and Me* High Note

L. Subramaniam & Larry Coryell, *From the Ashes* Water Lily
This record was done in the middle of the night in Santa Barbara, California, with material that had been composed by L. Subramanian the previous afternoon. He and I play well together with just violin and guitar. "Mani" drove us up to the date from L.A. and got a speeding ticket on the way. He was going really fast—like, around 100 mph. I never forgot that.

## 2000

*The Coryells*, with my sons Murali and Julian  Chesky

> Emotionally, this was a bit rough because it was a family thing—but we got it together and I am *so* proud of the way my sons played and sang on this record. It was also good to have two close friends, Brian Torff (bass) and Alphonse Mouzon (percussion), to round out the group.

Larry Coryell, *New High*  High Note

## 2001

Larry Coryell, *Inner Urge*  High Note

Steve Marcus, *Count's Jam Band Reunion*  Tone Center

Hari Prasad Chaurasia, *Music Without Borders*  Navras

> Recorded live in San Francisco with V. K. Vinayakram (percussion) and George Brooks (saxophones).

## 2002

Ronu Majumdar, *Moonlight Whispers*  Our World

> This was a carefully rehearsed and recorded victory for Indo-jazz fusion, done in Hamburg with a savvy Iranian-born producer. Ronu and the other guys (two great drummers) are exceptional musicians. Some of the slow movements from this recording are truly sublime, as is the dexterous use of odd time signatures.

Cedar Walton, *Cedars of Avalon*  High Note

> I had always wanted to do something with Cedar, and this was a gift from Joe Fields, who made the date happen. "Theme for Ernie" was one piece I had wanted to do since I had jammed it back in Seattle around 1963 with my old friend Sarge West. Tunes like that never lose their luster. That's the great thing about jazz—it's not trendy.

Larry Coryell, *Birdfingers*  Universe

> A compilation of previous Vanguard tracks.

Larry Coryell, *Inner City Blues*  Past Perfect

> A compilation of previous CTI tracks.

## 2003

Larry Coryell, *The Power Trio* with Paul Wertico and Larry Gray  High Note
This was recorded live at the Jazz Showcase in Chicago, and I have to thank Joe Segal for providing me with an unfettered, relaxed atmosphere for improvising. Live records are good, because they capture the stretching we do when we're in front of a friendly public. This was the first master of my music that I ever owned, and instead of trying to release it myself I placed it with Joe Fields. We did pretty well with this record.

Larry Coryell, *Shining Hour*  Savoy Jazz
Re-release of the 1989 Muse recording.

Kazuhito Yamashita, *The Ultimate Four Seasons*  RCA
Originally released in Japan in the 1980s. All I remember about this record is how amazingly this young Japanese guitarist played. It was fun, and a great opportunity for me to do the music of Vivaldi, of all people.

## 2004

Larry Coryell, *Tricycles* with Mark Egan and Paul Wertico  Favored Nations
This recording captured my main contemporary group—we've been together for quite a few years now. It was done on the road in Germany. We were all sick with the "grippe," but that didn't stop us from documenting the tightness we had developed as a trio—and the German engineering was clean and clear. This was originally released on In and Out Records, the company of my old friend, Frank Kleinschmidt.

## 2005

Larry Coryell/Victor Bailey/Lenny White *Electric*  Chesky

## 2006

Larry Coryell, *Laid Back and Blues*  Rhombus
This is the second master I've owned—again, a live record. This time, though I'm keeping ownership of the master, I'm licensing it to a distributor, Rhombus Records. This was recorded at the Sky Church at EMP in Seattle with three friends who are great players in that town: Mark Seals (piano), Dean Hodges (drums), and Chuck Deardorf (bass). It was done as part of a series called Jazz in January, and I have to thank Jeff Hauser and the late Jim Ray of the No Wasted Notes Foundation for making it happen. The fourth track, the blues

with Tracey Piergross singing the lead, marked my return to singing after a long absence—and I sang the blues pretty well, by golly. Tracey is at her best here, and when people hear her on this track they say, "Baby, where have you been hiding?"

Larry Coryell/Victor Bailey/Lenny White *Traffic* Chesky

# *Acknowledgments*

Thanks to Wes Montgomery for listening to me and to Charles Mingus for encouraging me. Thanks to all my music teachers: John LaChappelle, Danny Love, Jerome Gray, and my classical teacher, Leonid Bolotine. Special thanks go out to Francisco Mendez for his recording expertise in the studio and for putting together the CD audio portion of this book, under pressure and rather quickly. Thanks to Mike Mandel for giving me accurate remembrances of the "Jack Bruce and Friends" tour. Big thanks to Richard Johnston and Jim Roberts for the tediousness of editing and the heroic job of dealing with my last-minute corrections and additions. Also thanks go out to everyone at Backbeat Books for this wonderful opportunity. Thanks to Chris Bou, Rick Sowden, and Daniel Mesa for reading through the early portions of the manuscript and helping with time-line information. Thanks to Julie Coryell for helping me "remember when" and also to Joseph Tangels for all his photo-hunting research . . . . "Here's to you, Norton." Also kudos to Paul Santa Maria for finding some of the lost *Guitar Player* columns.

I would like to thank my cousin, Dorothy Horner, for helping me with the early history of my family in those first few years in Galveston. Also a big thank-you to my sister, Gloria, for clarifying facts about our mother, Cora, and her husband, Gene Coryell. To my daughters, Allegra and Annie, and my sons, Murali and Julian, for their unconditional love and support. To my brother, Jim, for being there for me at all times and for being such a big jazz fan. To my three grandsons, Zach, Charlie, and Jackson, for the happiness that comes from being a grandfather. Last but not least, thanks to my little wifey, Tracey—all my love and thanks to her for endless typing, putting up with the late nights and early mornings, and for keeping me honest.

# *About the Author*

A prime mover of jazz-rock fusion, acclaimed guitarist Larry Coryell has recorded more than 60 solo albums and has appeared on numerous recordings by artists such as Stephane Grappelli, Gary Burton, Herbie Mann, Randy Brecker, Charles Mingus, Jean-Luc Ponty, John McLaughlin, and Chick Corea. He has written two instructional books for Backbeat: *Jazz Guitar: Creative Comping, Soloing, and Improv*; and *Larry Coryell's Power Jazz Guitar: Extending Your Creative Reach*. A resident of Orlando, Florida, Coryell continues to record and tour worldwide in musical settings that range from blues and straight-ahead jazz to classical and world music. His sons, Julian and Murali, are accomplished guitarists with growing lists of solo and sideman credits, including the family outing *The Coryells*.

## *Improvising* CD Tracks

1. Intro / Scale Routes in E Minor / Picking Exercise
2. Right Hand Independence Exercise
3. Left Hand Prowess / "Addendum Blues"
4. Melodic Minor Lesson / "Paco's Melodic Minor"
5. Lenny's Lesson / "Lenny's Lesson Composition"
6. Harmonizing the Phrygian Mode Exercise
7. Scale Routes Example in C / "Lines"
8. "7-11: Hector Meets Igor"

*Total Time:* 41:00

**Note:**

The stereo is split hard left and right so that the listener/student can turn down either channel and play along with the Master.

**Credits:**

The following "compositions" were created by Larry Coryell:

"Addendum Blues"—copyright © 2006
"Paco's Melodic Minor"—copyright © 2006
"Lenny's Lesson Composition"—copyright © 2006
"Lines"—copyright © 1967
"7-11: Hector Meets Igor"—copyright © 2006

**Recorded and mixed by:**

Fransisco Mendez at Xcyrus Studios, Orlando, Florida

**Publishing:**

EL-CEE Music, BMI